DEVELOPING

EXECUTIVE TALENT

DEVELOPING
EXECUTIVE TALENT

Best Practices from Global Leaders

Jonathan Smilansky

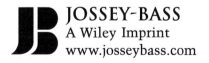

JOSSEY-BASS
A Wiley Imprint
www.josseybass.com

Other Wiley Editorial Offices

John Wiley & Sons Inc., 111 River Street, Hoboken, NJ 07030, USA

Jossey-Bass, 989 Market Street, San Francisco, CA 94103–1741, USA

Wiley-VCH Verlag GmbH, Boschstr. 12, D-69469 Weinheim, Germany

John Wiley & Sons Australia Ltd, 42 McDougall Street, Milton, Queensland 4064,
Australia

John Wiley & Sons (Asia) Pte Ltd, 2 Clementi Loop #02-01, Jin Xing Distripark,
Singapore 129809

John Wiley & Sons Canada Ltd, 6045 Freemont Blvd, Mississauga, ONT, L5R 4J3,
Canada

Wiley also publishes its books in a variety of electronic formats. Some content that appears
in print may not be available in electronic books.

Library of Congress Cataloging-in-Publication Data

Smilansky, Jonathan.
    Developing executive talent : best practices from global leaders / Jonathan Smilansky.
        p.   cm.
    ISBN-13: 978-0-470-03318-0
    ISBN-10: 0-470-03318-5
    1. Executives–Training of.   2. Executive ability.   3. Leadership.   I. Title.
    HD30.4.S646 2007
    658.4′092 – dc22

                                                                              2006028047

British Library Cataloguing in Publication Data

A catalogue record for this book is available from the British Library

ISBN 13 978-0-470-03318-0 (HB)
ISBN 10 0-470-03318-5 (HB)

Typeset in 11.5/15pt Bembo by SNP Best-set Typesetter Ltd., Hong Kong
Printed and bound in Great Britain by TJ International Ltd, Padstow, Cornwall, UK

This book is printed on acid-free paper responsibly manufactured from sustainable forestry
in which at least two trees are planted for each one used for paper production.

CONTENTS

ACKNOWLEDGEMENTS

I am grateful to my Hydrogen Partners, Valerie Fairbank, Emily Heller and Ian Lloyd, who worked with me on numerous talent management assignments and helped to develop some of the key concepts in the book.

I have spent many hours with my friend and colleague, Brian Sullivan, thinking about executive talent. His ideas on assessment, potential and the hierarchy of management positions have had a major influence on my thinking and are fundamental to this book.

Avivit Schpizisem, Tali Avigdor, Miki Glikman and Nurit Berman have worked with me to implement these concepts in the international arena. Mark Byford, from Egon Zehnder International, and I spent a lot of time talking about talent management and how to assess and develop executives.

Edgar Bronfman Jr encouraged me to develop talent management practices within the context of a global business.

Francesca Warren, as my Editor, saw the potential in this book and helped to make it a reality.

My brother, Shaul, gave me very useful feedback and support throughout this journey.

Andreas Eracleous made this book a reality through his dedicated typing and feedback, while Emmeline Skerrett contributed similarly to the original report on 'The Systematic Management of Executive Talent'.

And finally, I am so grateful for the love and support of my children, Shirra and Alexander.

CHAPTER 1

WHAT IS THIS BOOK ABOUT?

*T*his book is aimed at three different types of readers – first, a Chief Executive, Division or Function Head who wants to develop the managerial talent in his or her business.

Many Chief Executives find that when there is a job opening because a person retires, leaves or is let go, they can only think of a handful of names internally and none of them seems to fit the bill. Therefore, when there is a vacancy, you may need to go outside, hire expensive headhunters, spend 6 months searching for the right candidates and, in the end, take a risk on an unknown person who is not familiar with the culture of the organisation and who you hope will be able to do a good job.

Alternatively, if you had a systematic talent management process in place, then you would have been able to anticipate this course of events. You and your direct reports would have identified senior executives with the right potential to fill a variety of key jobs and you would have developed and nurtured that potential so that candidates were available internally when the time came.

The second type of reader for this book is the Head of Human Resources or the person who is already responsible for talent management in an organisation. Talent management is a new field and most Human Resource professionals who do this type of work were, only a few years ago, responsible for Learning & Development or were HR generalists looking after a broad array of topics. While you, as an HR executive, may by now have developed a great deal of experience in the talent management area, this book will still provide a much broader array of input from the experience of leading businesses in the USA and the UK about what they have done in this area. The book provides actual quotes from Heads of Human Resources describing their experience and concerns. It also includes specific tools and describes key processes that are used by large businesses to identify, develop and manage their senior executive talent. These tools may not necessarily fit your requirements. They will, however, provide a framework that you can compare to what you are doing and, thereby, enable you to create even more effective talent management processes in your organisation.

The third audience for this book is you, the reader. As a senior executive, you know by now that no one will manage your career unless you do so yourself. Many organisations have started to put in place talent management processes. These are designed to help your boss and you to identify what you are capable of, to assess your suitability for more senior positions, to help you to build on your current strengths and to reduce the negative impact of your weaknesses. They should also help to identify possible job opportunities within the company that will enable you to stretch your capability and to take on larger and larger challenges.

All this is excellent, where it does exist. But, as you will see from our examples and interviews conducted in many leading organisations, even the best businesses are still far from being perfect in these areas.

If you want to further your career and utilise the best resources that your organisation has to offer, then you need to educate yourself about what is available and also to encourage your organisation to use a broad array of tools to help you to develop. This is a win–win situation since you can help the organisation to develop its talent and, thereby, to reduce the need to recruit externally, while at the same time helping yourself to develop the most fruitful long-term career path. Achieving this win–win objective will happen when you understand what can be done in the talent management field and what the best organisations are actually doing today. This will help you to become an 'educated consumer' of talent management services. It will enable you to get the most out of what is available and improve the quality of existing practices.

The material in this book is based on my experience, and that of my partners in Hydrogen Talent Ltd. Hydrogen was founded as a sister company to Oxygen: a boutique executive search firm which has a significant number of large businesses as clients. It was founded by partners who left large search firms in order to be able to work with clients more closely.

As executive search consultants we have seen our clients become more concerned with the quality of their existing executive teams. We have been asked to conduct a number of benchmarking studies, comparing the quality of internal executive teams to what is available in the marketplace. We have also recruited for a number of talent management roles for large corporations that have, for the first time, appointed a full-time executive to oversee this critical area.

As part of these initiatives we started to work in conjunction with business psychologists, such as myself, in order to ensure that we have the depth of professional expertise required to conduct senior executive assessment, benchmarking and development assignments. The growing focus on this area led us to create a new venture – Hydrogen – which is focused on the development of executive talent.

In many ways, the developments that we have seen are a reflection of an overall trend in the business environment. While the economy is generally positive, there is still a great deal of pressure on businesses, including very well-established ones, to improve their performance. This pressure tends to translate into a focus on the Chief Executive and the senior executive team, and an increased need to ensure that they have the leadership capabilities required to compete in the marketplace.

From a Human Resource perspective, this focus on executive talent represents an expansion beyond the traditional Training & Development input that tends to focus on entry level staff and on junior and middle management. The new focus is on key executives who are in positions of significant influence. The Human Resource (or Human Capital) function is increasingly asked to develop means to assess senior executive capability, examine their performance and potential objectively, help senior executives to understand their development needs and, thereby, ensure that the business has the best players in pivotal executive positions.

Since talent management is a developing area for many organisations, there is still a lack of consensus about what is involved and a variety of approaches have been adopted. A number of our clients have asked us about what we see in the marketplace and what would represent best practice. Most are aware of the GE model but that is generally viewed as an extreme approach, which does not necessarily fit the culture and style of many organisations.

I decided to write this book in order to convey a more coherent picture of what businesses are doing and what they are concerned with. The work is based on in-depth interviews that I conducted with Heads of Human Resources in large organisations such as: AXA and Aviva (in the insurance field), Allied Domecq (in the drinks business), Amerada Hess and Centrica (in the energy sector), Argos (a large retailer), Ashurst (a legal firm), BAA, BT, Barclays Bank, Compass (the world's largest caterer with over

400,000 employees worldwide), Dell computers, Electricity de France, PricewaterhouseCoopers and others.

When I approached our clients to talk about this talent management project and to see if they were available to be interviewed, the level of positive interest surprised me. Of the organisations that we approached, only one Head of Human Resources said that he could not participate at the time since they were going through significant restructuring (even though he would be interested in talking with us about the findings, once completed). I believe that the high level of interest in this area represents people's perceptions of the importance of talent management to the competitive positioning of their businesses. In my interviews I asked about:

- The importance of systematic talent management for the long-term success of their business.
- The objectives of their talent management efforts.
- How they assess and develop their senior management group.
- How they deal with the need to have effective succession for their current senior managers.
- How they engage in talent scouting in the external environment.
- How the business systematically identifies future executive talent in terms of objective assessment of future potential and development of that potential.
- The relationship between talent management and diversity in terms of enlarging the executive talent pools that are available within the business.
- The nature of internal and external branding that is associated with attracting promising executives from inside and outside the organisation.
- How hard or soft is the business in terms of facilitating talent development.
- How integrated are all of these talent management initiatives in terms of providing a coherent process.

In addition to these interview results, my partners and I have worked with a large number of international businesses to help them to improve the effectiveness of their talent management processes. That experience is summarised in this book. I have also interviewed a significant number of senior executives about their personal experience as 'consumers' of talent management processes in their respective organisations. What they say will help us to understand the expectations that senior executives in diverse businesses have from talent management efforts.

This book is also based on the professional literature that summarises what we know about talent management and its implications for business effectiveness. Appendix 2 includes brief abstracts of key books in the area. When reviewing articles in professional journals I found that some of the key topics have been the subject of significant investigation while others are less prevalent. The topic of succession management is presented by Guinn (2000), Huang (2001), Kakabadse and Kakabadse (2001), Byham (2002), Behn et al. (2005), Cantor (2005), Clutterbuck (2005) and Sambrook (2005). Their findings are incorporated in Chapter 6. It is interesting to note how recent all of these publications are, reflecting the emergence of talent management as a key business imperative. Other topics within the field have been subject to significantly less research and the book includes their findings in the relevant chapters. Specifically, Hiltrop (1999), Pollitt (2005) and Stainton (2005) discuss the significance of talent management activities. Kransdorff (1996) reviews the importance of on-boarding processes. Watkin (2003) and Dulewicz and Herbert (1999) discuss the importance of competencies in reviewing executive talent. Approaches to executive development as part of talent management efforts are presented by van der Sluis–den Dikken and Hoeksema (2001) and by Mighty and Ashton (2003). Executive career development is the focus for Hall (1999), Atkinson (2002) and Crawshaw (2006). Finally, the concept of an employer brand is a focus of research for Backhaus and Tikoo (2004).

There are a number of definitions of talent management in the literature and I chose one that I felt was appropriate for this book. I did not wish to adopt an approach where all employees are considered 'talented' (even though they are in many different ways). Otherwise, talent management becomes an umbrella term for all internal and external resourcing, as well as Training & Development and Performance Management (which would make it almost synonymous with Human Resource Management). For our purposes, therefore, talent management is defined as:

> An integrated set of corporate initiatives aimed at improving the calibre, availability and flexible utilisation of exceptionally capable (high potential) employees who can have a disproportionate impact on business performance. While these processes should be integrated in the 'regular' Human Resource management processes, talent management processes are designed to ensure that the business improves its competitive advantage through the effective utilisation of a small number of exceptional individuals in key leadership positions.

All of my work in the talent management area points to the fact that there is no one right answer or approach to achieving the desired objectives. Different organisational cultures with different levels of commitment, at different stages of development and within different business environments, produce a variety of specific approaches that match their particular circumstances.

In this regard the book examines the range of corporate approaches to handling the issues involved. My purpose is to give you, the reader, a map of the area, so that you can compare what your business is doing and identify other possible approaches that can augment your own current efforts.

My discussions have highlighted the fact that talent management is a new area for many organisations. A number of senior executives in very large businesses were candid in admitting that they have done little in certain areas and that they are just starting on this journey. The systematic management of executive talent is a key strategic initiative for most large corporations. The information presented throughout this book summarises the key activities and concerns of large businesses, mostly in the USA and the UK, that are focused around the identification, development and effective utilisation of executive talent. As an overview, the following paragraphs provide an executive summary of the main points.

Importance. Most of the organisations concerned viewed talent management to be one of their key strategic priorities. Competitive environments where talented executives are in short supply, plus the need to continue to grow their business, were seen as the main drivers for these initiatives. Most activities are focused on identifying talented executives early, developing their capability and 'utilising' them as corporate resources instead of allowing them to be slowed down by local considerations within individual business units.

Objectives. There was a wide range of objectives for talent management initiatives implemented by these businesses. The main ones focused on developing the best top teams in their competitive business environment, finding good internal successors for key jobs, enabling cross-fertilisation between business divisions, retaining talent through career opportunities, enlarging the internal talent pool through a focus on diverse employee populations, and building line management ownership of the need to have the best players as a key for future business success.

Developing senior executives. Most of our sample organisations were focusing significant efforts on developing their three top tiers of executives. The more sophisticated approaches included the use of external objective assessment of potential to augment the performance ratings that came from line managers. The data tends to be used to identify key strengths and areas for development with follow-up activities either tailored to individual needs or forming a part of a senior development programme usually implemented with the help of a business school. The key difficulties were around breaking divisional/business unit boundaries and creating real exposure for the best executives across the group.

Managing succession. The businesses in my sample tended to have an annual process (sometimes with a half-year follow-up to review progress on key action points and discuss problems). The main difficulty was in preventing a 'tick box' approach and ensuring a robust discussion of internal candidates and what needs to be done to help them to grow (versus always going outside while 'allowing' very lenient assessment of internal capability gaps).

External talent scouting. None of the businesses in my sample engaged in systematic external talent scouting. A number do this on an ad hoc basis and a few develop a talent 'bench' to be used for managing acquisitions or to address natural executive turnover. A small number of organisations are starting to initiate activities in this area, especially around executives from 'diverse' backgrounds, where a shortage of experienced candidates is already causing difficulties.

'Feeder' populations. Most of the organisations in my sample have systematic initiatives focusing on the early identification and development of talented managers who can be fast-tracked into executive positions. 'Regular' performance management processes tend to be used to identify high-calibre candidates and assessment centres provide objective data on potential. Development programmes (sometimes managed internally and sometimes through business schools) at different management levels seem to be the key to facilitating networking and ensuring a common base of knowledge. Most of these activities are initiated 'bottom up' and there is a concern about the lack of mobility across business units.

Diversity and talent management. Most of my interviewees look at diversity as a concern in terms of the size of the talent pool from which to draw corporate executives. The lack of female and minority candidates for senior positions is viewed as a block for the development of truly high-calibre senior teams. Key activities in these areas focus on research to understand what is preventing successful career development, input to senior executives to open their minds to a broader base of experience that could still be appropriate for key executive positions and planned networking to facilitate access.

Branding executive talent requirements. A number of the companies in my sample are heavily involved in branding their employer proposition for their general recruitment efforts. Only a few are already engaged in thinking through their proposition for executive talent development and in using that, externally and internally, to raise awareness about the kinds of people who can succeed in their business and about the career development opportunities that are open to the right people.

Being 'hard' or 'soft' on talent. Most of the executives in these organisations see their businesses as being on the 'soft' side and not having an 'up or out' culture. They did report, however, a trend toward more pressure on performance and less tolerance of a lack of performance at senior executive levels. Highly talented executives are viewed as being in very short supply. Organisations seem to be 'tolerant' of solid players and do not feel that they can have the luxury of insisting on talent (meaning the potential for taking on larger jobs in the future) as a criterion for maintaining a long-term career.

Integration of talent management initiatives. Most Heads of Human Resources agree that it is highly desirable to present an integrated set of corporate initiatives so that executives can understand how the various processes support the need to have the best players in key executive positions. Many of the talent management initiatives are already in place at my sample businesses and the real challenge is to integrate them into a coherent picture that includes reward and performance management together with the softer side of things.

Current state of play. The experience of the businesses in my sample enables us to generalise about the state of talent management initiatives in the USA and the UK. The data suggests that, while most organisations consider this to be a critical area to enable future growth, there is still significant scope for development. The basic Human Resource processes are in place in most organisations (performance management, succession planning, identification of high-potential individuals at junior and middle levels, training programme input, individual coaching etc.). On the other hand, there seems to be a degree of hesitation to put in place what is really required in order to have a bench of truly capable, 'edgy', assertive executives who are available to take on significant opportunities for business expansion. We seem to be missing:

- Real rigour to ensure that only high-potential executives occupy key corporate roles.
- A clear definition of what is required in terms of capability and breadth of experience in order to be able to occupy key executive positions.
- Objective assessment of current strengths and weaknesses of those that are in key executive positions as well as those that are nominated by their managers as having high potential.
- Strong and transparent career management processes that ensure that high-potential executives get the breadth of experience that is really required at the top (and, thereby, break business unit and functional boundaries).

- A system where senior executives receive 'feedback with consequences' around their strengths and development needs.
- Real recognition of the need to establish diversity at the top, not as an ethical issue but as a true business requirement.
- Feedback from the most talented executives about how they can be better 'utilised'.

These challenges are stated within the general context of businesses recognising the need for change and investing significantly more in talent management initiatives. There is, therefore, room for optimism that in the next few years we will see a continuing trend to 'harden' talent management practices and, thereby, to improve the quality of leadership at the top.

You may want to read this book in one go, following the order of the chapters here. Alternatively, I suggest that you start by reading Chapter 2, which highlights the importance of talent management initiatives and Chapter 3, which provides an overview of key processes in this area. These chapters will also highlight the key concepts provided in the book, and thereby enable you to have a conceptual framework through which it will be easier to understand everything that comes later.

You may then want to 'jump around' and go to those chapters that address your immediate needs. This book is very practical in its orientation and each chapter should help you to see what others are doing and to review the tools that help them to do things well. Some readers may want, for example, to focus on issues around the senior executive group. Chapter 5 describes how talent management processes apply to that population, which in many organisations does not receive any developmental input since they were considered to be beyond the need for development.

Other readers may want to jump directly to Chapter 8 and focus on what leading-edge organisations are doing to identify young executive talent, help these people to develop their capability and then facilitate their rapid career progression throughout the business.

Alternatively, you may want to jump directly to Chapter 17 and focus on your own career development and how talent management processes within your own organisation can be used to leverage your own rate of growth.

Regardless of the path that you, as the reader, choose to take to best utilise the information that is available in this book, you will find along the way both direct quotes describing how others approach key issues as well as concrete tools to work with.

The following brief chapter descriptions provide the menu that will help you taste what is available here:

Chapter 2: The importance that large businesses attribute to the systematic management of executive talent. What can you do in your organisation to assess the importance of this topic for the future success of your business? How do you convince your top team about the importance of managing executive talent systematically?

Chapter 3: What is involved in the systematic management of executive talent? What are the key steps in implementing an effective process? This is the overview and key concepts chapter.

Chapter 4: Focuses on using strategic business objectives to drive talent management efforts. How does your business strategy define requirements for executive talent and what needs to be done to focus on that?

Chapter 5: Is focused on talent management in critical jobs. We usually think of executive talent as a personal characteristic but this chapter describes why the process should start by looking at key jobs.

Chapter 6: How do organisations identify possible successors for the current senior executive team? What needs to be put in place in order to ensure that realistic candidates are available internally instead of always having to engage executive search consultants to look outside?

Chapter 7: How do large businesses identify external executives who are exceptionally talented and can add to their team's capability? How do the concepts of 'bench strengths' and 'talent scouting' apply when building senior level executive capabilities?

Chapter 8: What is done by leading-edge businesses in order to identify young managers who have the long-term potential to become senior executives? How can we understand the different requirements for talent at each management level and use that to identify executive potential?

Chapter 9: Focused on career paths, this chapter discusses how organisations have changed and what needs to be done to map career paths systematically and help executives to choose what fits their potential and ambition.

Chapter 10: This chapter focuses on the development of executive capability. Once we have identified individuals with long-term potential, how do we help them to build on their strengths and reduce the negative impact of their weaknesses?

Chapter 11: Deals with breaking down silos and ensuring that executive talent can be developed and utilised beyond the boundaries of a single business Division or functional area.

Chapter 12: Diversity is an issue that has a significant impact on talent management. How can organisations ensure that their talent pools include a diverse population that enables them to benefit from the range of potential available in the business and match the characteristics of their consumers?

Chapter 13: How do organisations create an awareness of the type of leading-edge executives that each business has and is looking for? How can that 'executive brand' be used to attract, develop and retain the kind of executive talent that is required for success?

Chapter 14: This chapter relates talent management to other Human Resource processes focusing on the need for integration in order to present a coherent process to client executives.

Chapter 15: This chapter focuses on talent management as it applies to 'exceptional performers'. How do we identify, develop and motivate executives who may not have the potential to take on significantly larger jobs in the future but who are exceptionally capable in terms of their performance in their current jobs?

Chapter 16: A focus on what needs to be done to build support from the top of the organisation will ensure that talent management is viewed as a key business process and not just a bureaucratic Human Resource initiative.

Chapter 17: What can an ambitious individual executive learn from the talent management practices of leading-edge businesses? What should I look for in choosing a business that will further my career? How can I build my own brand and use available talent management processes in the business that I am working for to develop my capability and further my career?

It is now time to jump in and see what you can find. As stated earlier, I would recommend that you continue to read Chapter 2 and then develop your own path through the rest of the book.

CHAPTER 2

THE IMPORTANCE OF TALENT MANAGEMENT FOR LONG-TERM BUSINESS SUCCESS

*T*alent management is an important concern for many companies and the senior executive teams that lead them. As part of writing this book, I interviewed Heads of Human Resources in large international corporations in order to get their perspective about the importance of talent management for the long-term success of their business. Organisations that were involved in this survey included among others Allied Domecq drinks, Amerada Hess in the energy sector, Argos retail, Ashurst which is a large legal firm, Associated British Foods, Aviva Insurance, AXA Insurance, B&Q retailers, BAA, Barclays Bank, BT, Centrica (who own British Gas), Compass Group, who are the world's leading catering business with over 400,000 employees worldwide, Dell computers, Electricity de France, PricewaterHouseCoopers who are the world's largest accounting firm, Smith Group which is a high-technology manufacturer and Taylor Woodrow who are commercial and residential property developers. The degree of consensus among interviewees in terms of the importance of executive talent management was high. Almost all the companies surveyed report that talent management is perceived within their organisation to be one of the most important corporate efforts, essential to enabling them to achieve competitive advantage.

The following quotes represent a selected sample of responses:

> Very important. In the context of our growth and our view of expected acquisitions, the retention and recruitment of talent is one of the main barriers to our growth. That is a huge challenge for us. The people are the only thing that makes this business successful. The cost of entry to our business isn't high. Having better people who do things just a little better is what makes a difference. This could be seen as glib, but it is actually fundamental to sustaining our success. (Large retail company)

> It is our number one priority, other than keeping our customers happy. If you looked at the performance management reviews for our businesses, once we finish talking about financials we move immediately to talk about succession planning at the top. Last year we dedicated 11 hours of our full Executive Board to discussing our top talent, business by business. It is important: we want to be able to grow people within the business who will stay with us. If we don't do that then we'll spend money on people and they won't stay and we will constantly have to go outside to hire expensive talent who don't really know our business. We are a diverse business and really need this talent. (Public utility)

> It's the number one item. In the context of a company that is one of the largest employers in the world and still growing, the leaders of an organisation of this size need the internal capabilities to grow and this puts huge demands on people. Also, we operate in a highly competitive labour market, and we must stay ahead to be able to attract and develop senior level talent. In this business we depend on service delivery as our product and, for that, the leadership is key. At this stage of our development we need to become more systematic in moving and developing senior people. We have realised that it is time to benchmark ourselves against other businesses

of our size. We want to retain the entrepreneurial, risk taking culture that brought us so far, and combine that with systematic talent management processes that are needed for a business of our size. (Large services company)

It's our number one issue. The Group has good products and a good sense of processes but, so far, we have failed to systematically address talent management as an issue. We are in the market for scarce critical skills and unless we manage it systematically then it becomes a lottery. (Engineering company)

In talking about the importance of talent management, I also had a number of mixed reactions from my interviews that differentiated between what is stated to be important and what the behaviour of the organisation really points to. A number of respondents highlighted the fact that, while talking about talent management, their organisations did little of a systematic nature to assess, develop and manage the careers of high-potential executives. The following quotes illustrate this situation:

We, including the CEO, find it important but we don't really demonstrate it in our actions. We talk about it and have some activities in place but do not really do anything that is 'joined up'. This is because we keep saying that people should own their own development but we only tick boxes. Also, we are in a tough market and the energy goes into managing the numbers. Finally, we are an international business and every country's definition of this is different and we have never had a common function looking at this across the group. That is why we have just appointed a head of Global Talent Management, and we will see how that goes. The commitment must be there otherwise we would not have made the appointment but the proof will be in the action. (Financial services company)

It's critical because we are a highly structured, left brain type of organisation. So if you don't structure a systematic process then the senior executives don't grab the issue. So creativity comes gradually but we needed a systematic process to sell it internally, and that is what we developed. Interestingly, now that they have bought into the process, they are ready for more flexibility. (Financial services company)

Systematic is the differentiating word. I have only been here for ten months. Talent management has been seen as important and there are processes to deal with it. We have a competency model, which links into a 360° feedback model, which links into assessment of performance and also into potential. So we have various models and frameworks which we use but not in a joined-up way. But there is hope, because people are interested and see how they could be used. (International airlines)

It is of fundamental importance. But we have not done much – and you can't half tell! I have been here some 12 months and am making some headway – I have a plan but we have a long way to go. (Public utility)

A recent survey on the importance of talent management for UK organisations was conducted by the Chartered Institute of Personnel and Development (CIPD). In their 2005 annual survey, they introduced a section asking participants to describe attitudes relating to talent management. Over 630 organisations responded to the survey. 51% of respondents had undertaken some form of systematic talent management activities. The development of high-potential individuals and growth of senior managers were reported by two-thirds of respondents as the main objectives for their talent management activities. In-house development programmes, coaching and succession planning were also common activities. 94% of survey respondents believed that well-designed talent management activities can have a positive impact on an organisation's bottom line, and the vast majority of the sample organisations agreed talent management was a business priority for their organisation (87%). Figure 2.1 illustrates the main objectives of talent management activities.

A third source of information that in many ways started the focus on talent management is the original research conducted by McKinsey consultants and reported in the book (and the *Harvard*

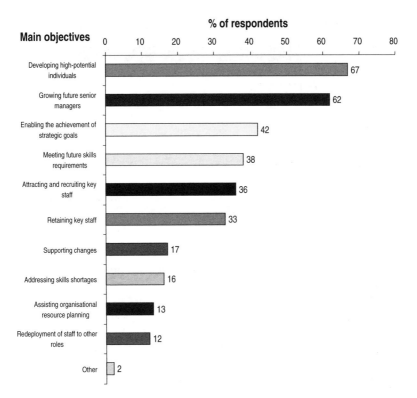

Figure 2.1   Main objectives of talent management.

Source: This material is taken from 'Reflections on talent management' by CiPD, 2006, with the permission of the Chartered Institute of Personnel and Development, London.

Business Review article of 2001) under the title *The War for Talent* (see Appendix 2). Their data from the USA showed how 13,000 senior managers perceive the way that their company manages talent.

As we can see from the data in Figure 2.2, only 19% of managers agreed that their company brings in highly talented people, only 3% agreed that their company develops people quickly and effectively, only 8% believed that their company retains almost all high performers, only 3% agreed that their company removes low performers, while only 16% reported that their company even knows who the high and low performers are. In their book *The*

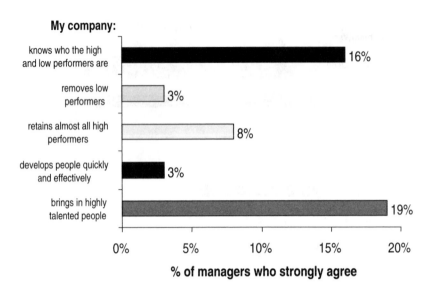

Figure 2.2   Most companies are poor at talent management.

Source: McKinsey & Company's *The War for Talent*, 1997 and 2000 surveys combined. Taken from 'Talent Management; A critical part of every leader's job.' (2001) *Ivey Business Journal*. Reproduced with permission.

War for Talent, the authors state that the main reasons that companies manage executive talent so poorly is that many leaders do not realise that the success of the talent-building process depends on what they do. The executives are those that make the hiring and firing decisions, they are the ones who create the culture of the organisation, they evaluate performance and they provide feedback and coaching support to the people who work for them. Even though it is the executives in the business that control the effectiveness of the talent management processes, in too many organisations, executives expressed a belief that building a talent pool and developing executives is the role of Human Resources and that people-handling issues are a distraction from what is really important in the business. In fact, when carrying out the research for their book, only 18% of respondents in the USA survey strongly agreed that senior executives view talent management as an important part of their jobs.

Another, more recent, report on the importance of talent management and talent development in the USA is by the Conference Board. In their December 2005 report, they state that a majority of companies in their survey want to accelerate the development of global talent. 77% of the 81 companies they surveyed in the USA report that they are seeking a variety of approaches to improve their global talent development. Providing feedback on performance and potential was cited by almost 50% of survey participants as being the most effective tactic in developing global talent. In general, they report that well managed businesses are more likely to accelerate global leadership development by giving global talent access to highly targeted development and, thereby, providing greater opportunities for global networking and using assignments to facilitate the breadth of talent development.

As we can see from the findings in my own in-depth interviews with Heads of Human Resources in large businesses and from survey results in the UK and the USA, organisations have become much more focused on the need to develop systematic talent management processes that will identify who are the best performers in their business, which executives have the potential for long-term career development, and how the business can facilitate this process of development.

The importance of talent management is due in large part to the reduction of the stability of senior executive teams. In the past it was common that once individuals became part of the senior executive team in large businesses their career was very stable and they could expect to stay in their position until retirement age. This situation is no longer true. In the USA and the UK, the life expectancy of senior executives has been going down steadily. Shareholders have become more assertive in their expectations and in the degree of pressure they exert when their expectations are not met. Table 2.1 shows the mean tenures of departing Chief Executives in various countries.

Table 2.1 Tougher at the top: mean tenures of departing CEOs (years)

	1998	2004
North America	10.2	8.8
Europe	7.2	5.6
Japan	6.9	6.1
Asia/Pacific	6.5	4.9
Global average	8.6	6.6

Source: Booz Allen Hamilton from 'Who's top of the pay pile?' by Andrew Saunders, featured in *Management Today*, September 2005, pp. 42–49. Reproduced with permission.

In their 2006 report, Booz Allen Hamilton report that:

Global CEO departures reached record levels for the second year in a row, and may be peaking, according to the fifth annual survey of CEO turnover at the world's 2,500 largest publicly traded corporations released today by Booz Allen Hamilton. Globally, 15.3% of chief executives at the world's 2,500 largest public companies left office in 2005, a 4.1% increase from 2004, and 70% higher than 10 years before. All regions experienced high turnover: Japan reached a record level of CEO turnover, at 19.8%, whereas the other three regions all recorded their second-highest turnover levels, with North America at 16.2%, followed by Europe, at 15.3%, and the rest of the Asia/Pacific region at 10.5%. One-third of global CEO successions were performance-related, defined as where the CEO was forced to resign because of either poor performance or disagreements with the board. In 2005, North America experienced a record level of performance-related turnover, with 35% of all its departing CEOs leaving involuntarily. Europe, at 42%, experienced near-record levels in performance-driven departures. Asia/Pacific followed with 28% of its CEOs leaving involuntarily; Japan's rate of forced turnover was 12%. From 1995 to 2005, the departure of underperformers quadrupled. As a result, only 51% of outgoing CEOs globally left office voluntarily, with successions resulting from mergers comprising the difference.

While we see differences between countries, there is a significant reduction in Chief Executive tenure during this 6-year period. Similar data from the UK point to the fact that the average period in office for FTSE 100 chief executives during 2005 was 4.7 years. That's according to the latest annual FTSE leadership survey from Cantos.

It is common today to expect Chief Executives in large businesses to remain in their post for fewer than 5 years and then be pushed out when company results are not in line with shareholder expectations. As a result, businesses have now started to treat the executive team in the same way that sports teams around the world are reviewed. The belief is that the success of the business is to a large degree impacted by the quality and performance of its executive team. When business performance is not in line with external expectations, the rapid response tends to be to replace the Chief Executive and/or a large number of the senior executive leadership, with the assumption that new people with different capabilities will be able to guide the business more effectively. As a result, while previously organisations talked about business concepts such as 'total quality', 'just-in-time', 'targeted marketing', etc., the discussion today is less around a new business formula or innovative approach that once implemented will improve the success of a business. Many organisations and shareholders believe that it is the quality of the leadership team that will determine the effectiveness of what the business will do. Moreover, there is a belief that different business environments and different phases of development of a business may require different kinds of leadership. It is important, therefore, to understand the relationship between the business strategy and the kind of leaders that would best lead the organisation towards making that strategy a reality. As a result, the importance of effective talent management activities has surfaced as one of the key tools in impacting the success of the business. Jack Welch, in describing his success in leading GE, has probably single-handedly provided a focus on the need for senior executives to devote a very large percentage of their time to put in place the right leaders for every part of the business, to continue to review the effectiveness of these people and to change them on a regular basis as required when they are perceived to lack the kind of leadership that the business needs.

The focus of this book is on what an organisation can and should do in order to understand and translate its strategic business requirements into a clearer definition of the kind of leadership that is required to guide the business forward. This clarity of purpose can then be translated into systematic talent management activities that will focus on assessing the effectiveness of current leadership, on identifying talent pools that can step in to provide the required leadership, on developing the underlying capabilities of the highest-potential executives within the business and on career management that will ensure that they are motivated and that their capability is best utilised by the business.

Most organisations in the USA and the UK are focused on the importance of talent management. As a reader, one of the first steps is to collect data about the importance of talent management in your business. To what degree are executives engaged in these kinds of activities or do they only leave this to the Human Resource function and participate reluctantly in what they perceive to be a bureaucratic process?

An interesting example of the information that is useful for understanding the current importance of talent management is a survey that I carried out for a large international business. They decided that in order to influence their Executive Board it would be useful to ask the 'consumers' of talent management activities to provide feedback about what they see as the key strengths and weaknesses of the current approach. Instead of quoting from *The War for Talent* and other general surveys, or providing recommendations by the Human Resource function, our clients felt that it would be more useful to interview the top 30 senior executives in their business (who report to the Executive Board) and to get their input about what is and is not working effectively in the talent management area. I interviewed these executives and summarised the results in a report that focused on the effectiveness of various approaches to development. At this point it would be relevant to quote what my interviewees said about the value and effectiveness of current talent development processes in their organisation.

Without exception, these 30 senior executives felt that it was very important for the organisation to review the executive talent that was available across the business and to use that information in order to develop talent effectively. Everyone, therefore, agreed that the process was essential for the long-term success of the business and that it was very good that the Company was committed to having it.

On the other hand, respondents felt that the current process was not as effective as it could be. From their experience, a great deal of time and attention was invested in talking about key people within their own business units and, as a result, the quality of the input to the process was good.

There was, however, a general consensus that very little concrete action resulted from all of these deliberations. Interviewees felt that the organisation did not have a proactive process for creating job opportunities for talented executives. Career opportunities resulted from a job opening because someone left and the decisions about nominations were done informally rather than as a result of a systematic process. This was especially true about cross-business-unit opportunities.

Moreover, respondents did not receive feedback from the talent management process and they felt, therefore, that they did not know what had been discussed. Some interviewees did get informal feedback from their manager but they felt that this was not necessarily reliable nor did it represent the 'official' view of the business. Most interviewees felt that they miss out on the opportunity to understand what they can realistically expect in career terms and how they can develop their capabilities to enable them to maximise future opportunities.

A number of interviewees talked about the fact that the organisation lost a few very talented senior executives and they felt that a more effective talent management process with direct, proactive feedback to individuals would be a useful tool to develop and retain executive talent.

The difficulty in implementing an effective talent management process may be related to the difficulty that executives experienced in having direct and sometimes difficult conversations with members of their teams. Many of the executives interviewed felt that they would appreciate an in-depth conversation and that, at this level of seniority, transparency was fundamental. This was especially true for effective executives. Some have raised the fact that it may be demotivating to tell less effective executives that they do not have a long career path ahead of them. But, if the organisation is not transparent and concrete in terms of future opportunities when dealing with high-potential executives, then they feel that they must go out and develop their career elsewhere.

The following quotes present a sample of what executives said in response to the question about the effectiveness of the 'Talent Development' process. Each quote is categorised by a (+) if it suggests a positive response to the question; a (−) if it suggests a negative response to the question; and a (?) for a mixed response.

1. What is the value of the Talent Development process for your business?

(+): It forces a discussion about the capability of the team and its weak spots and skill deficiencies and makes you confront hard choices about what needs to be done.

(+): It is very necessary. We have a talent shortage across the company despite the various mergers. So we need to spend time getting a shared understanding of the people and it is most important that we do something about the results and that is the area that is least developed. We need to give people development, help them to identify what they need to develop, and move them around.

(+): It is extremely valuable if executed properly. These conversations at the business unit level provide an open forum to talk about people and that is excellent if there are no personal agendas. We have to ensure that the tone of the debate is open so that we get actual quality data into the process. This process is one of the key enablers to build trust across the Company. People need to trust what they are getting. The high-level Talent Development needs to be backed up with the fact that businesses can free people to go to other parts of the organisation. This develops our future capability but we see large differences across the group where it is effective in some parts while handled politically in others.

(+): It forces me once a year to think about my people. Who are the key people and their development and succession? I would not do that without the Talent Development trigger.

(+): The Talent Development process has a value since it should give the organisation data about talent, career development, and focus on individuals who won't make it in the future.

(+): It is a good idea to create bench strength and ensure that it gets developed. We have been looking outside for a large number of jobs, which is because we don't have internal people who are ready.

(+): It became more valuable. It is only as good as the quality of the data and how well people know individuals. It is helpful in forcing a debate but it is more of a tool rather than outcome-orientated. The value is in creating the conversation and that has become much better.

(+): It is a valuable process and it is good that we have it. But it could be significantly enhanced. There is a tendency not to be transparent with the candidates. People want their leaders to be honest with them so the Talent Development could be greatly improved by more transparency and that means that we need to be slightly more robust. The discussions are highly valuable but we have to share with people where they are.

As a business we got progressively worse at developing people since we don't spend the money on that. Through the '90s we moved to a 'managing your own career' mode and I think that the company should be more active; otherwise we lose good people. We should also set targets for investing in people. This would be a truly positive message.

(+): It is critical because it makes us think about the people working for us and it levels our view across teams. The risk is that we move people around too much and lose our skill base.

(+): It is a really good idea when it works properly since you have facts and opinions about your best people and you can act on that by encouraging the best and pushing the worst ones out. I don't know how things work in the Company, but in my business unit I would give this 8 out of 10. In other business units they just move the deckchairs without involving real change so I assume that the Company process is not very effective. Their top team has not changed for years so why haven't they spread their team into the other businesses that are struggling? Are they protecting their 'flock' or is there no option to move good people to other businesses?

(+): It is a great process that does work well.

(?): We go through a Talent Development process once or twice a year. It is most important when we go through a restructuring but it is a mainly subjective process and opinion-based. Not clear that it really is used in making decisions about people.

(?): It is a uniform process of gathering data to assess people across the organisation and it uses a common language, which is positive. It is data for a useful discussion but it does not go beyond the data gathering; it is bureaucratic. We don't really think about what we need to do to develop people and what do we need to do in the recruitment market. Not enough intensity in the discussion. Talent Development at the top is not a real agenda. We don't invest in real people development. Also the process is federal; each silo does its own thing and the cross-business interaction is sterile. No Group level thinking and ownership of talent management issues. We can do it and we do it in some cases (like recent reorganisation) but we don't usually do it.

(?): It is an under-used process. It creates visibility and measures of individuals. I am involved in two Talent Development processes in my function across my business unit. This works well but the one for my function across the Company does not work well even though we use the same data. That is because there is no process to move people across business units. And that lack of process prevents Talent Development from being effective. There is a process within the business unit but not across units.

(?): Not very much. I had an open position but there were no good candidates identified internally despite the talent management process and that is especially true for international positions since we don't handle these assignments well.

(?): It is extremely valuable. It is the opportunity to evaluate your talent pool and assess when people are ready for a move, people at risk, and a framework for succession planning. But, it needs to be transparent and not a conversation behind closed doors. It needs to be seen to direct succession movement rather than just a conversation. It needs to be visibly seen as a form for execution, not just monitoring. Now most promotion decisions are made outside this process. We have done the hard part of having a Talent Development process and we have the Chief Executive interested. But now it needs to be seen to be operating well. More time needs to be devoted to it to make it more alive.

(?): It is a good discipline for us but is too over-engineered and too paper- and process-driven. Knowing the people and talking about them is key. Too much paper filing reduced effectiveness. But if you test the effort versus outcome, there is not much impact. Key people here have left since they were not clear about their future and no one did anything about it. Talent Development should be less paper and stronger commitment to implement the changes that are needed.

(?): It is valuable because it is better than not doing it, but it is flawed. It is not regular enough; the data collected is strange (too many numbers and letters) so no one knows what it means. It is too UK-centred and it is hard to get international businesses on the map. Finally, most of the job opportunities are filled outside of the Talent Development process, based on informal processes.

(?): It is at times extremely good. Works well where we are looking at an important role; gets people to focus on who is good and who is not, what is best for the company, and some parts of the organisation are willing to give up talent for the interest of the company. When we are doing a lot of changes, then the subjectivity of information does not help; people rate others very differently. We don't use bell curves or assess people objectively and we could do much more in this area; it is just too subjective.

(?): It is very effective. It is a continuous initiative each time when managers articulate who their 'stars' are, and how they are developing and their needs. My only concern is that we don't give feedback at the end of the process. Good at inputting in the process, less effective in terms of outputs.

(?): It is a good process. In the past we did not know who we had across the group and we did not plan for future changes. This process makes you think. I only do it for my team so I don't know how it works beyond that and what happens with my input.

(?): The important thing is the discussion on a small number of key people. It is an opportunity to exchange views on the top management of the company and that is key.

(?): The success of Talent Development depends on the reviewing group being familiar with the people being reviewed otherwise it is meaningless. We try to create situations that will enable the reviewers to get to know the people and when that is there then the process works well.

(?): It gets some consistency of perspectives on people since HR provides the norm and without that process we would have this information. But we spend a lot of time and I am not clear that it has real outcomes. No feedback mechanism around it and it disappears in space.

(?): The process is a great process since it forces managers to look at their people. Locally it is taken seriously and it is an opportunity for us to review local talent, highlight development, and discuss careers. Regarding the global process, I am not sure that it leads to real people outcomes.

(?): I don't know. I provide a report about the people who report to me but I have no understanding of the process after that. I don't know what happens with the information that I provide and I don't know the impact of the process. I don't feel that it is as important as the day-to-day informed process.

(?): It is all about the 'grandfathering' process, to ensure that we make the right decisions about people. We are not using this sufficiently for talented management. There are a few successes but not enough, given the talent in this organisation.

(?): At times it can feel bureaucratic but if you really identify high-potential people, then you have to develop them and similarly focus on the low performers. So it can be useful but only for the top and bottom 5%. Often though, the Talent Development review is not sufficient to move people across areas within the business.

(?): The principle is a good idea but it is not deployed effectively. It is important to understand the potential of our key people and what they may be able to achieve. This is important in decisions in recruitment, succession and development. In practice we don't use the information and don't have an overall plan of how to develop our talent.

2. What has been your personal experience as an individual who is reviewed in the Talent Development process? Did you receive any feedback?

(+): Yes. I don't see the forms that go in but I do get feedback following the discussion.

(−): None.

(−): Practically nothing and I don't trust it. Everyone gets positive feedback informally but it is not what really happens. We have an aversion to bad news and we think that people don't want the truth and we are afraid that they will leave us if we tell them the truth. Personally, I think that is wrong and that people at our level want to know where they stand.

(−): Nothing ever came back to me as a result of the Talent Development process.

(−): None. I assume that it happens but no one ever came back to say 'this is our view of you'.

(−): I have had no feedback at all on me and how I am perceived as part of the process.

(−): No. I never had any feedback telling me what was discussed at the Talent Development. I heard informally from people who should not have told me and that was nice but really not the right way to do it.

(−): No, never.

(−): No, I never received feedback. I have always been surprised at the lack of use of my skills within the organisation. I have been in my business unit for many years but have never been used beyond its boundaries. I joined since I thought that there are opportunities across the Group internationally. I have languages and cultural awareness but no one ever talks to me about why it never happens. And that attitude (very little movement between business units) has given us succession problems. I am doing very well here but why not use me in a broader context?

(−): It is mixed. Some of my managers have talked with me about how I am perceived but in general it is a secret process. I don't really know what is said about me. You should have a constructive discussion about this. At the moment, feedback is not systematic and holistic.

(−): I did not get any feedback.

(−): Not directly; informally and it feels that you need to read between the lines. Also feedback comes from various sources and not only from the Talent Development process.

(−): No one has ever spoken to me about it. I never got any feedback.

(−): I don't know what is going on with my Talent Development process. If anything it is very superficial feedback like 'you are a good man'. No one sat me down to say this is what you need to do to become a chief executive, since this is what I would like to get to. It is nothing systematic and I know that I am a 'good guy' but what else is there for me to do?

(−): Very limited. I have never had a conversation with my manager about Talent Development, only general conversations about what the organisation thinks about me, but even this is not a consistent and structured feedback.

(−): No, I have not received any feedback. We are not encouraged to talk about it.

(−): No, never at the Company level so I assume that they don't talk about me. At my business unit, I assume that they do talk about me in positive terms. If they did discuss me at the Company level, I think that my boss would try to kill it since he doesn't want to lose me, but I don't think that they do.

(−): No.

(?): Directly I have not received feedback. But indirectly. I probably know since it should be similar to the performance management process, where I do receive feedback.

(?): It is the quality of the conversation versus expectations. It is a very slow process and I did not have good quality, in-depth conversations about my future. I got very good general input. But as an organisation we are afraid of telling people how they are viewed in case things change. Afraid of an adult conversation since we need to be too sure. That is a shame since people are grown up and can understand that it is not a promise. But we don't help people like me by talking about what I can do in order to develop.

(?): I have received positive confirmation that I am a valued person, but not clear how my career expectations will happen. Everyone knows what I think but not clear that anything is happening. I am direct about these things – they listen to me and at the same time it may become overdue for action. We will see.

(?): Yes, I have had feedback and since my first 5 years here I have had several big moves. But for most people it is a black box. It has inspired me since my boss used the process very well.

(?): I have received feedback. I asked my manager and he has been good at doing that, much better than my previous boss. The process has structure in putting things in, but not structured in what comes out at the end of the process. It is done too ad hoc.

(?): I got no direct feedback in a formal way and that part of the process is not working well, even though I am happy on an informal basis. We need to establish better rules for this game.

(?): Not explicitly, but I have inferred some results when I had asked to go on the 'Leadership for the Future' course. And I was pleased since I inferred that something positive is being communicated.

(?): Yes, I did receive feedback. People were positive but I assume that if it were negative I would not have heard anything anyway.

(?): Yes and no. My manager was very good in giving me feedback about future directions and I got some of the flavour from the Talent Development conversation. So I got it but it was because I went and asked for feedback. There is no systematic process of feedback and discussion.

(?): Yes I did get feedback. My boss has been really good in giving feedback on how I am perceived but not necessarily because of Talent Development. So it is informal and has no formal transparency.

(?): Yes but I feel that we are not adult enough around feedback. People say nice things and don't mean it, or they make conclusions without talking about the reasons.

3. What is the impact, action that resulted from the Talent Development process? Did it relate to your personal development plans?

(+): Nothing in any formal way focusing on my development but there have been discussions about the next role that may be for me. It is an open, transparent and inclusive process for me so I don't feel that I am being pushed into positions that I am uncomfortable with.

(+): Yes, we have seen a number of internal appointments as a result of the Talent Development process.

(+): For me yes, a few years ago I made a move and the Talent Development process opened that opportunity.

(+): I assume that some of my career moves around the Company would have been linked to this.

(+): I could say that there was action that resulted from the Talent Development process but also probably because of my own visibility.

(+): Yes, I have been promoted.

(+): I did have a conversation and the Company gave me a free choice about my career and that is fantastic.

(−): No, never personally.

(−): Maybe I got my previous job as a result of a Talent Development process but they did not really need that process since they know me well so I did not see any action there.

(−): No.

(−): No, I don't know of any action that came from it.

(−): No since I don't hear anything specific from it.

(−): Nothing that I know of.

(−): Does not really relate to any of my development activities since they are more self-starting things rather than something that the organisation helped me with.

(−): I don't think that action resulted from this process. I have great support from the Executive but this has nothing to do with the Talent Development process.

(−): I don't know.

(−): I could not tell you if anything came from this process since I never received feedback but I have had many career development opportunities, so maybe.

(−): Not overtly but implicitly. I have been given more responsibilities and assume that it comes from that but I don't really know.

(−): Nothing ever changed for me until my boss changed and then the new person encouraged me and opened up new opportunities. This had nothing to do with a Talent Development process though.

(−): No, not that I am aware of. I have had a number of job changes that have helped my personal development but I don't see the cause and effect from the Talent Development process.

(−): Something somewhere must have been decided but I don't know what that is.

(−): I never received any feedback about development needs – either because there is no need for me to develop or because no one thinks about this with me systematically.

(−): No, I have not seen any action.

(?) Yes, for me it has certainly resulted in action, but I have been very fortunate and it is rather unusual from what I know about others.

(?): Over the last 9 years I had four different roles, each larger than the other so I assume that the organisation thinks about me. But it is not consistent or a structured feedback process.

(?): I don't know. My previous boss had a good opinion of me so I had no issues but now we will see.

(?): I was given a choice about what job I could have but I don't know if that was a result of the Talent Development process.

(?): I have been promoted a few times which is good. I have gone on various development programmes and all that is excellent. But I am missing the individualised engagement. I don't have a senior mentor outside my own business unit, just one example of fostering cross-business ownership of the talent pool.

4. Talent Development is the process that should involve discussions about your personal development, career and future roles in the organisation. Did someone have an in-depth discussion with you about these issues?

(+): Yes, I have had this. We talked about where I want to go and how realistic that is.

(+): Yes it has and my recent move was a result of those discussions.

(−): Nothing was ever communicated. There is no honest feedback on that. There is no openness or transparency on HR's work in this area.

(−): I am not present at the Talent Development meeting to know but I believe that it does that. But, the organisation does not have a succession plan that will describe what will be the shape of our future leadership. We are too reactive.

(−): You don't take part in your own Talent Development. You inform HR and your boss about what you want to do; but that is input and there is not any output. There is not a process where development recommendations follow the discussion. The Talent Development processes are one-sided since we don't have much movement of staff so usually others can't add to the discussion.

(−): It is done well prospectively. I have that discussion with my direct reports and my manager has that with me. But we are less strong about the Talent Development output and we need to focus on that.

(−): No, never.

(−): No, no one talks with me about this. Maybe since I am in this job only two years so it is not relevant.

(−): Very limited. No one has talked with me about my career with a Talent Development process leading on to the discussion.

(−): It is mixed. There has been a flurry of activity with various people leaving us recently. But in general there is an assumption that people know. I don't need a lot of pats on the back. A few more conversations with people who are not just my boss, maybe Group HR, would have helped though.

(−): No one has talked with me about it. No one has ever reviewed my strengths and weaknesses and organisational needs and career prospects with me. If you want that you have to initiate that yourself.

(−): I have had conversations about this and it led to my taking on my current role. My concern is that the organisation does not have a long-term discussion about where I could go to next and that opens me to approaches from the competition. I have no emotional attachment to the organisation since they have not used the Talent Development process to create that for the key people going forward. It is a lost opportunity.

(−): No, the Talent Development process for me has been about my evaluation of my team not about me and my future.

(−): I have not had this type of discussion as a result of the Talent Development process. There is no formal feedback about what others think of you.

(−): Not in a systematic way. Different bosses talk about this differently. My current boss is better, I don't feel in the dark but still, it is not really systematic.

(−): No one has ever discussed my career progression with me; nothing about what I wanted to do, could do or need to do.

(−): No.

(−): I don't believe this is embedded in the design. The Talent Development process is an entirely behind-the-scenes review and it may focus on development but does not demand a discussion with the individual.

(−): I had a conversation with my boss at the time when we restructured our executives here. A very good conversation but it took 18 months to happen and his views were different from those of others around here. So there was no systematic process that I could trust. That means that there is no agreed-upon consistent view, even though I got very positive messages from everyone.

(−): Managing Directors and Chief Executives are the worst to provide feedback so I have not had anything other than an appraisal. No one has sat with me in a systematic way to talk about my career and where I am going.

(−): I used to have that in my previous role but never with HR or with someone at the executive level; even though they know that I am at risk. Actions with no rewards speak louder than anything. And I am very disappointed about that since it tells me that they don't value me and don't care that I am at risk. Therefore, the Talent Development process seems to suggest that they don't care and that the process does not generate any action.

(−): Not consistently; it is a sort of 'hit and miss'. The organisation has been good to me but conversations really happen right before they are ready to move me. We don't do long-term career planning. It is not part of our culture since we don't plan with people and just assume that opportunities will happen.

(−): No.

(−): I have had these conversations but they came across as part of my performance appraisals rather than any Talent Development process feedback.

(?): There have never been in-depth discussions or meaningful inputs. It is nice to know that I am well regarded but what else is there that I could do?

(?): Not as an overt part of the Talent Development process. The subject may come up as part of annual appraisals but not formally. No one has ever asked me 'Would you want to work in country X?', or talked with me formally about future opportunities.

(?): Yes on an ongoing basis with my line managers. I have a good understanding of what senior people think of me. I don't know if there is a 'collective corporate view' and what it is. I know what I know but don't know what I don't know!

(?): Yes, absolutely. It happens regularly and I get much support and confidence, but this is due to my boss and his personal style. Those who run the Talent Development process in my business unit don't feel that they have the licence to be transparent with their team but they should be. The share options are also a problem since there is no transparency in that so it does more damage than it is worth.

5. What can we do to improve our Talent Development process?

(+): People need to be told if they are on a track and what kind of career path could be expected and then you would know if you have done something wrong and then you could do things to improve. That helps because you know where you are.

(+): The process works well for people who get a role but not for the others. What is my future path? What should I do now? A good organisation should be assertive in doing this with their high-potential people.

(+): Reengineering of it to be more effective as measured by real action that results from it. It is a dead, dutifully completed process. We need less bureaucracy and more proactive action — use the Talent Development process to be proactive to change things.

(+): We should do this more regularly; go through the output to see who are the good people, identify opportunities, and share likely vacancies. Create a forum where these things are discussed, maybe quarterly, and bring the international elements into it. This will transform the Talent Development process from an HR-driven process to a business-driven process. Also need to simplify the information that goes into it.

(+): We should have those uncomfortable conversations, ranking people and thereby getting more objective conversations to challenge why people have been rated. It takes time but the benefits will be enormous.

(+): Nothing more than what we discussed earlier.

(+): Some feedback would be great. I provide input on my team but have never seen anything happen to them as a result. This is similar for me.

(+): Framing my contribution into the group's requirements and then giving me feedback about where I am now and any future opportunities. Also input on what I need to do to develop. This is a fairly adult conversation to have but we should not sweep it under the carpet. It is important that I understand myself and have a realistic understanding of the company needs and that conversation does not happen today to me under the Talent Development process. The key motivation at this stage of my life is not money; it is about recognition and career opportunities, so the Talent Development process could be very important if done right.

(+): It is about using it more and being transparent about how we use it. Not a terrible situation since if you want something then you could get it. The perception is that it is more proactive and impactful than it really is.

(+): The crucial thing is that for the top 20–30 we should have someone at the Executive table that is a sponsor, and focuses on my career. That would create an emotional attachment and a trust that the organisation really values me and will demonstrate that.

(+): A candid feedback of the results and knowledge of the complete view would be helpful. I have selective feedback about what I do well and less well and it would be helpful to understand that more clearly. Obviously, no one can give me certainty about the future but I want to be confident that everything is said openly.

(+): More actions need to come out of it and a decision about how transparent we are going to be with our key executives; what is motivational and what is not. So it is a tough call but we have to be clear on what people need to work on.

(+): This sort of Talent Development process requires managerial skills and we are not sufficiently capable. Feeling embarrassed and not wanting to give bad news and discuss personal things. So we could work on that and improve this capability. And it gets worse as you get more senior. So it is the senior people who really need to learn how to do this.

(+): We should disconnect the Talent Development discussion for an individual from their line managers. The quality of input would be enhanced since the line manager has a bias depending on his needs. Then that external person could facilitate an objective career development discussion.

(+): There should be more openness and thinking about what this is telling us. I am sure that there are common themes if we look across – weaknesses in skill sets and specific development needs. It is an annual event not really embedded in management with a clearly communicated output about actions to follow.

(+): We should have feedback and it should be a transparent process.

(+): Events change and people change so we need to keep that in mind and the process needs to be more transparent and people must have better conversations that focus on what people need to do to develop. But we need to ensure that the feedback is not mechanistic.

(+): My boss should be supported by something more systematic; a facilitated process. Maybe a key person from HR or an external facilitator should sit on an annual basis with me and my manager and then support the development actions that come out of these meetings. We need an annual process with follow-up and proactive support not just waiting for me to ask.

(+): It needs a fundamental re-look. It is a very bureaucratic paper-based process, not dynamic and does not focus on a few key actions that we need to do. It is a process in a locked room without transparency and no agreed way to focus on action. We need openness, dynamism and need to focus on value and not paper-filling.

(+): A process is a process and it is about what we do with the data. We don't use the data to spot gaps and do something about that. It has become an HR-led process. So where does this sit in our business priority then?

(+): The current appraisal process is focused on current jobs. It is function-specific and the development discussion is vague. At the senior level it would help to say what I need to develop to be a true senior executive and focus on broader things like networking. It is OK not to promise specific future roles but it is important to say what I need to develop in order to be a Group level resource. And that could focus on the top 10–15 people, maybe with a common framework of what is required at Group level.

(+): Where do we do the needs analysis? There must be common needs at my level in the organisation. Somebody has to identify this and then design some input as a result. That is how we got 'Leadership for the Future' but that was a few years ago so we need to continue with that. I have been very fortunate since my development has been done through increased responsibilities. I have been stretched but not backed up with focused development. Now I need to understand more about Group issues, approaches, and thinking, which will increase my effectiveness in my business. Involvement in a rich debate around key strategic and financial issues would help me.

(+): It would be good to have someone independent from the Company to talk with me about where I am going and what I could do to support that.

(+): I would like to have some sort of senior person talk to the senior guys in each business and then work with them and move them around and help them to think of their development.

(+): It could be applied more consistently at senior levels; we still tend to go up through the silos and not cross-fertilising across the business. There is not a closed door now but it could be done more proactively.

(+): Less focus on the paperwork and more on real fact-based discussions on people. Greater pan-organisational involvement. The flow of people across business units is low compared to other major organisations. Our internal strategy is not clear and that prevents us from thinking about people. Some companies have an international cache of managers; where are we compared to that? Every one of our businesses is on their own. We don't develop people to be able to move around and each business unit holds on to its good people.

(−): Nothing more than what we discussed earlier.

(?): It is currently done in a black box. I don't share it with my people and no one shares it with me. If it was more open then people would know what to do but it would also introduce more risk. So it may be better not to say things. People get feedback through the performance appraisal process but not the Talent Development process.

(?): We need to take a step back and review how we want to develop talent and then put the process into that context. Who owns managers, how do we develop people, what do we do when a role becomes open? The Talent Development process will only work well if it is part of an overall talent development system. Even the current ratings are confusing, for example what do we mean by potential? So it is the basic stuff.

As you can see from these interviews, this senior group of executives in a large international business believes that systematic talent management processes are key for the success of the business. The current process, however, while being systematic, was, in their opinion, too bureaucratic and did not provide in-depth feedback to the individuals. It also did not provide systematic career management processes that enable the company to utilise their available talent in the most effective way.

A survey like this has a number of potential impacts. First, it enabled the Executive Board to understand what their direct reports felt about the opportunities that were provided to them. As a result, the company's Executive acted rapidly to create more effective talent management processes because they could see that those were required by their people as opposed to being a good idea put forward by their Human Resource function. Moreover, the in-depth interviews with senior executives in a company open the door to creating a more effective culture, where talent management and capability development activities were highlighted as important. This enabled the Human Resource function to implement a whole array of initiatives under the support of their clients, as opposed to trying to put forward interesting ideas and attempting to 'sell' them in terms of their potential impact on the bottom line.

As a reader who wants to implement or improve the existing talent management activities in your own organisation, the interview results present an effective approach for entering this topic. Instead of just talking to the senior team about what could have been done or what would be helpful to improve talent management activities, asking your entire senior executive team to provide feedback about their experience as 'consumers' provides data that is irrefutable.

The success of talent management activities depends on two components. First, the business needs to put together something that is systematic and that addresses the main blocks that prevent successful talent management from being implemented. In parallel, it is critical to ensure that senior executives and line management understand that the management of executive talent is a key component of their work. These expectations form a key part of a leader's task in day-to-day terms.

In determining the best way forward for developing more effective talent management processes in your organisation the most important perspective is to think of senior executives not as decision makers who have to decide about talent management activities for more junior people within the organisation. Realising that every executive as an individual is very focused on themselves and how their talent is being developed opens a new avenue for influencing the business. It is important to get individuals to talk about what they feel the organisation has done for them, in a systematic way, in order to help them to understand their own strengths and weaknesses. What has the organisation done for them in terms of providing a corporate view of possible career moves? How has the organisation helped them to understand what they need to do in order to improve their capability and, thereby, the likelihood of achieving the next move and becoming more influential in the overall context of the business?

In my experience, every individual wants to develop their own capability and senior executives are exceptionally motivated by career development. Many senior executives are in their 40s and 50s and they know that they are reaching critical junctions where either their careers would continue to progress as they had in the past, or they would reach a stumbling block and at best, will be stuck at their current levels or side-tracked as others continued to progress around them. Senior executives, therefore, tend to be very focused on what they can do in order to progress and these talent management processes are more important to them than short-term financial rewards. By engaging with a breadth of senior executives across the business and understanding what they as individuals want, you can create a collective vision of what needs to be done in order to create effective talent management processes that address the needs of the business and its senior executives. The chapters in the rest of this book will outline data from a variety of businesses in the USA and the UK in terms of what they have done to put together effective talent management processes. The more you get data from the senior executive 'consumers' in your business, the easier it will be for you to tailor what you do to develop talent management practices in your organisations and to make it effective within your business context.

CHAPTER 3

AN OVERVIEW OF TALENT MANAGEMENT PROCESSES

*T*his chapter provides a brief description of the main processes required for effective talent management. These will then be discussed in more detail in the rest of the book.

Most large organisations did not have systematic talent management processes until the last few years. Young graduates went to training programmes when they entered the business and then rotated to different parts of the organisation as their career developed. At various key junctions, such as moving from junior management to middle management or from middle management to senior management levels, individuals would go on a training programme which was believed to be the main input that they required in order to perform effectively at the next level.

Waves of reorganisations that took place in most large businesses during the 1980s and 1990s had a significant impact on the regularity of career development processes within organisations. Most of the career paths that were based on gradually enabling executives to climb the ladder in a systematic way had been torn apart. Cost-cutting initiatives were focused on taking out whole layers of management, thereby eliminating the organised career ladders within each part of the business. In addition, organisations started to become less patriarchal and thought that the main responsibility for development should be moved from the organisation to the individuals themselves. Managers were able to participate in development activities or to manage their own careers as they saw fit with the assumption that the best people would rise to the top as part of an internal free market of opportunities.

In the last few years we have seen a reversal of this trend. Large international businesses realised that this haphazard process, where an internal talent market was based on the activities of individual executives, resulted in the organisation not having the kind of executive capability that it required. When the business needed to grow and new areas had to be developed, recruiting managers found that they had to go outside the organisation in order to find the executives who were capable of leading this kind of growth. As a result, organisations such as IBM, GE, 3M, Johnson & Johnson, and other mostly American businesses started to develop systematic processes to review the executive talent that existed in the business and to make sure that the best executives were developed and promoted within the system. This US-led process gradually expanded to other countries. Today it is very common for most large businesses in Western countries to have a systematic talent management process that reviews the requirements for executive capability across the business, and discusses individuals and how they fit what the business needs in terms of its plans. While the systematic management of talent has, therefore, become much more of a high-priority item for company Boards, talent management processes in many organisations tend still to be very bureaucratic without necessarily having impact on business performance. Jack Welch is often quoted with reference to the processes that he used within GE and how senior executives in that business spent a very large proportion of their time devoted to identifying and developing talent. However, in most businesses, talent management processes are organised by the Human Resource function and the executive team do not focus on those in the same way that they focus on the use of capital or the development of new products and services.

TALENT MANAGEMENT PROCESSES

In most businesses, while there is a system where the senior executive team meets once or twice a year for a day to talk about talent, the information that is brought into those discussions is usually collected bottom-up. Managers within a business unit rate the capability of the people that work in their teams as part of the performance management process. In addition to rating current performance, managers also rate their direct reports on their potential, which is their ability to take on significantly larger jobs in the foreseeable future. People who are identified by their managers as high potential are described to the next level of management, thereby gradually going up to Divisional management and finally to the Executive of the company as a whole. In addition, the organisation tends to identify succession plans where all executive-level jobs in the first three or four management tiers will have successors identified for them. This usually includes names of two or three people who work below that level and the time frame by which these people are expected, by the current job occupiers, to be able to take over in case that person leaves.

The information about managers with high potential and successors to senior management jobs is presented annually to the company executive team and they try to identify areas where further development of talent is required and to talk about the implications of the findings. In most organisations, however, this data is collected bottom-up within organisational silos and, therefore, lists of successors and high-potential individuals are referred to only within those silos. There is not a systematic process that is used to identify talent across the business, to develop or to move people to enable them to gain a breadth of experience that is preparation for the next executive level.

In addition, while the data for talent management tends to focus on middle and upper-middle level managers and their capability to move up to executive levels, there is little attempt in most organisations to use the term talent management to review the capability of senior executives who are already in roles and are expected, in the immediate term, to contribute to the performance of the business. As a result, most of the talent management activities are long-term strategic efforts that focus on people who may provide a return for their development within the next 3 to 5 years. Development of senior executives in posts would have an immediate impact on performance but in many organisations executives in the top two or three tiers are perceived to be beyond the need for input and, therefore, there is little systematic effort to identify their strengths and development needs and to do something about that.

ASSESSMENT

A number of organisations have attempted to provide objective assessment of the capability of senior executives. This tends to happen when a new Chief Executive comes in, or when the organisation is trying to go through a culture change process and the assessment procedures are used to select the best people from the existing team in order to then augment them with significant executive talent from the outside. Few organisations invest systematic efforts to continue to evaluate and develop the capability of their senior executives, even though that population has a disproportionate impact on the performance of the business. As a result there is often the need to bring in senior talent at the top of the business from the outside since there is not sufficient certainty about the capability of the people who are below the senior executive team. Objective assessment is used today in many large organisations, but that is usually to identify the needs of middle or senior managers to move into the top two or three tiers of executives in the business. This assessment is usually based on efforts to identify the key competencies that are required for success within that business environment and then to provide input through 360° feedback from colleagues and/or through business psychologists who have external experience looking at talent. This assessment data is then used to provide feedback to the organisation and the individual in terms of what they need to do in order to improve their capability. The advantage of systematic assessment is that it enables the organisation to be clear about what it is looking for in terms of capability, and also individuals receive concrete feedback about their strengths and weaknesses which enables them to focus on key development areas. It is, therefore, useful to extend the use of objective assessment techniques to the senior executive population, thereby helping them to develop their capability. A broader discussion of systematic processes to assess potential is provided in Chapter 8.

CAREER DEVELOPMENT

It is still quite rare in most organisations today to have systematic processes for career development focused on executives who have potential (as identified through the assessment process). Most businesses do not have a map of possible career choices and, therefore, high–potential individuals are counted on to build their own network within the business and to identify what would be future jobs that they should be able to go for. When interviewing high–potential executives they say that there is a talent review process within the business and that they know that their names are being discussed. But the reality, or at least their perceived reality, is that real career decisions are made on the basis of individual contacts and that the most important thing is for them to network with the right decision makers so that career opportunities will be open to them. Moreover, most career progression decisions are still made within silos and, therefore, it is up to an individual's boss or boss's boss to spot the talent below them and to enable those individuals to progress rapidly. The problem with this model is that it is psychologically unrealistic to expect a manager to look at the people who report to them and to think that some of these people can replace them. If I have five or six direct reports it will be very hard for me to say that one or two of them can replace me immediately. It will be even more unrealistic for me to say that one or two of these people can actually progress above my level and become my boss within the next 2 or 3 years. As a result, this bottom-up system prevents rapid movement of people with high potential because they are limited by the horizons of their own managers. The main challenge for effective talent management is to open up silos and to create a relatively objective view across the business that will identify people with potential, provide them with objective assessment and then move them into positions of influence through judgements that are made centrally.

Finally, when thinking about talent management, one of the problems that we see in most large organisations is that when talented people move on to the next level within the business there is little systematic attempt to help them to develop the new capabilities that will be required for success. In many organisations there is an assumption that the competencies required for senior management are similar across the group and that most senior management positions in the top three or four layers require very much of the same competence profile. In reality, as jobs become more complex from a managerial point of view, individuals who perform well at one level need to perform in a very different way in order to be effective at the next executive level. However, without systematic input individuals tend to use the behaviours that were useful for them and contributed to their success at the previous level. A broader discussion of building career paths is provided in Chapter 9.

The next segment of this chapter will focus on five elements that are required for the development of effective talent management processes in large organisations. These include: jobs that have direct impacts on business performance; the development of talent pools with high-performance candidates who have the potential to take on significantly larger jobs in the near future and then using these pool candidates to feed succession planning; assisting high-potential executives to develop their capabilities in line with possible career paths; facilitating cross-business–unit familiarity with executive talent that can be used to reduce the impact of organisational silos; and finally building development processes that focus on exceptional performers who may not have the potential to progress significantly beyond their current positions.

CRITICAL JOBS

Our tendency is to think about talent as an individual attribute and therefore to think that talent management processes focus on individuals who have the largest amount of executive talent since we want to utilise them in the most effective way. However, it is usually more important to start the talent management processes by thinking about jobs. There are hundreds of job types within large organisations and talent management is a process that is designed to focus on key people that are in key positions. Therefore, the first part of any talent management process is to identify management positions which have a significant impact on business performance. Those positions would obviously include a majority of executive positions within the top tier. However, as you go down individual silos, you will find that there are a number of key positions that have a direct and immediate impact on the profitability of the business. These would include large store managers in retail organisations, large branch managers in banks, managers responsible for effective distribution in manufacturing, project managers in high-technology companies, etc. Any talent management process would have a significant impact on performance if it focused on those positions as opposed to focusing on other positions that are important for the ongoing running of the business, but do not have a direct and immediate impact.

Once we identify management positions with significant impact, we need to be clear about the competence that is required in order to occupy them effectively. Most businesses would have a competence framework but it would be helpful to ensure that it is relevant to these critical positions and in some cases we would need to adjust the framework to fit the different requirements for different positions. When we think of talent management we usually think of medium-term investment in people development that one day, if everything goes well, will bear fruit. However, one of the key issues in talent management is to identify the existing talent that is 'driving the ship' at the current moment. Therefore, the first task for talent management is to use the competence framework to assess the current incumbents that are occupying key executive positions with significant impact on business performance. That data can sometimes come directly from performance management information, but in many organisations that is not enough since managers are reluctant to give low performance ratings. Therefore, when you look at the distribution of ratings you will find that most of the people sitting in key management positions are rated high and there is no real differentiation.

We will talk about the systematic assessment of talent later on in this book but at this point, as a general introduction, it is sufficient to say that data about current incumbents has to either reflect a real differentiation in performance ratings through the performance management process, or there is a need to use more objective assessment processes that will really identify the strengths and development needs of people who are occupying critical positions and, therefore, have a direct impact on the performance of the business. The talent management committee meetings once or twice a year would be well used to start the discussion by looking at the current talent that is occupying key leadership positions within the business. This makes it possible for the Executive team to identify competence gaps and to discuss their implications in terms of business impact. Addressing competence gaps can sometimes be based on tailoring individual inputs to improve the capability of critical job holders. In other cases this may involve moving current job holders to less critical positions and moving those who have much stronger capability into more critical positions that have direct impact on business performance. Alternatively, it may be required to go outside if it is not possible to identify people who can fulfil these positions very well. Once again the key issue is that when focusing on critical positions, input on talent management will have an immediate impact on the performance of the business because it will ensure that the organisation has the kind of exceptional players that can lead it to the success that it requires. Finally, the focus of succession planning processes would best be used not as a hierarchical process where all senior executive positions have successors identified for them and therefore the process becomes just part of the annual bureaucracy. When succession is focused only on critical positions, everybody understands the implications of not having the right successors. A much broader pool of candidates can then be used to focus on a very small number of key executive positions that have a disproportionate impact on the performance of the business as a whole. A broader discussion of talent management in critical jobs is provided in Chapter 5.

TALENT POOLS

In the traditional succession planning processes, every executive job has a number of identified successors and there is an annual process of ensuring that these names are updated. The rate of change in most businesses today is so rapid that organisational structures change. As a result, a succession plan that was created a year or two ago for an existing structure would not really reflect the needs of the business as we move into next year. As a consequence, a number of organisations have changed from creating individual succession plans for all management positions to a combination of focusing on critical jobs and identifying talent pools. A talent pool is a group of individuals with a breadth of capability at a certain level, who are perceived to have what is required to move into a range of positions at the next level. There isn't a need to provide a specific succession plan since one individual can fit four or five alternative positions. Talent pools are designed to provide a flexible resource at a certain executive level that can be used to fill gaps that result from movement from the level above, from changes in business structures or from new business developments or acquisitions.

Most organisations would need to develop three different talent pools. The first would include candidates for those executives who will be on the company top team. These will usually be people who are in charge of large Divisions and the heads of functions. In most large businesses you can assume that there will be a pool of around one hundred candidates who could move to the most senior level of the organisation. Of this potential population, the organisation should be able to identify up to ten individuals (if they are lucky) who would have the potential to be candidates for the next executive level. The key is to ensure that these ten exceptional candidates from the top one hundred are developed to be able to take on board an array of possible positions at the next executive level, as opposed to creating a rigid individual succession plan that says which individual will take on which position. While sitting within the pool, each of these top ten individuals should be developed to ensure that they gain the breadth of expertise and develop their potential so that they will be ready to take on the required position when the time comes.

The second pool would include candidates for critical senior executive jobs (heads of smaller Divisions, business unit CEOs, functional heads within large Divisions etc.). We are now talking about a population that in large organisations will include the top five or six hundred individuals. Again, the idea is to identify around fifty people who will become a pool that could fill a broad array of second tier positions across the organisation, one level below the executive team. As with the first pool, second tier pool candidates need to be developed in order to have breadth of experience and well-rounded capability so that they can fit the requirements of a number of senior positions as opposed to the traditional way of looking at succession in terms of one individual for one possible future job.

The third pool is a more long-term investment. It would include middle managers who are perceived to have the potential within the next 5 to 10 years to get to the most senior executive ranks. While the population to feed this pool is exceptionally large and would involve a few thousand people, the pool itself should not include more than one hundred candidates. Those middle managers with exceptional potential should be the subject for exceptional development opportunities and career planning processes. If there were to be significantly more than one hundred people within this pool then the business would not have the resources to really focus on them, and they will just become names on spreadsheets.

In most organisations, pool nominations would still be based on a manager's submissions to the talent management committees as part of a process that tends to be attached to the annual performance management cycle. Individuals who are identified as having high potential then need to be discussed and reviewed by the next tier of management and to go through more systematic and in-depth assessment by the Human Resource people who will be driving the process. The key is to make sure that managers do not stop the progress that is available to their direct reports. Therefore, it may be ideal to create a distribution of nominations to ensure that only a small number of people are identified as having exceptionally high potential and that those people become the focus of attention.

The next process in the development of talent pools is to put in place an objective assessment of potential that will go beyond the input that is provided by an individual's manager or even the manager's manager. This assessment is usually done by external people who have the capability to understand what high potential looks like and to compare the executives in your business to those whom they see across a variety of other organisational settings. Usually the assessment of potential for the first and second talent pools is done individually where the executive spends a day with a business psychologist. The assessment of potential for the third pool tends to be done through assessment centres where individuals participate in relevant exercises and are observed by external assessors and senior executives from the business who will identify the requirements that are critical for success in their environment.

It is not enough to create talent pools: they have to be used in practice. The organisation has to ensure that all executives across business silos are familiar with all the individuals that are sitting in the various talent pools. This familiarity should be deep enough so that when there is an opening in a unit that is critical for business success, management will be willing to take a risk even though they have not worked with a specific internal candidate directly. This issue will be discussed in more depth in later chapters but it will suffice to say that every executive appointment has a risk associated with it and it is important to create systematic familiarisation processes between pool candidates and recruiting executives at the levels above so that the risks associated with internal recruitment will become significantly lower than the risks associated with external recruitment at senior executive levels. A broader discussion of managing succession is provided in Chapter 6.

DEVELOPING HIGH-POTENTIAL EXECUTIVES

Once we have executives in various talent pools we need to develop their potential based on the objective assessment of strengths and weaknesses against the requirements for a certain position in the next step up the managerial hierarchy. I will talk about development in more depth in Chapter 10, but for this overview of the process, it is sufficient to say that individuals and the organisation need to 'own' potential career paths and the development requirements that are associated with them. The Human Resources function should have a clear definition of what the available career paths are and then help high-potential executives to understand where they can go and what they need to be able to do to progress in those alternative directions. As a result of 'owning' the career plans, the individual will be able to begin to form a map of what they need to do in order to develop the capability required in the future. Coaching, mentoring and participating in Group-wide strategic forums tend to be the best ways of developing senior-level executives. This will be discussed in more detail in Chapter 10 but the focus here is around individual tailoring. Just as career paths need to be related to the individual and their own capabilities and desires, input also needs to be provided in a way that enables them to choose the input that they will find useful and that would help them to develop in the direction that they would like to. Management development in a talent management context is not the same as the general development processes that the organisation will be using with all of its management populations. Development is a good and useful input for everyone, since everyone in an organisation has certain talents and it is useful for the individual and the organisation to develop these talents. However, as we have discussed in Chapter 1, talent management processes focus on a small number of individuals and on key positions in order to ensure that the best people fill the most critical positions and, therefore, provide the leadership that enables the business to move forward effectively. As a result, it is important that a disproportionate amount of development activities are focused on a small number of high-potential executives and that these individuals are 'fed through' a career management process into critical jobs in order to ensure that they have a disproportionate impact on the success of the business.

BREAKING DOWN SILOS

Every large organisation is characterised by silos, which typically include business Divisions or functional units within the overall structure. In some cultures, there is a fundamental belief that each part of the business should be left autonomous and the business, from an integration point of view, only acts as a financial catalyst that enables each part of the business to perform as its leadership sees fit. In other words, there is a much more integrated perception of capability. In other organisations, different divisions are expected to work closely together and there are strong functional units at the centre which exert a great deal of influence in terms of Marketing, Finance, Human Resources, IT, Research & Development, etc. across the business as a whole. Even highly integrated organisations, however, tend to have strong business unit and/or functional silos that prevent the best use of executive talent across the organisation. People are recruited into one part of the business and their careers tend to be managed within that part until they rise to the top (if they have the right potential, motivation and luck) of that silo. It is rare to see individuals recruited into one part of the organisation who then move into other parts on a regular basis so that by the time they reach the top they have covered most of the different parts of the broad business. Silos prevent the best use of executive talent because they restrict career paths. Individuals are promoted since they are best within their silo as opposed to being the best across the whole business. In addition, if most of the career progression is managed within the silo then, when an individual is ambitious and has the potential to move up and they look at their career path, they see a very restricted future because, unless their boss dies or one or two other people decide to leave the organisation, there will be no prospect for progression in the next 3 to 5 years. In these cases, highly motivated and talented individuals will look outside because they will see a very broad array of opportunities externally, while internally there are only restricted ones. Career paths should, therefore, be mapped within a talent management process across business units. As a result, individuals will see a whole array of opportunities that go across the business and will not be restricted to their own silo. A broader description of what can be done to break down silos is provided in Chapter 11.

EXCEPTIONAL PERFORMERS

The final section in this high-level overview chapter relates to 'exceptional performers'. Everything I have outlined so far under the talent management heading has related to a small number of key individuals who have the potential to move up the managerial hierarchy. There are many other people within the organisation who are extremely capable and by focusing on a small pool of high-potential individuals we do not want to lose exceptional performers who are also critical to the success of the business. Exceptional performers may not have the potential to take on significantly larger jobs but they do contribute and have the capability to add significantly to current performance. Their motivation and development is also key to ensuring business success. Just as an organisation is systematic in its talent management efforts focusing on key jobs and individuals with high potential, it is also important to be systematic in identifying and developing exceptional performers. But this does not include everyone. The 90% that were not identified as having high potential include another 15–20% who can be identified as exceptional performers who do not, however, have the long-term potential to progress to significantly larger jobs. These are still not the general, average population but, rather, another key group to focus on. Exceptional performers should be identified through the performance management process and while in this case there is not necessarily a need for an external objective assessment, their names should be validated through the talent management processes. Each part of the organisation, Divisions and Functions, should identify their exceptional performers. Executives at the next level need to understand who these key contributors are today and what the organisation needs to do to keep them motivated and developed. The talent management process should also identify the needs of exceptional performers in terms of what they require in order to become even more effective in their current jobs. In talking with exceptional performers, it is clear that many of them would like to expand their responsibility, become experts within their own speciality area and be recognised beyond their individual business unit. Enabling people to contribute in a breadth of areas while keeping their current position would motivate them, help them to increase the depth of their expertise and become even stronger exceptional performers. From a motivational point of view, competence development provides people with recognition. They will feel that the organisation develops them and they will want to continue to invest in it. A broader description of what can be done with exceptional performers is provided in Chapter 15.

SUMMARY

Chapter 2 provided an overview of what is involved in the systematic management of executive talent. This overview should give you, the reader, a perspective of what will be discussed in much more depth throughout this book. Should it be required, Appendix 3 at the back of the book has a PowerPoint presentation that outlines the main ideas that have been described in this overview chapter. It can be used to discuss the issues with your team or to present them to key decision makers. In summary, talent management and succession planning processes should focus on key jobs and key individuals. These are jobs and individuals that are critical in ensuring that the business is profitable in the short- and medium-term that have the potential to contribute to the long-term success of the business. I have also talked about the need for objective assessment in order to ensure that the judgement about individual potential is unbiased by the perspective of a person's direct line manager. It is important to provide objective assessment of the people who occupy key positions and to use that to help them to become more effective or to enable others who are more capable to step in and take on key responsibilities across the business. I also talked about the fact that the assessment of potential should focus always on the differences in demands between the individual's current job and future managerial requirements. As jobs become more complex it is important that the individual does not carry on doing what made them effective at the previous level. Understanding the hierarchy of management positions will enable effective career path management across the business and will provide the basis to reduce the impact of business silos and, thereby, increase the probability of managing talent across the business in the most effective way. I have also discussed the idea of creating talent pools instead of doing a bureaucratic succession planning process. Talent pools with high-potential managers at different levels will enable a much more flexible approach to internal resourcing and will develop people with a breadth of capability that can be placed into a broad array of positions at the next level. Finally, I talked about the fact that it is important to not only focus on key jobs and key high-potential individuals, but also to be systematic in managing exceptional performers and ensuring that their capability that is currently available in the business is maintained and highly motivated in terms of ongoing requirements.

CHAPTER 4

USING STRATEGIC BUSINESS OBJECTIVES TO DRIVE TALENT MANAGEMENT EFFORTS

*I*n my interviews, I asked Heads of Human Resources what they saw as the objectives of their talent management efforts. Instead of comparing a variety of different lists, it would be more useful to look at the complete set of talent management objectives that I have put together from those provided by each of my interviewees:

■ Develop top teams that are the best in the competitive environment.

■ Find successors for key executive jobs, who are at least as competent as current job holders, and ready to step in.

■ Enable cross-fertilisation of executives from different functional, geographical and business backgrounds to foster innovation and best utilise existing internal resources.

■ Develop real and perceived career opportunities that retain and draw in the best executives.

- Build a culture that pushes our best executives to perform at the edge of their potential.
- Ensure opportunities for the most talented employees to rise rapidly from the bottom to the top of the organisation.
- Promote a diversity of executives (gender, ethnic background and age) in key jobs, reflecting customer/client characteristics and a broad talent pool.
- Establish processes for the assessment of potential that go beyond the limited perspective of an individual's manager.
- Build line management ownership of the need to have the best players (versus 'OK' ones), to open unlimited opportunities to exceptional people (versus forcing them to follow the normal path) and to develop individuals for the corporate good (versus hiding them within their own business or functional units).

In looking at this wide range of objectives for talent management efforts, the key is to try to understand how talent management fits within the overall efforts of Human Resource functions and businesses to improve their business performance. It is interesting in this context to quote from *The War for Talent*, which states that only 18% of the corporate officers that they surveyed in the USA, through the McKinsey survey, agreed to the statement, 'Our annual talent review process has the same intensity and importance as the budget process'.

The starting point for any talent management effort is for the top executive team to discuss the importance that the business attributes to having an especially effective management cadre within their business. This sounds like a trivial question since obviously it is useful to have high-quality executives leading the business. However, in reality, most businesses are relatively happy with 'OK' people. There is an expectation of a normal distribution so that some of our executives will be exceptionally capable, others will be 'OK', and some will be 'not great'. However, it is only in exceptional cases that businesses do something about this distribution. One of the most famous cases is the GE model that has been described at length by Jack Welch in his book *Jack: Straight from the Gut*.

GE's all about finding and building great people, no matter where they come from. I'm over the top on lots of issues, but none comes as close to the passion I have for making people GE's core competency. In this case, while it may seem contradictory, the system plays a very important role in making it all happen. For a guy who hates bureaucracy and rails against it, the rigor of our people system is what brings this whole thing to life. In a company with over 300,000 employees and 4,000 senior managers, we need more than just touchy-feely good intentions. There has to be a structure and logic so that every employee knows the rules of the game. The heart of this process is the human resource cycle: the April full-day Session C, held at every major business location; the July two-hour videoconference Session C follow-up; and the November Session C-IIs, which confirm and finalize the actions committed in April.

We build great people, who then build great products and services. While we have a system, with its binders and clear-cut agendas, it is by no means static.

No matter what we put in our books – and we put everything in them – it's not simply the binders that count. What counts is the passion and intensity everyone brings to the table. When managers put their necks on the line for their direct reports, you learn as much about them as the people you're discussing. Sometimes we can debate for an hour over one page. Why are these sessions so intense? One word: differentiations. In manufacturing, we try to stamp out variance. With people, variance is everything. Differentiation isn't easy. Finding a way to differentiate people across a large company has been one of the hardest things to do.

In the GE business environment they considered the quality of their executives was one of the key levers that would determine business performance. Therefore, as part of their annual talent reviews those executives rated at the bottom percentage of the distribution in terms of performance were asked to leave the business in order to open up places to bring in new talent and to gradually bring up the standard of leadership provided across the business. This is a harsh model and few businesses have the resolve, tenacity or belief that this approach will actually improve their performance. A number of large consulting businesses also have an 'up or out' philosophy since they assume that the quality of the consultants that they provide to their clients has to be exceptional. Individuals who cannot demonstrate especially effective performance would be asked to leave in order to open up opportunities for 'fresh blood'.

This 'survival of the fittest' approach to leadership is not perceived by many businesses to be the kind of culture that they would like to create internally. As a result, in most businesses, when you look at the distribution of annual performance appraisal ratings across the entire management group you will discover that on a range of performance ratings from one (low) to five (exceptionally high) the vast majority of executives will be rated at the top two categories. Accepting this lack of differentiation suggests that the top team is happy with the quality of executives that they have, that these people are the best that they could expect and that they feel no need to differentiate between exceptional and average performers within their business environment.

Some organisations have implemented what is called a forced distribution in performance appraisal ratings in order to ensure that managers use the entire range of performance ratings. Thereby, they create a distribution and differentiate between exceptional executives in their team and those who are just average (even if they feel that the average people within their team are good enough). Discussions around the need to create differentiation and, in the extreme, the need to weed out people who are less able, in order to free space for people who may prove to be exceptionally capable, are all part of a philosophical debate within the top leadership team of the business about the importance of leadership. In this context, sport analogies are interesting in their philosophical underpinnings. When looking at sports teams in football, basketball, cricket or baseball, it is unthinkable that the club will not see a direct relationship between the effectiveness of its players and the quality of the outcomes and between the effectiveness of the outcome and the profitability of the club. As a result, clubs spend a great deal of time and effort comparing their existing players to alternative players who are in the market. Sports clubs use their resources to continuously upgrade the quality of the players whom they have because they understand that any step improvement in the quality of their players will have a significant impact on the performance of the sports club as a whole. In business, many senior executives tend to cloud this causal relationship. While there is a great deal of pressure on organisations to focus on annual growth and achieve business results that are better than their competitors, when this gets translated into a comparison between the leadership teams that exist in one business and those of the competition, the discussion rarely comes up at Board level. This is due, in part, to the fact that while there is a general belief that leadership is important, the quality of systematic effort to describe the kind of leadership that is required, to measure the leadership that exists in the business and to be active in improving the quality of leadership is a much less systematic process within businesses than it is in a sports environment. Some of that may be due to the difficulty of measurement, but a lot of it is due to the fact that we have only recently translated external competitive pressures to direct pressures on individuals that lead large corporations. Until recently, senior executives and Chief Executives of large businesses could expect to spend their entire career in a single business. When they reached the top two or three layers in large corporations they would expect to have the luxury of remaining in their positions until they were ready to retire. This is no longer the case. The average tenure of a Chief Executive in some of the largest corporations tends to be less than 5 years. When a Chief Executive is forced to leave because the shareholders are no longer happy with the growth in business results, a new Chief Executive tends to replace the majority of the people in the top team and that process starts to cascade down the organisation. Therefore, in most large businesses in the USA and the UK, management teams go through rapid change processes and senior executives are well aware that their life-expectancy within a single business has shortened dramatically. If everything goes well then they will expect to move from one business to another on a regular basis, assuming that their marketability will be maintained. This direct attribution of the relationship between business results and individual executive performance is quite new. On the other hand, understanding the implications of this direct impact and translating it into the need to do much more systematic and hard-nosed thinking about the quality of the team that leads a business is only in its initial phases. Talent management processes exist in almost all large businesses in the USA and the UK, but for many of them these are annual events that are somewhat bureaucratic and are based on reviewing long lists of names and discussing succession maps that do not really challenge the capability and performance of individuals and do not result in rapid impact (positive or nega- tive) on the careers of individuals in the top two or three layers of the business.

In deciding, therefore, on the key business objectives that should drive talent management efforts, it is important for the senior team to start with a philosophical discussion about the importance of having the best players in the management cadre. Are they committed to invest serious efforts in ensuring that sys- tematic, transparent and hard-nosed decisions are reached in order to ensure that the best players exist at every level of senior man- agement teams and that 'fresh blood' is available across the business to replace people who may be 'OK' but are not good enough in respect of the performance standard the business sets for itself? This discussion has to start with the strategic positioning of the business vis à vis its competitors and the importance that a continuous, aggressive, growth strategy has to the growth prospects of the business and, thereby, the survival of the senior executive team. In many cases, senior executives hesitate to have this frank discussion even amongst themselves, because it is easier to deal with the day-to-day and not deal with the threatening question of 'What is our probability of remaining in the driving seat of this business for the foreseeable future unless we make some hard-nosed decisions?'

Talent management efforts, therefore, have to start with a definition of a talent standard:

- What level of capability do you expect from executives who lead your business and where would that be in comparison to your main competitors?
- How important is it for you to continuously scan the environment internally in terms of managers in more junior positions who have the potential to rise rapidly?
- Externally, which executives who work for your competitors could provide you with a significant boost to your team's capability?

This initial, somewhat philosophical discussion will provide the foundation to begin to set up a process of measurement that will enable the business to start to quantify where people are in terms of their strengths and weaknesses. This will provide individual executives with frank feedback about their strengths and development needs and focus the business on ensuring their rapid improvement or on freeing their positions for other executives who have the capability to make things happen. Defining a talent standard in visionary terms makes it possible to specify a set of leadership competencies that the business considers to be fundamental to success in its competitive environment.

Most large businesses define what they consider to be leadership competencies that are required for success. Appendix 1 includes a number of samples from very different business sectors that illustrate the competencies that organisations find useful in this area. The key is to ensure that management across the business shares a language that defines what we mean by the sub-components of leadership. When we say that one manager is performing well and another manager is performing less well, we usually talk in terms of their achievement of business objectives. But when we want to understand why that person is performing or not performing we need a language to explain their profile of achievement. No one is excellent in all aspects of management and when we need to compare two executives we want to compare them across the range of managerial competencies required for the job. In my experience, a number of common factors form the basis of most competence frameworks across many different business settings. The main factors that seem to appear include:

- The ability to have a vision and long-term strategy.
- The ability to manage operations effectively.
- The ability to lead a team.
- The ability to co-operate with others and create effective partnerships.
- The ability to initiate and manage change and innovation.
- The ability to focus on customers/clients and their needs.

In defining the objectives of a talent management effort, we need to use competence language as a foundation to create a common core that will enable us to look at who are the most capable people in the organisation.

Businesses have a hierarchy of managerial positions and while competence domains such as those described above may be common at every level, the specific behaviours that define success and failure at each level would be very different. Having a vision and strategy for the manager of a sub-business unit is a key requirement. But it is very different from having a vision and strategy for the organisation as a whole or from having a vision and strategy for a diverse business conglomerate that includes a number of different companies within it. Therefore, in order to understand talent management, we need to have a concept of job levels and competence requirements that differentiate each one of these levels.

The competence definition by levels is the foundation for the 'normal' performance management processes that are carried out in every organisation. However, when we are thinking of talent and individuals who have the capability to progress to significantly more senior positions, then we need to focus on potential and not only on performance in the current job. Therefore, most organisations create a two-dimensional grid where managers are asked to rate both the performance of the individual and their potential to take on significantly larger jobs. This creates a 3 × 3 table (Figure 4.1) where a manager can plot those individuals who are high in

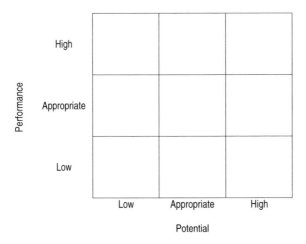

Figure 4.1   Two-dimensional performance–potential grid.

performance and high in potential, those who are low in performance and low in potential and all other permutations. Asking managers to rate potential is usually done in a relatively undefined fashion using the type of rating scale shown in Figure 4.2.

The problem with understanding what is required for a person to make one- or two-step increases in their jobs goes back to the identification of the competence levels and how these are specifically different when one proceeds from one level of management to another. Therefore, it is important that managers understand that when they are judging potential they need to know what the requirements for the next level of jobs are. This requirement will be discussed in much more depth as part of Chapter 8 where I present key managerial transitions and how they require different competencies from the executives that go through them.

Everything that we have seen so far tends to be similar from one organisation to the next. As we saw, most competency frame-

Rating of executive potential for input into the bi-annual talent review	
GREEN – READY NOW	Ready for a move, if available, within the next 6 months. All competencies demonstrated. Evidence of core and development skills provided with next level skills starting to develop. Will have a high performance rating. The jobholder is unlikely to have been in role for fewer than 24 months. Appropriate move specified in commentary.
BLUE – READY WITHIN 12–18 MONTHS	All role competencies demonstrated and some evidence of development skills provided. Anticipated to be ready for a move in 12 to 18 months' time. Potential next move specified in commentary.
YELLOW – CONTINUOUSLY DEVELOPING WITHIN ROLE	Evidence of core skills and role competencies provided. Continue to develop in current role. Future aspirations captured. Typically 80% of population will be here.
RED – OPPORTUNITY POSITION	Core role skills and competencies are not demonstrated. Not suited for current position or performance. Issues to be addressed.
WHITE – NEW POSITION	New to position; too early to tell. Less than 3 months' service.

Figure 4.2   An executive potential rating scale.

works, while they may be based on feedback that is solicited from senior executives in a specific business environment, tend to come up with very similar competence domains and quite similar behaviours under each of those domains. In effect, when we ask senior executives what is required to be an effective leader in a business they come up with a common framework, which is driven by a generalised vision of management or leadership as opposed to by the specific business circumstances in which their organisation is operating. However, if we want to create a truly effective talent management process, it is critical that the criteria that are used to review talent are not based on generic management competencies and on generic ratings of potential by line managers. We need something that is directly linked to the business strategy and that is, thereby, intended to provide true competitive advantage for this business within its own competitive business environment.

As a result, it is important not only to use a generic list of competencies by levels as we have seen above, but to review this list in light of the strategy of a specific business. For example, in some businesses, future growth is associated strategically with opening up international expansion opportunities. If that is one of the key components of the long-term business strategy then individuals with high potential will have to be able to operate in a multicultural environment not only in terms of managing significant business units in cultures different from that in which they grew up, but also in terms of interacting with executives and clients from other business environments and understanding the impact of cultural and business practice differences across international boundaries. This strategic requirement can be translated, therefore, directly into a talent requirement that should be used to select individuals who have the talent that will be required for long-term progress in the business. Such a strategic focus brings us back to the initial discussions in the introductory chapter regarding the difference between talent management and general management development efforts that are implemented in different organisations. It is important to develop the capabilities of managers across the business and enable them to build on their strengths, reduce the negative impact of their weaknesses and thereby improve their contribution to the business. That is what we call 'learning and development'. However, as mentioned earlier, talent management practices are designed to focus on a small minority of managers in your business. The idea is to look at maybe 10% of the most capable people and to invest disproportionately in their development. That does not mean that you will not continue to invest in everyone else and their capability as a way of upgrading the competence levels of all of the managers in your business and, for that matter, of all of its employees. What the talent management models are saying is that in addition to the overall investment in people, we need to invest disproportionately in those people who have the potential to have a disproportionate impact on the performance of the business. Therefore, to go back to the business strategy, when we talk about the 10% most highly capable individuals at each level of management, it is critical that we select that 10%, but not just in terms of their capability to function with today's competency requirements in today's business environment. They also need to have the potential to lead in a strategically impactful way. Therefore, it is not sufficient to select highly talented people by asking managers who has the best potential to rise to the next level. We need to be more focused and ask what the business strategy is and how that will drive future performance requirements. For example, retail financial services in the last few years have become much closer to general retailers. As a result, the key strategic development for retail insurance businesses and retail banks has been to expand their marketing initiatives, in terms of product development and of marketing based on consumer segmentation, and to introduce a much more fast-moving, creative, diverse and assertive process for handling their relationship with various subgroups of clients. One of the key strategic planks for one of my insurance clients has become, therefore, to continue to develop its capabilities as a fast-moving and creative retailer of diversified insurance products, as opposed to seeing itself as a product-driven insurance company that is only focused on risk and product development from an internal technical perspective. This strategy has many implications for the kind of senior executives that will now, and definitely in the future, be required to lead this business. Just as we stated earlier when we talked about international expansion, also here, the most talented 10% of managers at different levels in this business need to be identified in terms of the degree that they possess this ability to be creative, to take on a very dominant consumer perspective, to have the flexibility and fast-moving decision-making processes that characterise successful retailers. In terms of external recruitment, this talent strategy means that my client is bringing in marketers from the retail sector and teaching them what is required to be an executive within an insurance company (instead of trying to turn actuaries into FMCG marketers). Similarly, in terms of developing their own internal talent, the focus has changed towards people who have these strategic capabilities that characterise effective leaders in a retail environment. What we see, therefore, is that it is not enough to define competencies and management levels and to ask managers to rate the performance and potential of the people who work for them, thereby identifying the top 10% of executives at each management level. It is critical to work with the senior executive team in your business to translate their medium-term business strategy into three or four key capabilities that will characterise exceptional executives in the medium term as the business strategy unfolds. That strategic definition then gets translated into each competence domain and, thereby, enables you to create key behaviours/characteristics that are fundamental for the selection of the top talent in the organisation.

EXAMPLE OF THE OUTPUT FROM INTERVIEWS WITH SENIOR EXECUTIVES (Business Requirements and the Characteristics of High-Potential Executives)				
Strategic Dimension	Global accounts/bids with global relationships and implementation	Process improvement to take out costs and improve margins	Service quality with customer and employee focus	
Experience in managing depth of business accountability	• Projects with budget of £X million • Multi-location projects without direct day-to-day managerial contact	• Budgets of £Y million reduced by Z% – to demonstrate ability to lead efficiency drives	• Managing X employees in client positions	
Professional experience	• Financial analysis to understand long-term cost and profitability implications • Multi-location contract negotiations	• Significant cost-reduction exercises	• Measuring customer satisfaction • Measuring employee satisfaction	
Personal work exposure	• Working in different countries with different work cultures			
Personal capabilities and characteristics	• Financial acumen • Building long-term client relationships • Cultural sensitivity	• Financial acumen • Willingness to confront difficult situations	• Customer orientation • Team leadership	

KEY ACTIONS

1. Interview senior executives to assess strategic initiatives required to enable future growth.
2. Translate each of these requirements in terms of implications for talent development. What level of business do they need to manage, what specific professional accountability do they need to have, what should they be exposed to work-wise, and what personal characteristics and capabilities do they need?
3. Focus the discussion on individuals, not jobs. What experiences are required to enrich their capability? This will create bench talent that is ready to take on a breadth of jobs across the business.
4. Define a career ladder. Identify key positions across the business that can provide the required levels of accountability and experience. Use these key jobs to build the capability of high-potential executives, leading them rapidly to the top bench (assuming success in each step of this experience 'ladder').

Figure 4.3   Strategic business needs and required leadership characteristics.

SUMMARY

In this chapter we have seen that businesses differ in terms of the importance that they attribute to having the most capable leadership cadre to drive the business forward and the degree to which they understand that by having a strong team at each management level when compared to their competitors, the business will be able to propel itself forward and maintain or expand its leadership position. We have also seen that the business environment has changed dramatically. As a result, there is regular turnover in senior executive teams as more assertive shareholders expect to see significant changes in leadership when businesses do not perform according to market expectations. This shift in the degree of pressure on the senior team to perform at exceptional levels has, in a number of large and successful businesses, translated itself into having more systematic and 'assertive' talent management practices. Instead of having bureaucratic HR-driven policies that identify successors and focus on business school based training programmes, organisations have shifted gear and are taking a much tougher look at the quality of executives that they have at each level in the business and ensuring that their leadership teams are the best in the marketplace. In order to drive effective talent management practices the organisation needs to be clear about the profile of leadership capabilities that are required to be a member of the most talented team within their business environment. While most businesses ask for managers to rate potential in very general terms, we have seen that it is important to understand potential in terms of the differing requirements from one management level to the next. The main focus of this chapter has been on the relationship between business strategy and talent. The more the business is clear about its own strategy and how it expects to gain and maintain competitive advantage in the marketplace the easier it will be to translate that strategic focus into a clear definition of talent. The 10% most talented executives at each level in an organisation need to be leaders who have characteristics that are going to be a core requirement for implementing the business strategy. Therefore, we have seen that it is critical to start any development of significant talent management initiatives with a highly focused understanding of how the business strategy impacts the key criteria that will be used to differentiate the top 10% from the other managers within the business.

CHAPTER 5

TALENT MANAGEMENT IN CRITICAL JOBS

Whook hen we think of talent management our mind naturally focuses on individuals. The organisation needs talented individuals and invests disproportionately in their development and progression in order to benefit from their capability. From that perspective, everything is about defining, identifying, selecting and developing the most talented people in the business. The problem with this focus on individuals, however, is that it tends to be a long-term process. Organisations go to the best business schools, identify some of the most talented graduates and hope that by developing them they will create a cadre of future leaders for their business. This is an extremely long process and organisations change dramatically all the time so our needs today may be very different than when these graduates will finally mature. Moreover, we know that early signs of success in academic achievements are only very partial (at best) predictors of success in business. Other characteristics that have to do with tenacity, interpersonal capabilities, long-term vision and determination seem to be more important than some of the key abilities that people demonstrate at a top university. Even when focusing on the identification and development of middle managers who have the capability to eventually get to senior executive positions we are still involved in a process that, at best, would last over a three- to five-year time horizon. As a result, since most executive teams are focused on the here and now and have to deliver quarterly results that demonstrate year-on-year progress, it is very hard to get them to focus on what needs to be developed within this more long-term horizon. The majority of talent management efforts, therefore, tend to be led by the Human Resource function that has the accountability for more long-term development, while the rest of the management team are focused on what needs to be done in order to perform significantly better in the present.

From a business perspective, talent management should really be focused on the development of leadership capabilities that have a direct impact on today's performance. At any moment in time there is a small number of executives who are occupying critical positions in the business and their capabilities to focus on what needs to be done in light of key strategic objectives, to drive operational results, to lead their team effectively, to build relationships across functional and business unit boundaries, to relate to consumer/customer needs and address them effectively and to initiate change and innovation, is absolutely fundamental to the competitive performance of the business today. Therefore, in this book when I talk about talent management I am focused on the maximisation of existing talent within the business in the immediate term, and only secondarily on the development of long-term talent that will one day hopefully step in and take over from some of the existing executive talent that is leading the business today.

My interviews with Heads of Human Resources in leading-edge businesses provide interesting data about their efforts to assess and to develop the capabilities of senior executives who are already occupying influential positions in their business.

The organisations where I conducted my interviews were in different places regarding the assessment and development of talent at the very top. There are a few who still do not 'touch' executives at this level since they have 'already arrived'. However, most are trying to do something with this senior group. Some businesses have initiated the use of external assessment for their most senior executives in order to develop an objective, benchmarked view of their capability and potential. Others have followed that up with systematic development actions (usually individually tailored) to address the needs of this group.

The following quotes give a flavour of what is being done in this area, starting with those organisations that are advanced in addressing the needs of their senior executive group:

> We have about 100 in the most senior executive group – leadership of our major lines of business and key functional groups. The top 100 historically were the least measured people in the organisation: after all they were already there. But when the business faced a more complex environment we used an external supplier to benchmark our top 100. It was an opportunity to focus on the development of these people. It created a lot of anxiety in the organisation though we were clear that it was a development exercise. The feedback was very direct, but well accepted as a foundation for development. We haven't done it again since, but have become more rigorous about our scorecard. This actually extends to the top 200 people. The scorecard focuses on business and personal objectives and these are hardwired to bonus payouts. In general we have become much tougher about the process. We probably don't need to do another external assessment exercise of that magnitude again but we are using an external supplier to assess potential internal and external candidates for major roles. Also, people who are identified as 'talent' are assessed. So, in general, we use much more rigour than we used to, but still have a lot to do. (Large retailer)

We have defined a common vision of what we expect from our top 500, which includes intellectual capability, making things happen, etc. We demand that these people will be rated by their own bosses – no special process just the normal process to rate people. Initially around 80 people from this 500 were identified as talent – now it's around 100. These 100 have a variety of development opportunities but it is completely tailored to the needs of each individual. Not just academic development but learning by doing. We have a Talent Development Forum, which is a panel of three Executive level people, one of whom is the Head of HR. They meet three times across the year for a half-day with each of our high-flyers (two people at a time from the Executive Team give one day per month to sit on this panel). That helps them to get to know our best people. The panel meets these 80–100 executives and the discussion focuses on insight (what they learned about themselves), impact (what do they want from the panel) and innovation (new ideas). HR spends a lot of time in preparing these people for their panel meeting. The biggest issue is about their aspirations and how realistic they are. This can be hard for some people since the panel sends feedback to their boss after this meeting. In general, this is a very good process since it is backed by objective external assessment of the potential of each participant. This process gives visibility to our most promising senior executives through their direct contact with the Executive Team and, therefore, this becomes a real foundation for succession management (instead of just ticking boxes). (Financial services business)

We would include about 100 people across the group. We see them as a talent pool that works across different parts of the group. Our succession plans focus on these people as being the key success driver. We have three large businesses and, realistically, we have only developed systematic talent management processes in one of them. There we have a twice-yearly process to assess performance in current role and also potential: what kind of role could they move to and what role they need to develop in to do that. We offer the entire group the use of a personal coach. We use external assessment for all external recruitment at this level. We also extend this process, with a development focus, to the high-potential people in the top 100. Half-day structured interviews supported by psychometric tests and then feedback; all done by an external supplier in order to maintain objectivity. We hope to extend this across the group with the three companies, now that we have seen that it is successful in one. (Public utility)

A number of organisations that I interviewed have systematic processes for the senior executive group that are similar to those they use for other levels of management. Typically, this is an annual performance management cycle where managers are rated on the achievement of business objectives as well as on their 'behaviour' as managers. This performance management process is coupled with a review of potential that is sometimes done at the same time but, in many cases, is done separately. The business uses that review to discuss possible successors for key jobs and to identify executives who have the potential for further career growth.

The difference between this approach and that described earlier is around the importance associated with talent management at the top. The use of external assessment and benchmarking for this critical group of executives brings an objective 'hardness' to the process, which makes the results more credible.

On a more subtle level, there seems to be something of a 'tick box', HR-owned process that comes through when talent management for very senior executives is applied as part of the routine of the annual performance management cycle. The following quotes illustrate this approach:

Three times a year we have a Management Development Review where all senior executives who report to the Board are judged on a nine-box matrix of performance and potential. That is designed to drive differentiation among these 50 people but it is really the same process we use for all managers. The Board has the judgement based on their observations. They all have clear sets of business objectives that are used to judge performance. We have a compe-tence model that is simple and is used to judge potential. We also try to look at experience that adds to this. It is true that we could go deeper here, especially on the development at this level. We have an external assessment with psychometrics for executives when they get into that top group so we know that they have the capability. (Large manufacturer)

Everybody is performance managed in our business, all the way to the top. We agreed a set of competencies that apply to our executives. We put in a new process that goes across the group replacing a range of processes that were in place in different parts of the business. We rolled it out last September and are now collating all that information with the aim of using that data for our Management Talent Review. We focus on four key competencies plus technical competencies. Our CEO and executive team review the information and establish succession; three levels down, which we feel is deep enough. We try to examine performance against business objectives. Bonuses are tied in to these objectives with very tough criteria. Also you get a potential rating that comes in addition to that, whether they have one or two job levels ahead of them. There are two different processes, one for performance and bonuses and the other for potential and succession; each done at different times. We use a matrix of performance by potential focusing on people in the bottom left box, who need to improve rapidly or leave. But we need to focus much more on the upper quartile population. Hiring people who have the potential for two steps within the business and working with our current senior people to see if we can ensure that at least some have the same potential for future growth. We need real calibre for the long term. For our very senior level people, we don't have other sources of data yet, in addition to these internal judgements. We are starting to roll out 360° but not everyone is happy. On the other hand there is now growing commitment and we are moving towards that 360° and towards objective assessment. But we are not yet really ready for benchmarking existing people against the external market, or for doing something more powerful with our really talented executives. (Financial services company)

We use the same talent processes throughout the organisation via performance management. There is nothing special for the top team. We have a twice a year cycle: how people perform against their objectives plus their behaviours (how they achieve these). We are very numbers focused, but now also focus on behaviours. Numbers are the entry ticket, but 'How' is the key to success. We have a set of leadership competencies, and individuals self-assess. Then their managers assess against general competencies plus function-specific ones. These ratings are the basis for their individual development plan. This is done systematically as well but we focus more closely when we go up the organisation since these are more critical people. When looking at development we also look at talent: Where is this person going? Is this someone who is very talented? What are potential succession moves and timescales? And this rolls up throughout the organisation. We are a US-led business and these processes are very systematic. (Consumer goods company)

For a number of my interviewees, talent management at senior levels is still a very new process. Most of their efforts are focused on running a senior executive training and development programme that is usually put together in co-operation with a business school.

However, this training input is still not tied to an in-depth diagnosis of individual development needs. Some of these organisations are just starting to use objective assessment of executive potential and to collect more than just manager feedback. Our respondents recognise that there is a real need to differentiate the assessment of performance from the assessment of potential and that line managers do not necessarily have the perspective that will enable them to assess if one of their direct reports has the potential to progress one or even two levels up the organisation's hierarchy.

While recognising the importance of these issues for building a cadre of exceptional senior executives, these organisations are still in the early phases of this journey, as illustrated by the following quotes:

We have a core set of competencies for the top 500 (those who report to the Board and to country MDs). They go through a performance management process led by their Manager. We also have a succession planning process in each division – which is reviewed by the Board two days a year. We have a Leadership Development

Programme focused on these 500 people, which has been very successful. We focus both on generic work and personal development focused on the needs of each person. There is a five-day programme for 80–90 people mixed geographically and functionally, which is run by internal and external business school people. It's a very big investment but it facilitates networking of people in the top 500 from around the world. We now want to cascade this process down a level to their direct reports. The programme also allows people to work on an MSc in business leadership – 53 people are involved. That is key to keeping people – it gives very senior people a lot of pride in their own development, so it's a great motivational tool. In terms of potential, we are now focused on identifying two different populations: business-critical versus high-potential. We are not rating everyone, but take nominations, which are brought to the Board and discussed in depth. It is easier to focus on individuals rather than ratings to avoid a box-ticking exercise. The differentiation between performance and potential is very difficult for a boss to do. We are successful in getting the Board engaged in this process and that is the most important part. (Consumer services company)

I have been here 11 months and two things have taken up my time: pensions and talent. I have tried to focus on the top two levels – direct reports to the Chief Executive (10), their direct reports and their Level 3s – a total of about 150. We started a process we call succession management (not planning) since it is not about filling in boxes, but about managing a process. It is a combination of leadership development and succession review. We started to profile these people using external assessment expertise. This includes assessment, feedback to each person and development plans. We need time to take people through the process to ensure that it's effective and to get to all 150. We don't want an elitist process – telling people that they are chosen. There are a lot of people in the middle, not high-flyers, who are very important to the organisation and we want to invest in their development. We want to sell the idea that development is about improving people's value to the business and themselves, not just about going up the ladder. On the other hand, we have to be candid with people about how they can be most productive and add the most value – while not giving a negative message about how far they can go. We are in the early stages of this (around 20% implemented) – then the divisional people will put in place development plans. The long-term aim is that in a generation's time the Board will not face the problems we are facing now. (Large retailer)

Finally, a number of interviewees were either doing very little talent management for their senior executives or what they were doing was half-hearted. As discussed earlier, there tends to be a difference between what organisations say and what their actions demonstrate. A certain level of frustration with this state of affairs comes through in the following quotes:

> We have a business school programme for 30 of the top 100. It has 12 modules, four to five weeks a year, with a lot of personal development. We haven't really done any systematic assessment of potential or individual development for these people though. We are not really ready culturally for that. (Public utility)

> We have a worldwide definition that includes the top 200, based on the fact that they have CEO in their title or sit on an operating company Board. At the moment we do little with these people. We do use external suppliers to do objective assessments across the Group but not really systematically. Usually new people entering this group will go through the process but nothing systematic happens with that. Development opportunities at that level depend on one's relationship with one's boss. In the last nine months we have started to finalise talent management discussions and, as a result, people will start to be sent to a business school Senior Management Programme. But still, when you look at that group of 200, we lose a lot of them in any given year. So, clearly the activities don't seem to be motivating or stopping these people from leaving. We want to improve and the heart of the President and his commitment is focused on this, so I am hopeful. (Consumer services company)

What we see from my interviews with the Heads of Human Resources is that while there has been a lot of development to build capability within the senior executive team, there is still a long way to go in this area. Therefore, as a first step in devising an effective talent management strategy for your business, it is essential to look at the current leadership that is driving the business forward and to assess the talent that each one of them has in light of the strategic business needs that are critical for competitive advantage for your business.

Before we try to develop future generations it is important to examine the strengths and weaknesses of the people who are currently in high-impact positions, and to determine what can be done to ensure that the leadership of the business is the best that is available in the marketplace. As a result, talent management initiatives need to start with a systematic mapping of the critical managerial positions within the business. Once we understand what the most important jobs are, then we can start to assess the talent of the individuals that are occupying these jobs. We can either develop those people or put in their place executives who already have capability that is significantly higher than the existing job occupant. A focus on talent development in terms of individuals is, therefore, the second step to a focus on the critical positions where those most talented individuals should be sitting.

How do we identify management positions that have a significant impact on business performance? In general, one could argue that every position within the organisation has impact on the performance of the business, because otherwise that position would be eliminated. That is correct to a large degree. But when we are talking about talent management, we are focused on investing in a disproportionate manner in positions and in individuals that have a disproportionate impact on the success of the organisation. Therefore, if we use our usual 10% rule then the first step is to identify, across each of the management layers, the 10% of 'managerial seats' that have the most significant impact on the performance of the business. This will naturally start with a focus on the senior executive team. By definition, the top 10–15 executives in a business have a disproportionate impact compared to all the other managers within a business since they determine the direction in which the business is going, the culture that permeates the business and the operational performance that is characteristic of this business on a day-to-day basis. Therefore, all executives who occupy the top tier of a business would typically be the focus of our talent management activities.

When we consider the second and the third tier of executives, we would in most large organisations think of around 100 or 150 executives. We need to begin to show some selection in our choices when considering this group. At these second and third tiers there will be some executives who have direct authority over the key business activities that generate most of the revenue or that are responsible for the most significant elements of the costs that determine the profitability of the business. Therefore, people in key line positions are usually those that have the most direct impact on outcomes. What we are trying to do here is to identify individuals where a significant difference in their capability will result in a significant difference in the performance of the business. There will, however, be individuals within this top 100–150 executives who are important to the medium-term success of the business but have much less impact in terms of the performance of the business day-to-day. A number of senior specialist positions are typical in this respect. They are important to the success of the business, they require a great deal of expertise and experience and they involve executives with high earnings and status, but in reality, their impact on the business is much more medium-term and indirect since they influence the activities of other people who in turn may influence the performance of the business. Therefore, usually in the second and third tier we will select around one-third of executives as critical for the immediate competitive performance of the business and two-thirds of them would typically be important but not necessarily a key focus for today's performance improvement efforts. Once we get to the third and fourth management levels, even within a large business, we would typically see much stronger differentiation. We will find that maybe 10% of the 500–700 people that will be in these management tiers will have immediate impact on the performance of the business while many others will be supportive and provide internal service roles. The key here is to identify positions/'seats' where an exceptional executive will have a significant impact on the performance of the business in the immediate term when compared to the impact of an average executive sitting in the same position.

Reviewing executive positions from the most senior team to the middle of the organisation in the fashion outlined above will enable you to identify, even in very large international corporations, about 100 or so 'seats' or executive positions that together have a disproportionate impact on the performance of the business in the immediate term. Our talent management activities should focus on these 100 'seats' which represent around 10% of executive positions. These are not the top in terms of the salaries of the job occupiers or the importance of their title, but they are in terms of the direct impact that these positions have on the immediate-term performance of the business. If we can design talent management activities that have a significant impact on the capabilities of the occupiers of these 100 executive positions then we will have a very significant impact on the performance of the business in the immediate term. In this sense, by focusing on executive positions and not individuals we are able to transform the impact of talent management activities from being a medium-term activity that may bear fruits in a 3–5-year horizon to an activity that has an immediate impact on the performance of a business.

Once you have identified the critical executive positions within a business you will need to evaluate the capability of the current job incumbents in order to see how they are in comparison to what an ideal executive would be able to do in that critical position. With this objective in mind, we can go back to what I described in the previous chapter, which is to focus on the key competencies that define success within each job. If we have an effective performance management process, we can review the critical executive positions that we have identified and examine the distribution of performance appraisal results for the executives that sit in these posts. Ideally, we would like to focus our attention on those individuals who are performing exceptionally well in exceptionally influential positions in order to invest disproportionately in them. They are our most capable talent and, therefore, by improving them we improve the performance of the business as a whole. Similarly, if we find that we have average or even worse performers in critical positions it is imperative to move them to less important posts, although not necessarily out of the organisation, since these executives may have sufficient capability and experience that is useful in less critical positions. This discussion, around the current capability of job holders in critical positions, is a very high priority for the executive team of the business. Just like they want to be updated monthly on how the business is performing financially vis-à-vis its key financial targets, or operationally vis-à-vis its key operational targets, they would be very interested to know to what degree the most important executive positions are filled by people who are exceptionally effective and can be characterised as the best players in the marketplace.

The problem with this very logical approach is that you will discover in many organisations that the performance management system does not really differentiate effectively between exceptional and average performers. Most managers find it difficult to give negative feedback and they do their best to avoid differentiating among their direct reports (since they don't want to have to explain why they are not treating everyone equally). It is hard to tell someone that they are not doing as well as they could be doing since that could get you into an argument. That assessment may also reflect badly on me as a manager if I say to my boss that some members of my team are not exceptional.

To counteract this lack of differentiation, the business needs to create an incentive that ensures that managers do differentiate between the people who work for them and, thereby, provide some form of assessment that makes it possible to ascertain the degree to which the current players in key managerial positions are the best players that are available in the market for these executive positions. The key here is around the motivation or the perceived need to do this task effectively. Once the senior executive team is helped to focus on the 10% of executive positions which have a disproportionate impact on the success of the business, then they themselves will be interested to ensure that people in those positions are the best people that are available in the marketplace. The business can be more lenient, understanding and considerate in the quality of the executives and the harshness of its Human Resources decisions when it is looking at 90% of the management across the business. However, when we focus on the top 10% of critical positions, then we need to ensure that our best players are sitting in these 'seats'. Once there is an agreement within the senior executive team as to which positions are critical then the road will be open to a much more objective analysis that goes beyond the hesitancies of existing managers across the business. Also, since we are talking about a relatively small number of executive positions, then it is possible to invest in an in-depth definition of what competence is important for successful performance in each one of them and then to gather a broader group of senior executives to review the capability of current job occupiers in these critical positions. Usually there will be a number of viewpoints that are independent of the view of the direct-line boss and together it will be possible to use a rating scale that focuses not on a general discussion of whether somebody is good, bad or indifferent but on a comparison of the current job occupier in competence terms when compared to the rater's knowledge of the players that are available in the marketplace.

Some businesses have used a forced ranking process to differentiate among executives. They can then examine critical executive positions and see if their job occupiers are rated highly in the forced rankings.

A number of businesses have gone further than clarifying the criteria and facilitating a top team discussion that brings in diverse viewpoints about executives that occupy critical positions. They use external assessors who have a broad view of the talent that is available in the marketplace in order to provide an in-depth perspective about the capabilities of the people who occupy these positions. In some cases, these assessments are done by executive search firms who can bring objectivity to a process by reviewing existing job holders in comparison to what is available in the marketplace. In all talent management activities we are focused on a very small number of executives who occupy a small, though critical, number of senior positions. A mass assessment of all of the top 300–500 executives that manage the business would be a very culturally sensitive exercise that would generate a great deal of individual and team reactions that may actually slow the business down unless there is a real business need to create a significant cultural change. What I am suggesting here, as part of the ongoing annual talent management process, is to focus on a small number of key jobs and to ensure that the people who are in these jobs are still the best players that are available in the marketplace. In most organisations, the top team will agree that some of these players are good but that there are better people out there who can do these jobs more effectively. Therefore, it would be possible to take a good executive who may not be absolutely a top performer and move him/her to a sideways position that is less critical for the immediate success of the business and put somebody else internally or externally into those critical driving seats. By focusing on critical executive positions, talent management activities suddenly become urgent and high-priority actions for the senior executive team. We can then provide ongoing feedback processes to what degree the executives who are sitting in these driving seats are peak performers who are performing in the most effective way. If not, what could be done immediately to ensure that peak performers are actually in those positions either by developing and helping the existing job holders to achieve rapid improvement or by replacing them with others who can step in and increase the pace. This focus on key positions is in addition to more medium-term activities for talent development that will be described in the next few chapters. It is important to grow and develop people who will over the next few years be able to step into critical positions and I will discuss in-depth how that can be done. The first step, however, is to ensure that talent management activities are a top priority for the senior executive team and not just a 'nice to have' Human Resource process. This will happen by focusing on critical jobs and thereby ensuring that there is an immediate impact of talent management activities on what is done today.

Once you have a process of identifying critical positions and describing the key competencies that are required in order to perform at an exceptional level and once you have assessed the performance of the current job occupiers, the senior executive team will be able to review capability gaps and discuss their implications. This should start with a focus on the senior executive team itself, as the people who report directly to the Chief Executive. Any issues at that level that represent gaps between the top performers that are available in the market and the current performers who occupy these top 10 or 15 positions need to be addressed immediately. In addition, it is important to review other executives that sit in the next few layers of management and again in critical positions. We are therefore talking about a highly focused review process of anywhere between 40 to 100 executives. Even in very large international corporations with hundreds of thousands of employees, these people are occupying critical positions that have an immediate impact on the performance of the business. Every quarter or six months, the executive team should receive a review of the performance and capability of current job occupiers in these positions to enable them to discuss what it would take to ensure that each of these key players will be a top performer in the overall marketplace and not just within your specific business. This diagnosis should come not only in competence terms, but in terms of the underlying causes that prevent an individual from being one of the top performers in the competitive marketplace. This diagnosis will focus on the degree to which the gap in capabilities is due to:

- underlying intellectual or interpersonal abilities of the executive that is sitting in this position
- level of motivation and resilience that he or she has
- their experience base

It is important to get to this diagnosis of the underlying causes because the diagnosis would enable you to understand the course of action that is likely to produce the desired result. If an individual has a problem because they do not have the underlying abilities that are required in order to be an exceptional performer, then it is unlikely that those abilities will be developed in the short timespan that is required in order to have a leading player in a leading position. If there is a problem of motivation then it is very important to understand what is causing that executive to not exhibit the degree of motivation that is required for effective performance in that critical position. Is this something that is happening in their personal life? Is this something that relates to their interaction with their manager? Are there political issues that are happening around the business, etc.? Finally, sometimes executives in critical positions do not compare well with others in the competitive marketplace because they don't have the breadth of experience that is required in order to perform exceptionally in this critical position. The question here is to assess to what degree this lack of experience can be augmented through focused mentoring processes with others in the organisation that have that experience, or to what degree that experience can only be achieved through long-term business experience so that the organisation cannot afford to spend the time and wait until an executive in a critical position will acquire it.

In general, therefore, by focusing on a very small number of key positions and therefore a very small number of executives, and by using an in-depth assessment of capability and a diagnosis of the reasons for any capability gaps, it is possible to create a focused action plan for each position and each executive that is sitting in that position. These action plans will point to the fact that some of the current executives are the best in the marketplace and therefore all we need to do is to help them to maintain their superior performance. It may be useful to go back to my sports analogies since even Olympic players receive very intensive coaching and practice in order to remain peak performers. A top sportsperson would not dream of dropping his coach or stop practising because he is a top performer and therefore there is no need to do that any more. Similarly, within a business context, our best performers would want to continue to receive input because they know that this will help them to continue to be the best in the marketplace. Through this intensive diagnosis focused on critical positions, you will find that there will be some individuals where it is clear that within a 2–3-month period it will be possible to provide them with the coaching or other types of input that would enable them to rise and become one of the key players in the competitive marketplace. This kind of input would be worthwhile since there are always some consequences when people in key leadership positions are moved around. Intensive, focused development will be worthwhile because, by improving the performance capability of the people who sit in critical positions, it will have a direct impact on the performance of the business. Finally, you will find that a number of executives who are sitting in critical positions will not be exceptional and there will not be a straightforward way to transform them into the best players in the marketplace. These executives need to be moved urgently into less critical positions in order to free up the space for people who are top players. They will come either from the outside, when we know that there are better players in competitor organisations, or from inside where, by developing succession, as we will see in the next chapter, we should have a pool of exceptional players who are ready to take on more significant responsibility. In a number of organisations I have found that it is also possible to find exceptional executives in less critical positions. Sometimes the business, for one reason or another, has taken exceptional people and put them in other parallel positions just because of lack of thought. Again, by moving those players who are exceptional into positions with critical impact, we can maximise their potential and, thereby, significantly impact the performance of the business as a whole. Taking a promising executive and putting them into a critical position requires not only their potential to be an exceptional player but also the intense on-boarding activities that will ensure that they will step into a new critical position in an effective way.

In summary, this chapter has focused on the fact that talent management activities do not have to be identified with a 3–5-year development horizon within which we can create another generation of leaders. Talent management activities should start by focusing on critical executive jobs that have a disproportionate impact on the performance of the business as a whole. By identifying those critical jobs, crystallising what it takes in order to be a superior performer in those jobs, assessing the performance of current job holders versus market standards and taking direct action, the business can transform its leadership profile in a process that will have an immediate impact on business performance. As we have seen throughout this chapter, the senior executive team will be interested in the assessment of individual executives, once it is clear that the focus is on critical jobs where the occupier has an immediate impact on the performance of the business, as opposed to general assessment activities that relate to all management jobs.

CHAPTER 6

MANAGING SUCCESSION

S uccession management is a Human Resource process that has been implemented for many years in most large organisations. Typically the Human Resource function put together a large book that includes most of the senior jobs in the organisation. For each job managers were asked to indicate who from among their direct reports could replace them in the foreseeable future. In addition, managers were asked to indicate when the person who could replace them, in their opinion, would be ready to do so and what input, in terms of training and development activities or project experience, would be useful to help their potential successors to be ready when the time came.

These succession management books were usually brought to the senior executive team once a year for them to review the recommendations. Sometimes the review focused on individual jobs and names and usually it was around key issues that needed to be dealt with on an organisation-wide basis. For example, when large groups of executives were approaching retirement the Human Resource function usually highlighted the fact that there would be a very broad transition process and that it was important to become more serious about the need to have adequate replacements on hand. Similarly, there were situations where a number of different individuals identified the same people as potential successors for their jobs and, therefore, a choice had to be made. Also, a number of jobs may not have had any realistic successors who would be ready in the foreseeable future to step up.

In all of these cases the process was based on an assumption that there would be a great deal of stability in an organisation and that individuals would need successors either because they would eventually reach retirement age or because of the famous 'bus scenario' which was more of an unrealistic occurrence where they would suddenly not be able to work. When these systematic succession planning processes were used there was no expectation that large-scale changes would impact the organisation significantly. Businesses lived in a world where executives were an extremely stable population and the structures of large organisations and the individuals filling key positions within them did not tend to change from one year to the next.

The reality today is dramatically different. The life-expectancy of chief executives in leading companies has shortened significantly. To quote from *Chief Executive Officer* magazine (2006):

The average life expectancy of the average CEO is now somewhere between 30 and 40 months. Whether a new CEO sees this as an adequate length of time to turn an ailing business around depends on the size of the business concerned. But one thing is certain: becoming CEO makes even the most confident business leader jumpy and inclined to glance over their shoulder. In the UK, in 2000, one in four CEOs of UK businesses with sales of over £500m left before they were supposed to. This is twice the early departure figure for 1990. And the trend is continuing.

When a CEO is replaced due to pressure by shareholders, the natural tendency is to bring in a whole new team of senior executives. As a result, we see in the USA and the UK waves of changes in the senior executive populations of large businesses. It is no longer useful, therefore, to have a systematic succession planning process that is based on putting individual names opposite specific managerial positions since in 2 or 3 years a position may not exist in its current form and the people who may be required to step up to a position if it does exist may themselves have moved to other places in the interim. As a result, succession planning processes in most organisations have become much more flexible.

In addition, during the 1980s and 1990s, most large businesses went through dramatic cost-cutting processes. In order to improve competitiveness within and across national boundaries large organisations took out significant costs associated with their management structures. Most of these cost-cutting activities involved large-scale delayering where whole layers of management at the top and middle of the organisations were taken out and the breadth of managerial accountability was extended dramatically. While in the past it was typical that each senior executive would have two or three direct reports who would look after large parts of their area of accountability, today it is not atypical to have 10 or 12 direct reports each looking after much smaller parts of the business. As a result, the gaps between managers' capabilities at each level have increased. It used to be characteristic of large organisations to have a well-defined career progression ladder where executives who performed even adequately could expect every 2 or 3 years to go up a step in the corporate hierarchy as part of their eventual climb to the top. As a result of large-scale delayering, most organisations have eliminated many of the steps in the hierarchy. Executives can expect to stay for much longer periods in their current jobs or to have a number of sideways jobs before they are perceived to have the breadth of experience required to make the move up a much steeper career hierarchy.

As a result of delayering and the change in organisational stability, we have seen in the last few years a dramatic shift in the nature of succession management processes in large businesses. Many organisations adopt a much more flexible approach that does not focus on individual jobs with identified successors for every executive in the business. Instead of producing large books that identify two or three successors for each job, organisations look at broad management bands and identify succession possibilities that are associated with those. The Human Resource function would typically report once a year on the senior executive band, identifying potential vacancies that may result from age and natural turnover. In terms of successors, organisations focus on the development of talent pools that include a group of executives who are perceived to have the capabilities to step up into a broad array of jobs at the next management level. The creation of talent pools enables flexibility in matching individuals to different jobs that may become open during the coming year and ensuring that talent is available to look at a whole level of executive positions regardless of the specific structure that happens to characterise the business today and may be completely different tomorrow. This increased flexibility provides senior management and the Human Resource function with a lot more options to look at the likely succession requirements and alternative ways of resourcing them internally and externally.

As part of my in-depth interviews with Heads of Human Resources in large international businesses I asked them to describe the systematic processes that they use to identify possible successors for senior management positions, to assess the strengths and development needs of these successors and to facilitate development actions in the areas identified.

Most of my interviewees reported that they are doing something to develop a high-potential pool of candidates that can be used as an internal resource for senior executive jobs. The difference was in how rigorous a process they put in place. In many businesses, this was an extension of the regular performance management process. Managers rated not only performance but also the potential of their team members and that data was used to identify a 'high-flyer' group. These people sometimes went through some form of executive development process (developed internally or with a business school provider) and were, at least theoretically, available when there was an opening.

In other organisations, there was an attempt to be more objective and to use external assessment processes to ensure that the people on the list were not just those whom their boss appreciated, but executives who actually had real long-term potential.

There was also variability in the degree to which businesses tailor development to individual needs and in how they ensure that the Board/executive team had the opportunity to get to know the most talented executives personally. This was perceived to be a key for developing an effective mentoring relationship and to ensure that high-potential executives were used as a management resource across business units. Typically, most of the assessment of potential is done within each business unit separately and it is difficult to expose executives to opportunities outside their immediate environment.

The following are quotes from some of the organisations that were most advanced in this area:

> This is where we get very systematic. We do it for the top 500 up to the Chairman. We spend hours with bosses to ensure they really have people that they would put into the top talent category. Real talent and high-performance people who are capable of doing a job two steps up; then one step up+ moves; lateral moves; blockers (need a plan for them); and technical specialists. The process helps people to do this and we are now going into the third annual cycle. We do this at the half-year as a checkpoint with a full day with the Board (together with other issues). Also, at year-end, for each business unit and then for the group as a whole. Discussions are not about people but about issues, such as succession profiles on certain areas like marketing, etc.; not hours spent talking about individuals.

But we can still be much better at this. (Financial services company)

We use a performance–potential nine-box matrix already described. We add to that a consideration of such factors as risk of leaving, mobility, ease of replacement, criticality of role, etc. We follow this through most rigorously where it matters most, e.g. for senior line positions. In terms of assessment of potential and development needs, we undertake psychological assessments, using an external firm to ensure objectivity. That is added to by our own internal competency-based interview and, at the middle management levels, an internal assessment centre. There is a 'sign-off' process at all levels. At Level 1, this would entail a sign-off process involving Board members. (Large retailer)

Succession management – we used to have a huge book and I threw it away. Let's focus only on the key jobs that are critical to the business, trying to get three senior names for each of these, and then what is the timescale for that. The key point is to ensure that they are realistic names. Typically, people are too optimistic or too pessimistic. Then there is a discussion about the best way to fill the gap. The HR people bring the names from the business units. We then bring line management in, to own it. This is done once a year by members of the Executive, Managing Directors and Functional Directors at big group meetings that follow earlier one-on-one discussions. We focus on 100 key jobs and who are the high-potential candidates and ensure that we have proper development plans for these people. (Airline)

A number of organisations that I interviewed have systematic processes for dealing with succession and 'feeder' talent but are still in the early phases in terms of having a process that they are really satisfied with. Sometimes there is no objective way to differentiate performance from potential; or they have just started so it is still too early to tell how things will develop. The following quotes illustrate this half-way stage:

I am only six months in the Group HR role so everything is new. We are not a very structured business, so we need to have something flexible. At the moment, we define a successor for each key role, rate performance and potential as two dimensions and identify a younger group of high-potential executives. We ask for this data from each of our businesses and collect it at Group level. The hardest question is about how to differentiate performance from potential since the person's boss does not have the right perspective. This assessment by each business is based on their performance appraisal process. The goal is to gradually improve the reliability of this process. We needed to move, even if it is not in a perfect way. So now we have a list of people and need to test if they are really high potential. We need to assess them both for the corporate need and for their own development. As a result, we will understand the organisation's strengths and weaknesses and also get to know these people in order to be able to use them for internal resourcing. Having objective data will also help to put in place the most appropriate development process for this group. We have just commissioned an external organisation to do that, using 360°, psychometrics and self-insight, and in-depth structured 3-hour discussions. The first tranche of about 30/40 people has been looked at and then we will probably expand to a larger population. We need to keep flexibility, since our businesses are very different, so that we can build on what each business already has. After this, we will sit with the external supplier to identify common themes, and thereby have something to feed back into the business, so that they feel that this was a useful process for them (line manager and HR). For these 30–40 people I will also share their development plans with the businesses since that is their primary relationship. I will then think about moving people across the Group – which will be a joint process for the HR Directors from the Group together with those from each business unit. These people will be good for the succession process. At the moment, once or twice a year, we sit with the Chief Executive and discuss people. He spends a few hours on each business and has separate meetings for functional areas. It is the same for the Chief Executives of each business so it's a large time commitment. So we now go through the entire succession process with Key Performance Indicators in this area –

to see if we have the right ratios. We now have the data and it's a good start. Gradually, we will have more action on people moves. Now we have open conversation about people's perspective on the big players and are gradually identifying people where we have gaps and we are starting to figure out how to bridge those gaps. (Large manufacturer)

We have a standard process across the group, bottom-up, a nine-box matrix including performance and potential. It is done annually and we have now started to do it twice a year to push people harder to take action on what they said they would do. Our process ensures that we have confirmed action on the people that were reviewed, not just talk. Our Board is very committed to spending half a day on these people – not a mechanical process, but real live debate. To measure potential, some parts of the organisation have defined clear criteria. We are still trying to reduce that into a short set of 2/3/4 things that are critical for being a Director of one of our large businesses. We try to get more and more internal debate so that people will share and understand. We want to develop a process where our most senior executives will get to know the next layers in each of our businesses personally. That will make the Group talent process have real consequences. You need to bring more objective data to the table via assessment, but that needs to be combined with personal familiarity so that we will be able to judge executives based on personal experience with them, not just data. Having the right style, chemistry, fit and edge which are all key to success. (Large retailer)

We have pure succession plans that go into a Management Development Review (MDR) process. We look at each job, likely departures (do we want them?) and then possible successors. We identify possible people and how long it will take for them to be ready. We look at both specific succession for each role and at a talent pool that could fit a variety of roles. This MDR process is an opportunity to have a conversation. In any one year there may be 20% turnover at this senior executive level and we try to fill half from inside. We have also created broad pay bands to be able to reward talent without job promotions. This is the whole top team that is being reviewed. Each is rated on the nine-box matrix, but it is up to the boss to what degree that will happen. That is a little bit of a problem since the boss may not always have the right perspective. In terms of development for those who may be able to get to the top: 80% of the development comes from on-the-job experience, giving them enough stretch and challenge. We supplement this with some other things. Executive coaching, sometimes business school programmes – but no 'sheep dip' programmes at this level. We don't intervene unless there is something important to roll out. It is up to the individual to own their development and some people tend to take on more than others. Usually, it's through coaches. This is not seen as a sign of a problem – it's acceptable that executives at this level use a coach as part of positive development – and they are free to use whomever they want. Coaches have been used to work on image, voice, performance issues etc. Maybe we could get more systematic with that. (Large retailer)

We have a very robust process to look at people with potential and to make the tough decisions when we do not see that they can make it one or two levels up from where they are now – and that is working. In some areas people are still too comfortable but this is changing since we clearly need to be harder. We still need to put in a more systematic process to assess and develop high-potential executives and to move them as a key resource around the group. But we are not GE, so we need to be more gradual and are still not clear on how to do it well. (Public utility)

We have a database to help with the management development process. At the end of the performance management process in each division, they fill our group database with all the relevant data that allows us to build profiles on the top 500 executives. We don't go below the 500 at Group level – the Divisions do lower levels. We do help the Divisions to work systematically but still from a decentralised perspective. Some organisations within our Group focus on succession for each job and others create a talent pool that can be used to fill a variety of jobs. There is job evaluation data to ensure that people are moved to job levels that are appropriate. In general, we have the data for each job, but it's not really a robust process. There is no systematic sign-off process. Our executives tell us that career opportunities are a key driver of loyalty. So now we are focusing on how to develop this process in a more effective way. (Consumer services company)

Finally, through my interviews with Heads of Human Resources I found that there are a number of organisations that are doing very little in terms of the systematic management of succession. In some cases the process is too bureaucratic, without real emphasis on action to improve capability at the top. The following responses illustrate this:

> We have had succession planning in place for some time as part of our business continuity plans. But, if I take all that information and look at individual files, you'll see no relation between personal appraisal and actual development efforts and career progression. The fear is that if people are not labelled as high-potential they will leave, so managers give very generous ratings. Also, in the past, review processes like this would be used to fire people so executives are worried, but we certainly need to move forward with this. (Financial services company)

> We analyse the situation as follows: Critical role? – Critical person? – Readiness – now? In 12 months? In 2 years? – Specialist? – Within 2 years of retirement? – Been in the role for more than 4 years and therefore potentially blocking others? – Needs a sideways move? So, we are working on it, but it is a paper-driven exercise right now. Though limited, it is still rich data – and, if there are no answers to the questions, then that speaks volumes in itself. The problem is that we don't use this data to do something real. (Public utility)

How do we make succession planning work in the new business environment? The key is to start with the reasons that we need succession planning in the first place. Organisations see a continuous pressure on performance that gets translated into the need to ensure that the executives that occupy key positions are the top players in the competitive environment and know how to mobilise the business to maintain and improve its strategic positions. As we saw in Chapter 5, the key to building competitive advantage is to focus on critical jobs and on ensuring that the executives that occupy these jobs are as effective as possible. Succession planning processes, therefore, in the new business environment, focus not on a hierarchical concept of management layers but on the critical positions that are perceived to be key for the business's success. Identifying those key positions and an in-depth review of their current occupants would create for your organisations a map of the risks associated with the current management. You will find that a number of incumbents are perceived to be exceptionally capable but that they are approaching retirement age and may not be there long enough to see the business through key performance requirements. Moreover, an in-depth analysis would show that a number of current jobholders are adequate but do not really possess the capabilities that will enable the business to transform itself in line with its competitive strategy. As a result of this analysis of executive positions, it will become clear that there is a need for a certain number of successors to be ready to step into key management positions. The best way to deal with these succession requirements on an organisation-wide as opposed to individual job basis is to develop talent pools.

A talent pool is a group of high-potential executives that are deemed to be ready to step into a variety of executive positions at the next level of management within your business. These candidates are perceived to have exceptional capability and to be ready to take on a relatively broad array of possible next steps. I will discuss the long-term view in Chapter 8 with a focus on the identification of future talent for the long-term, ideally a 5-year time period. For more immediate requirements within a succession management processes, the best practice in large organisations today is to create a number of different talent pools. First is a pool of candidates from the second and third tier of executives who are perceived to have the capability required to become a part of the top executive team. This is based on the assumption that some of the members of the top team will leave because of age, or because they will find alternative employment in competitor organisations, or because they will be perceived to be not good enough for the competitive requirements of their position. A talent pool at the second and third executive tier level would include typically eight to ten individuals out of a group of 100–120 possible candidates. These candidates would have been identified through discussions with the Chief Executive and each of the members of the top team would also identify one or two individuals who they think have the potential to become part of the top team within a maximum of 2 years. These initial impressions need to be verified through more in-depth assessment work, usually with externally objective assessors who can provide a market benchmarking view that places these top eight to ten candidates in comparison to equivalent people in the outside world. Development activities will then ensure that members of this senior pool are not matched as successors to each individual job within the top team but that they are perceived to have the capability to step into a number of alternative positions. This breadth of capability is key because we know that the structure of the top team and, therefore, the requirements for senior level positions are likely to change frequently as the business adapts to competitive pressures. Once individuals are selected into this top level executive pool, it is also important to talk with them about the fact that they are there. This transparency will ensure that they are motivated to remain in the business rather than look outside and take competitor positions that are offered to them by executive search companies. Moreover, the transparency about career prospects opens them to receive in-depth advice in order to be clear about their strengths and development needs and to develop their breadth of capability so that they are ready if and when the time comes to step into more senior positions. Development activities include involvement in task-force projects, mentoring relationships to help the individual to understand different parts of the business and exposure to members of the senior executive team. The key in utilising this top-level talent pool is to ensure that the Chief Executive and the members of the senior executive team become intimately familiar with the eight to ten individuals that are in it. Otherwise, while it is nice to have a list of names that are recommended by members of the top team, executives will be reluctant to enable a more junior person to step into the top team without knowing them in-depth. This risk is very hard to overcome when we are talking about the leadership of large companies. As a result, when a position becomes vacant at the top the natural reaction is to go to an executive search firm and ask them to look outside and get appropriate candidates that seem more attractive than those known internally. The dangers associated with bringing people from the outside into a management team are also significant. Therefore, it is important to provide an in-depth familiarisation process for the senior team with the candidates that are sitting in the top tier talent pool. That does not mean that external candidates will not be selected, but, at least by becoming familiar with internal candidates, senior executives could be sure that there are realistic internal alternatives for top level positions. If it is not possible to identify the required level of potential out of a population of 100 or 120 senior executives then the business is in a truly problematic state in terms of its current level of leadership talent. At that point, it is important to bring in external talent more rapidly into the second and third tier of executives who have been assessed as having the potential to join the top tier talent pool and become realistic candidates for the top team.

In addition to creating a senior level talent pool, effective organisations also create a second level talent pool that can be used to replace individual executives who are currently operating at the second or third tier. Usually the candidate population is now between 500 and 600 individuals and out of this number the organisation will choose 40 or 50 candidates who are expected to have the potential to step into the top 50 or 100 jobs that lead the business overall. This second talent pool is critical because it creates the backbone of decision making in the company and therefore the quality of people who sit in this pool will determine how well the business adapts to change over the next few years. As with the top-level pool, this second tier talent pool requires an investment of significant resources to identify the pool candidates, to ensure that they develop the breadth of capability that will enable them to step into a broad array of senior executive positions. We would expect in any given year that around 20% of the top 100 positions will be vacant through some kind of change and the talent pool from the top 500 has to be able to accommodate a significant proportion of that 20% turnover. It is useful for the organisation to bring in 'new blood' from outside the business and Chapter 7 will focus on talent scouting and how it can become an assertive, proactive, forward-looking process as opposed to a reactive, knee-jerk need when a position suddenly becomes vacant. But within this context of succession management it is important to have enough people in the second tier talent pool that will enable you to fill at least half of the positions when there is an expected 20% turnover in the top 100. Candidates in this second tier talent pool would be selected on the basis of recommendations from the top 100 who are then verified by an executive from the top team. Initial recommendations for candidates to the talent pool must be assessed through an objective process to ensure that selection does not become a political choice where people nominate others who have been loyal to them, as opposed to putting forward names of those who truly have the potential to step up to the top 100 level positions. External assessment is usually done by people who have seen a broad array of executives within the sector and, therefore, can provide an objective assessment of the capabilities of pool candidates when compared to what is available in the competitive marketplace. In my experience, more forward-looking businesses also do their best to identify two or three exceptionally talented individuals who come from a much younger age group and are expected to be able to jump two steps in their career and provide a truly fresh perspective to a top 100 position. It is obviously a risk to identify 35-year-olds and enable them to make those career jumps since they have a limited experience base to enable senior executives to be sure that they will be able to take on broad responsibilities. On the other hand, through an in-depth assessment by external experts and by focusing on a very small number of individuals who have performed exceptionally well in their current jobs it is possible to identify two or three young executives who provide a somewhat shocking perspective as members of the top 100 executive population.

The key in any succession management process is not just to identify good candidates for executive pools and prepare them so that they have the breadth of capability that will be required when the time comes; ultimate success depends on the perceptions of the recruiting executives. Most executives in senior positions have a relatively conservative view of the kind of people who are able to become effective direct reports. Individuals think that their own personal career path was the ideal one and, therefore, they would look for people who came up the same route. When provided with candidates who come from a different part of the business and do not have direct content experience in the area that they are dealing with, senior executives become risk-averse and are afraid to take on those challenges. Executives tend to assume their direct reports will come from one of the people who are currently reporting into one of their direct reports, and that provides a very restricted population of potential successors. When they cannot see an appropriate candidate in this restricted pool then they go outside to recruit.

It is critical to help recruiting executives to be willing to take on larger risks by going outside their own environment and looking at a much broader talent pool. It is not sufficient, therefore, to prepare pool candidates; a significant amount of work needs to focus on preparing recruiting executives to open their minds to exceptional candidates that come from diverse back-grounds. Usually we use the word 'diverse' to focus on women or on different ethnic groups. This topic will be discussed in Chapter 12. But when talking to recruiting executives the need to create diversity in their teams means to include executives who have experience from a different silo within the organisation, which typically they would not consider to be realistic candidates. In recruiting a new executive to succeed an existing job occupant the recruiting executive is taking on significant risk. A large part of his or her own area of accountability is going to be delegated to that direct report and if that person will not succeed they may threaten the continuing success of the senior recruiting executive. Therefore, it is critical for Human Resources to help the recruiting executives to focus on the real underlying requirement for success in critical jobs that report into them and to gradually broaden their perspective about what are the characteristics that will enable a candidate to become successful within that requirement. This can be achieved by meeting highly effective individuals from the talent pool and spending time with them to understand what they have done already and how they can translate their experience into a different content area. This interaction between senior executives and candidates in the talent pool who come from a different back-ground opens the way to broaden their minds about realistic recruitment sources. In some organisations the Head of Human Resources helped the senior executive team to be exposed to key players in the marketplace (from other businesses) who come from very diverse backgrounds in order to help them to internalise a broader range of resourcing possibilities. One of my clients is an international financial services company that is trying to become more like a fast-moving consumer goods retailer. They decided to bring in senior executives who have a retail marketing background to meet with their senior team in an informal dinner setting. This helped to open their minds to the advantages of bringing some-body from a completely different environment into their business, and to thereby facilitate a wave of creativity and innovation that could have a massive impact on the performance of the business. This is much easier to do at the top 100 level as opposed to bringing people with that kind of background into the top executive team directly where their lack of content expertise may be associated with too much risk. The key is to create informal opportunities for the top team to meet a variety of successful people from diverse backgrounds and help to open their minds in terms of the content expertise that they really need in their direct reports.

The final problem with effective succession management processes is that of ownership. In most businesses, executives 'own' their direct reports and the people who work for their direct reports. They decide who to hire, who to move from one job to another and who to fire. This 'ownership' creates a silo where executives feel that the people who work in their team or in the teams below them are their resource. They invest in the development of that resource as a way of ensuring that they have the leadership capability that is required for them to produce the business results that they are accountable for. This team ownership is a very laudable process and Human Resource professionals tend to see it as a positive step in ensuring that executives feel that the people they have are truly part of their team and together they can focus on achieving common business results. The problem of ownership, however, is in the fact that, if managers own the executives that work for them, then the career opportunities for these executives are extremely limited. As a high-potential executive my opportunities for career progression depend on my boss disappearing and, therefore, vacating his place for me. Alternatively, he or she can recommend me to someone else and thereby lose me, which would not be in their short-term interests.

If we want to create effective succession management processes for a large business we need to expose individuals to a broad array of possible positions that are outside their current business unit. This would identify high-potential executives that a recruiting manager would not typically see as part of the pool of potential candidates within his/her business silo. However, in order for members of the pool to be a truly available resource they have to be 'owned' at a corporate Group level and cannot be 'owned' by their manager and the specific business unit that they happen to be working in at the moment. In organisations that manage succession effectively, executives who become part of the talent pool, either at the senior level or at the second tier level, become a Group-owned resource. This enables them to be placed in a position by Group Human Resources and, while their line manager has the right of veto if he does not want them, that manager is not the one that will determine their next career move. If they continue to perform exceptionally well in this position, then after 3 years or so they will be moved to another part of the business in order to build a broad base of experience. This 'ownership' arrangement for the small number of critical positions and a small number of executives in the talent pool makes it possible to move very talented executives every 3 years across the breadth of organisational silos and, thereby, enable them to build a breadth of capability that is essential for managing key leadership positions at the most senior levels in the business.

Everything I have talked about so far has focused on senior executive positions and on the development of succession for those positions. In a number of organisations, however, the concept of succession management extends beyond senior executives into positions that require unique skills. Many organisations need not only very effective leadership but also a number of critical positions where the technical expertise of the people who hold them has a disproportionate impact on the performance of the business as a whole. In some financial institutions these would be traders who develop deep expertise in specific areas of content and their success or failure has a major impact on the success of the business. In high-technology companies these may be project managers who handle development-orientated projects that, if done effectively, could have a massive impact on the performance of the business. Project managers are also key to the success of infrastructure businesses. As a result, in those businesses it is important for the talent management efforts to focus on positions that require a depth of technical expertise and to ensure that those positions also have effective succession management processes attached to them. This requires a parallel system to everything that I have described so far in relation to senior executive positions with a focus on a very limited number of highly technical jobs. The organisation should identify two or three key specialist jobs that have significant impact on business performance, assess the capability of the current job holders in terms of specific competencies that are required for performing effectively and compare the capability of existing job holders to others that are available in the external marketplace. The business should then assess the number of employees in these technical positions that leave in a given year and use these turnover figures to predict how many new people will be required. In addition, the data about the capability of existing job holders compared to those available in the market will identify a number of people in these technical positions that may be acceptable, but are not at the level of performance that could be obtained by using the best people. As a result of this analysis, you may identify around 20% of the existing technical positions that are at risk in any given year. This becomes the foundation for building a talent pool of this 20% size that is available at any given time to step in if and when positions become vacant within the technical expertise group. It is hard to generalise here because in technical situations every job is different, but traders, project managers or people with specific IT capabilities are both available in the marketplace and can be trained internally if there is clarity about the nature of succession requirements that are likely to come up in a given year. The key from a talent management perspective is not to focus on all technical positions in the business and what is required for resourcing all of those positions, since that is part of the normal Human Resourcing processes. In the context of talent management you need to focus on succession for a very small number of critical technical jobs that have a disproportionate impact on the performance of the business as a whole. Only those positions need to become the focus of in-depth succession management processes to ensure that the best players in the marketplace are occupying them in your business.

SUMMARY

The concept of succession management has been around for many years where organisations have focused on identifying possible successors to senior management positions. As we saw, changes in the structure of businesses through delayering eliminated many interim management steps and it became harder to build the required talent to move up an organisational ladder. Organisations have also become much less stable at the top and frequent change in the structure of the business and in the individuals who occupy senior management positions has meant that highly planned succession management processes no longer worked. As a result, organisations that are effective in succession management have moved into much more flexible arrangements where individualised, highly focused talent pools are created to enable internal resourcing processes to continuously upgrade the capability of senior executives in highly influential positions. We also have seen that some organisations use the same kinds of methodologies to focus on critical technical jobs that have a disproportionate impact on the performance of the business.

CHAPTER 7

TALENT SCOUTING IN THE EXTERNAL ENVIRONMENT

*O*rganisations regularly look outside their own talent pool for senior executives to fill key positions. This is done when there is a specific job opening and the recruiting manager feels that there are no internal candidates that are good enough. When dealing with senior positions, external recruitment will usually be done through executive search firms that will come up with a list of relevant organisations in which potential candidates would be available, do research to identify a long list of individuals who are recommended by others, create a shortlist of people who have been identified as appropriate, go through a selection process interviewing candidates themselves and bringing them to the recruiting manager until the chosen candidate is finally selected. In some cases businesses are more active and look outside even when they do not have a specific vacancy. Sometimes individuals in posts are considered to be not good enough for the changing requirements of an executive position and, therefore, the organisation may go outside and see if there are better candidates in competitor organisations who could provide more effective leadership within the business. Also, a number of businesses in the last few years have identified a strategic need to create a fundamental change in the way their business is running and, therefore, they have brought a large number of senior executives from other businesses who were perceived to have the potential to become catalysts for significant change within what used to be a very stable management team.

The process of recruiting senior executives from the outside is handled by the recruiting manager together with relevant support from the Human Resource function. When briefing executive search companies, the focus is on a job description and on the cultural characteristics of the organisation so that potential candidates will fit in once they have been chosen. Businesses that are more advanced in terms of their talent management practices have a more sophisticated process for briefing external recruiters in light of the talent management needs of the organisation. As described in Chapter 4, these businesses would have a clearly defined talent standard that identifies the key competencies that are required for executives to be effective in key roles. They would also define the level of potential that would be expected from executives who are coming into the organisation. These businesses ensure that executive search firms get a brief, not only through a job description, but also in terms of the relevant competence frameworks that will be used when choosing among alternative candidates, for a given position internally and externally. This brief enables the executive recruiters to rate their potential candidates in terms of the competencies and provide a more detailed profile of strengths and weaknesses to match the requirements of the job. Internally, recruiting managers and Human Resourcing professionals can similarly use this competence profile to ensure that the new candidates for senior executive positions actually have the profile of capability that the organisation is seeking. All of these processes improve the external resourcing activities when the organisation interfaces with executive search firms and helps everyone involved to be clear about the profile of strengths and weaknesses that is desirable for a new position. But this process of selecting for talent in organisations that are highly focused on the issue extends beyond a job description and a competence profile into the broader context within which a specific executive recruitment is occurring. From that perspective, when the organisation brings in 'fresh blood' at senior levels, it is important that the newly selected candidate can not only perform the specific job for which they have been hired but also can augment the overall talent pool in the organisation and, thereby, become a key contributor to the medium-term success of the business. As a result, businesses that are focused on talent development will ensure that when executives are recruited from the outside there are also criteria that address the kind of medium-term potential that candidates should be able to demonstrate. Moreover, these businesses will create recruitment interview guides with specific questions that enable internal interviewers, including the recruiting manager, the business unit Human Resource executives and others, to focus on what the organisation thinks are fundamental requirements not only for the current position but also in terms of long-term talent development. These guidelines enable the recruitment process to have much more validity and to ensure that multiple interviewers are asking the same types of questions which make it possible to look at the total interviewing dataset and get a consistent view about each individual candidate. In general the clearer the recruiters are about the criteria for selection and the more consistent the organisation is across various interviewers, the higher the validity of the choice and the better the talent that will be recruited into the business. This consistency is very different from the typical recruitment process where a job description is used and individual interviewers ask their own questions and form their own impressions based on not very well-defined criteria. Their selection then tends to be more on the basis of gut feel and will, therefore, have much lower validity in ensuring that truly effective executive talent is brought into the business.

A number of my clients' organisations also ensure the validity of recruitment processes at senior executive levels by using external objective assessment processes. Business psychologists and in some cases assessment centre methodologies are used to ensure that there is objective data about the perceived capability of alternative candidates in light of specific competence requirements and that the best person is actually selected. Similarly, while in the past many businesses were relatively lax about taking references, today a number of them are clear about the importance of references and focus on the kind of questions that need to be asked of a broad base of referees to ensure that candidates do not control the quality of information that comes into the selection process. All of these processes, including clarifying competence criteria, focusing on long-term potential, providing interviewing guides, ensuring that a broad base of reviewers meet each candidate, utilising in-depth objective assessment processes and taking good references are there to ensure that the quality of talent that is brought in at senior executive levels is high. This is based on the fact that more sophisticated organisations understand the significant risks that are associated with bringing senior executives from outside the organisation and on the expectation that new people, if they are exceptionally talented, will have a significant impact on the performance of the business. Businesses that understand the importance of executive talent would invest, therefore, in having sophisticated processes for looking at a broad base of candidates and making in-depth selections when bringing people in.

Effective selection processes also need to be augmented by systematic on-boarding processes. Businesses that understand the importance of being effective in bringing talent into the organisation understand that selecting the right candidate is only the first step in ensuring that people succeed in their new positions. Even the most talented individuals have to make a significant change in the way that they operate when they move from one business environment to the other. It is important to prepare candidates before they join a new organisation so that they can plan effectively what to do. It is also critical to provide them with support during the first few months as they adapt to the new environment and start to exert significant influence. Similarly, it is important to prepare the recruiting manager for what he/she needs to do in order to facilitate the entry of a new executive into an influential position in the business. Moreover, it helps to work with the entire team on how they can accept a new member into their existing culture and ensure that the newcomer becomes an effective player within the team as rapidly as possible. The chart shown in Figure 7.1 identifies key steps in the on-boarding process.

An effective on-boarding process starts before the selected candidate comes to work (see Figure 7.1, Phase I: Pre-Entry), continues with activities that take place upon entry into the new organisation (see Figure 7.1, Phase II: Following Entry) and ends 3–6 months following entry when a more stable working environment has been created (see Figure 7.1, Phase III: End of 1st Quarter). The objectives of an effective on-boarding process are to think of the various elements that will enable an executive to enter into a new job in an effective way, prepare everyone to support this entry process (the person, their boss, other members of the team, key internal and external clients), solicit feedback about what actually happened during the entry process and use that feedback to help everyone to become more effective.

A famous statement suggests that 'you never get a second chance to make a first impression' and that crystallises the importance of making an effective entry into a new executive post. The more prepared everyone is, the smoother the transition and the faster the executive will be in terms of his or her on-the-job contribution.

Everything that I have talked about so far is focused on creating effective processes for bringing in external executive talent

The Challenge: Following recruitment, many Executives find it difficult to feel accepted in their new organisation. They tend to feel unwelcome, expected to make an impact too quickly, don't understand how 'things are done here' and encounter resistance to change. Recruiting managers (at senior levels) tend to become disappointed once the new Executive is in place because they don't see any real impact despite all the energy that went into the process. Management team colleagues may be apprehensive about the new recruit who thinks that he/she has all the answers based on their not-always-relevant external experience. All this is more pronounced when the organisation is not used to recruiting senior executives from the outside.

PHASE I: Pre-Entry
OBJECTIVES
1. Define key parameters required for job success.
2. Agree process for getting to know the business (meetings, reading).
3. Formulate entry strategy.

ACTIONS:
- Meet with the recruiting manager to agree Nos 1 and 2 above and to discuss pitfalls of entry phase and how to prepare for them
- Meet key executives who will have significant contact with the new person. Discuss how they can support an effective entry
- Help the Executive to formulate an entry strategy ('you don't get a second chance to make a first impression')

PHASE II: Following Entry
OBJECTIVES
1. Solicit initial feedback and share positive comments and concerns.
2. Agree realistic business objectives for first 3 to 6 months.
3. Establish mentoring/colleague support programme to facilitate 'bedding-in' process.

ACTIONS:
- Meet the recruiting manager to solicit positive and negative feedback. Help them to plan and implement a feedback session with the new Executive aimed at improving the entry process
- Meet with the new Executive to help them to prepare (in a non-defensive way) for the feedback session with their manager
- Identify 2/3 Executives around the business who can help the new person to understand how to get things done and get into the informal network. Facilitate these introductions

PHASE III: End of 1st Quarter
OBJECTIVES
1. Solicit more systematic feedback from the Executive, their manager, direct reports and key colleagues.
2. Use data to put together personal development plan.
3. Establish/reinforce mentoring and colleague support.

ACTIONS:
- Conduct 360° feedback process (using questionnaires and/or interviews). Discuss feedback with the Executive and agree development actions
- Help the recruiting manager to finalise business objectives and personal development plan for the new Executive. Ensure that this is followed by a meeting and that a 'normal' performance management process is in place

Human Resources can facilitate the entry process of a new Executive (directly or through the use of external coaches) and, thereby, help to ensure the success of the recruitment by helping the executive to function effectively within the new environment.

Figure 7.1 On-boarding.

into the organisation. A small number of organisations, however, have started to realise that it is important not only to bring in executive talent when there is a vacancy or when an executive in a specific position is not performing and will need to be replaced in the near future.

Some organisations have become much more assertive in ensuring that their leadership includes the best players that are available in the marketplace. The concept of talent scouting is very well known in the sports world where teams employ internal and external talent scouting agents that get to know the significant players that are available. They then help the sports team to think through its strategy in gradually upgrading the talent of their players by knowing where current players are in relation to those available in the field. A number of large businesses have started to use similar processes to augment their leadership talent pool. As you will see from my interviews with Heads of Human Resources, this is a new area for everyone. Most businesses do not think about external 'talent scouting' in a systematic way and these activities only occur when executive search firms use them to find external candidates for a particular job. A number of businesses, however, have started to initiate systematic bench-marking studies unrelated to recruiting for specific jobs. The following responses represent Heads of Human Resources who were interested in doing something systematic in the area of external 'talent scouting':

> Increasingly, as the Group is developing, we see that the really great people are concentrated in a number of organisations in the mar-ketplace who are some of our key competitors. I am thinking that maybe we should have our own in-house research team – a Talent Director whose role is to research people. We need to have a 'bench' that is prepared for acquisitions. We used to, but it is now empty since we bought a large business recently. So now we need to repopulate our subs bench so that we are ready for sudden depar-tures within the Group and, more importantly, for an acquisition.

We had a budget for this bench. This becomes a demonstration of 'edge' when someone is confident enough about their capability and potential to come into our business and sit on the bench. It is a demonstration of their willingness to take risks, which is what we want them to have. (Large retailer)

We are opportunistic and should be more systematic about it. When we have a need in a given area, then we do searches, but do not have a structured relationship with suppliers who do that job for us. We could certainly do better in this area. In the last few years we sometimes find an exceptional person and then tailor a job around them, but that is just the beginning. This is about the marketplace, which is now beginning to be much more competitive. This pro-activity will happen more and more as the market tightens up. My primary focus is as the internal headhunter. As the Group HR person, I will be helpful to the management in specifying the brief, but line HR managers handle the search. Sometimes we do calibrate internal with external candidates – that is when we are not sure about the internal people we have. In the past, top level resourcing also used to be here at Group level so that the resourcing job looked both internally and externally. We may need to come back to that in a different way if we really want to have enough people at the highest level of potential. (Public utility)

In our sector we know everyone in the competitor organisations and, given our success, we can cherry pick the executives we want. Looking outside our sector, to get people with a broader background, we don't do nearly enough of that – at least not systematically. Lately, we have brought in more external people (non-industry) than in the past. Systematic benchmarking – good idea but haven't done it. (Consumer services business)

We are terrible at this and have just recognised that we should do this but are thinking about it. Now external recruitment is 90% dependent on search firms but we want to move to 50–50 so that we will be tracking people who could be useful for us and we can go in when we need to. This is especially important for our diversity issues since everyone will want the same thing and it will be really hard to get the people you want if we are not prepared in advance. (Financial services company)

We employ good scouts through search companies plus some of us know good people from outside. We identified some good people but were too slow to promote them and then lost them. Still, this is a very limited amount of external scouting; we do it for a few positions that may become open. We haven't really thought about a talent bench that is ready to resource key positions due to acquisition or when someone isn't currently good enough. (Public utility)

Nothing in this area, I am afraid. Once we feel we need someone from outside, then we go through the assessment processes etc. as I already described, but we are not proactive. I am not sure why that might be; though it is true that we always have a number of people pressing to be promoted but, equally, we are aware that, as a result, we are not bringing in enough fresh blood. (Large retailer)

As you can see, Human Resource executives are only beginning to look at the concept of talent scouting when it applies to senior executives. We all know about talent scouting within the sports environment, but this is very new for corporate clients. In my own experience, I have done a number of projects for clients to benchmark executive talent across a sector. This executive search research is beginning to be more prevalent. Organisations are typically asking to understand who the key executives in specific types of jobs are across their business sector. In many business sectors there are four or five large players that dominate the market. Still, while executives in informal discussions would say that they know a lot of the key players in those businesses, that is usually not the case. Each executive may know two or three other people, especially in businesses where they have worked in the past. That knowledge is based on previous experience that is now a few years old or on very limited exposure to others within professional forums. These personal impressions are not done on a systematic basis and it is very hard to get an overall picture of what is available in the field. Moreover, in most business sectors, in addition to the four or five very large players that may dominate

80% of the field, there are still a number of significant niche players who focus on specific sub-sectors or specialist areas. Those may actually have exceptional executives who have a great deal of expertise but are outside of the main limelight in the field. Benchmarking executive talent across the main competitors in a specific area enables the business to place its own key players in the context of what is available in the competitive environment. It is not useful to benchmark all management positions in a large business because the data will become old very quickly as there will be too many individuals identified in this process. However, having a benchmark survey done by an executive search company is exceptionally useful when focusing on a number of critical jobs similar to the ones that we have identified in Chapter 5.

Benchmarking surveys have also expanded beyond the key competitors in a specific market. A number of businesses, when focused on critical jobs such as marketing, sales or even finance, are starting to open up to candidates that come from very diverse environments – financial institutions that look at retailers, chief financial officers that come from diverse industries and may be able to secure more creative funding arrangements or provide much more sophisticated use of financial resources, etc. As a result, some businesses are now beginning to ask executive search suppliers to provide them with benchmarking surveys that focus on a very small number of key jobs but identify individuals from diverse markets who are known to be exceptional within their own sector. These exceptional people are not viewed initially as candidates since there is no specific job opening at the moment. The Chief Executive and some of the key members on his/her team get to know these 'players' through informally arranged meetings. By getting to know people in depth, the business begins to open up its senior executives to understanding what could be achieved and to realise that maybe some of their current executives do not actually have the talent, and do not bring the breadth of experience, that it is possible to acquire in the marketplace. In general, getting to know very strong players from across diverse business environments impacts the perspective of the senior executive team on the type of talent that they could have and enables them to switch mediocre players with truly creative ones that can push the business forward much more rapidly.

The concept of talent scouting extends in some businesses to creating what they term 'bench strength'. This is a concept that comes from the sports world and the idea is that it may be advisable to bring in a few exceptional executives from the outside and put them in charge of project-type jobs or employ them as task-force leaders without having a specific executive position available. I have been told by one of my clients that if an exceptional individual is willing to take the risk and come into the business without having a specific role defined, then they have the kind of assertive and risk-taking characteristics that will be required for talented people in the long-term. This 'bench strength' enables the business to be ready for major acquisitions and to make internal organisational changes knowing that they have sufficient executive talent that provides them with the flexibility to move things around.

SUMMARY

Talent scouting is a very new process in the corporate world and, therefore, we know more from the experience in the sporting world than we do from business. My interviews with Heads of Human Resources in large corporations indicate that a number of them have begun to explore this area more systematically. But none of my clients has at this point in time a sophisticated process that you would find in every major league sports team. One can expect, from trends, that a small number of businesses that are highly focused on leveraging their executive talent are beginning to move in this direction. They understand the importance of having the best players in their leadership teams as a tool for advancing their competitive positioning and as a result they continue to become more educated about what is available in the marketplace. They have a systematic map of the executives that are leading their competitors and, therefore, they can have in-depth discussions about the benefits of bringing a number of significant players from the outside. I do find, however, that this is a new trend and a number of clients have started not only to map the environment, but also to create informal evening sessions where exceptional candidates from the outside are introduced to the senior executive team around the dinner table so that people get to know each other. This does not address a specific need, but it opens the thinking of both sides and gradually, if the chemistry is right, then, over an 18-month period, the senior executive team frees up opportunities and starts to bring in exceptional executives from outside whom they have by now become familiar with. This talent scouting process is an example of how the business environment in the USA and the UK has changed dramatically in the last few years. There is much more awareness of rapid changes within businesses and also much less loyalty of senior executives that have lost the fantasy that they will spend their entire career in one business. Everyone on both sides is clear that opportunities are available across the marketplace and that good candidates will not remain within a single business for more than 4 to 6 years. This more open executive marketplace makes it legitimate for senior executive teams to get to know key players in other businesses across the competitive environment and to gradually start courting processes that enable them to continuously improve their talent base.

CHAPTER 8

SYSTEMATIC PROCESSES FOR IDENTIFYING FUTURE EXECUTIVE TALENT AND ASSESSING POTENTIAL

*M*ost large organisations have a process for identifying future generations of talent who are expected, within the medium term, to become senior executives within the business. I asked Heads of Human Resources in large international businesses to describe what systematic processes they employ in order to identify young managers who have the potential to become senior executives. How do they assess the strengths and development needs of these people vis-à-vis future positions, and how do they facilitate development actions in the areas that have been identified?

Most businesses in my sample were doing something to identify and develop talent at lower levels, and to use the findings to identify 'feeder material' for senior positions. The most frequent approach was to have management-training programmes (development centres) appropriate for high-potential individuals. Some organisations recognise that managers may view these as 'prizes' and send people on the programme to keep them happy (rather than because they are genuinely high-potential). As a result, the businesses have instituted more objective processes to assess potential. Usually this meant that once someone was nominated as high-potential, they were assessed objectively to ensure their suitability.

The following quotes illustrate the more 'sophisticated' approaches used by businesses to identify and develop 'feeder' talent:

We cascade our Management Development Review process through the organisation on a functional basis. When we get box 9 people, we ask if this person could become part of the top team – they are nominated for 'the talent scheme' – then sent for psychometric assessment externally to ensure objectivity. If the report is positive then they become part of the scheme, and they get a lot of focused development. We have an annual development contract with each individual and their boss – looking at what they need to work on. This whole thing is an annual process – so not a 'bright graduate's scheme'. People drop out if they are not in box 9 next year. The aim is to keep it a pure scheme that only has really excellent middle managers. We have about 40 people in this pool. Development plans are personalised – it's not a 'sheep dip' programme. Each boss has to convince people in the MDR process to buy into their ratings. We don't have a forced distribution, but there is pressure on the team to keep the standards high. MDR is a lively discussion. At the moment there is no one at the bottom level since we have cleared these out – but gradually some people are labelled as weaker. We are trying to be creative in getting people to identify the weakest people. Some functions have tried forced distribution, but not everyone. In the future we may do that with our front line managers as a way to drive change in the organisation. (Large retailer)

Talent management at the junior level is, in our business, a sub-set of the same overall integrated process. HR will talk with managers at the lower levels of the organisation to identify talent early. They are identified individually, but participate in leadership development programmes that are aimed at their level of management. It's not really an open thing where people are labelled, but key managers know. We now have a software tool that we put on our HR system. This will push senior managers to be more open in their input. (Large manufacturer)

We are good at this. Each Regional Managing Director has six direct reports. That talent will be assessed through an assessment centre. People who want to be considered for Regional Managing Director roles get a chance, as well as feedback, which is then followed by help to think about development. It's interesting but not great. There are big gaps when looking at people to move from functional to Regional Managing Director roles. And this is not just because of the management; people resist moving from one functional role to another. We use a business school to provide the management training for high-potential people. (Property developer)

A number of businesses that I interviewed were active in the identification and development of talent at more junior levels, but still had significant concerns about the effectiveness of their approach. Sometimes their managers were too sensitive about 'rocking the boat' and afraid to upset their average team members who were not perceived to have high potential. In other cases the process was just not tough enough and people went to management training modules without a robust vetting process. These situations are illustrated below:

We have two programmes: the Academy project is run for us by a business school with a 1-year programme with modules focused around our operational and functional issues. Anyone expected to get to our top group is expected to go to that. A second programme (Advance) is more skills-based and focused on more junior people that will be feeders into the next level. These programmes are viewed very positively in the business. With both programmes we provide coaching by senior managers in the business to every participant. This helps them and also exposes them to senior people so they get to know them. In one of our businesses we put together a development centre to identify people at the lower levels of the organisation – they will feed the Advanced Programme. This is manager-driven based on appraisal. These people now feature on the succession plans. We are beginning to face a problem – i.e. a need to ensure that this is driven by managers based on potential and not as a consolation prize or something positive to give to people who are key performers. They need to understand that not being a candidate for a programme is not bad. This is a transparent process for people who go on the Academy programme. We 'force' managers to have an open discussion with people since their rating is related to pay. Unless you are performing well you will not have a discussion of future potential. We don't really want low-performance high-potential kinds of people since they are destructive. (Large retailer)

On the Leadership Development Programme we provide training for promising middle managers. We also have a linkage programme at more junior levels. This is done in major countries and helps us to identify people who can go further. Also the data management process that feeds up to us at the corporate centre highlights talented people. This is key since, given the size of our business, we need this future talent. We don't actively talk about people being on the talent list, except for the top six high-potentials and six business-critical people in each division. We do not have a fast-track type of approach because it doesn't fit our culture. We want to stay more flexible and entrepreneurial and don't want to create a bureaucracy in this area. In the last few years people have recognised that the appraisal process has become more important and the senior management is now more behind this and has embraced it. Now senior executives are looking for better ways to develop people because of the business necessity. We want to make this systematic to ensure that things are done effectively despite the size and diversity of the organisation. With such a rate of growth it's harder to know everyone and the process needs to compensate for this to ensure that we don't lose our best people. (Consumer services company)

We have talent round table discussions but it still depends on knowing the right people. Key people are mentored by senior people around the group. Once you are in this position then many opportunities are presented to you but not through a systematic talent management process. We think of talent in clearly defined boundaries. There are a number of things that we do, like other organisations, under a talent leadership banner. So we do it but really it is a tick-box process that doesn't add up to a real commitment. We still do things very much within the boundaries – functional, geographical, company, technical areas – rather than having a broad view that creates the breadth that people need to become really broad leaders for the future. We just introduced flexibility in reward at the top three levels so that starts to open things up. The other thing is: who owns the identification of future talent? It should be the Board but who helps these people to use complex data and to change their assumptions about people? Too many discussions are led by people who cannot do that. The business focuses on ticking boxes and we need to push them to get the truth out and then we can make real decisions. (Financial services business)

We do some of that. We attempted to take the Leadership Development Programme and cascade it down the organisation, starting this year. This is especially important in Southeast Asia and North Africa where we can't continue to use expats. So we stopped recruiting graduates here and started to recruit in Asia and move them around the world to give them experience. There is an important link between talent and the use of expats. Having more systematic talent management systems should help you to use fewer expats. Culturally, the Talent Management process doesn't work outside the Anglo-American concept. In Asia, individualism doesn't play well. It is a more consensus-driven culture and we found it hard to get people to differentiate, but even in the UK people are unhappy to differentiate overtly. Hard decisions are not popular. (International energy business)

The process of identifying future executive talent starts with performance management data that is gathered in almost all businesses on an annual basis as part of a formal performance appraisal process. In many organisations, managers are asked not only to rate the performance of their direct reports but also to rate their potential. That data is usually described in terms of their readiness to take on senior positions within the foreseeable future

Rating Management Potential

Please rate the potential of this manager to take on significantly larger jobs within the foreseeable future

Rating	Potential	By when?
5	Very high – has the potential to make two moves up the management hierarchy	
4		
3	High – has the potential to move to the next step within the management hierarchy	
2		
1	Unclear – has not demonstrated the potential to move to jobs that are significantly larger than his/her current position	

Comments (on the nature of future career paths):

Comments (on the nature of personal development required to build his/her potential):

Figure 8.1   Example form for rating management potential.

(see Figure 8.1). The combination of the performance rating and the potential rating provided by managers creates a nine-box grid as shown in Figure 4.1 (p. 77).

The information from performance management is brought up the organisation within each Division or Function and then discussed by the senior executive team as part of the annual talent management process. Usually people who are in what is called 'box nine', meaning rated both 'high' in performance in their current job and 'high' in terms of their potential, are discussed as being the high-potential pool of executives that can provide the leadership foundation for the future. In many businesses where more sophisticated processes are used, line management identify a pool of individuals rated in 'box nine' who are then assessed externally in a more objective manner to ensure that the ratings of line management are backed up by more objective data. This assessment is usually done individually when dealing with relatively senior people. But when dealing with more junior managers who are expected to have long-term potential there is usually an assessment centre that is used to provide objective assessment data about their long-term potential.

Figures 8.2 and 8.3 identify the 'strategic few' who are the focus for talent development activities, plus additional populations to focus on.

What do we really mean by long-term potential? When describing an executive's performance on the job most businesses don't only rate them as being 'high', 'medium' or 'low' in terms of their performance, since they have developed a language of competencies. These include areas of performance that enable a manager to understand the profile of strengths and weaknesses of the people who work for them. Even when describing a strong performer, instead of just saying that they are doing very well the description also states in what way. For example, they are performing very well in terms of their strategic thinking, in terms of their operational capabilities, in terms of how they manage people, in terms of how they manage relationships, in their approach to change and innovation, etc. This language of competence not only enables managers to describe performance in terms of the achievement of objectives, but also provides a diagnostic format that enables managers to help the people that work for them by building on their strengths and reducing the negative impact of their weaknesses in specific competence areas. When we are focused on potential, however, we do not have a similar language. Executives are asked to rate those who work for them as being 'high', 'medium' or 'low' potential, or as having the capability to

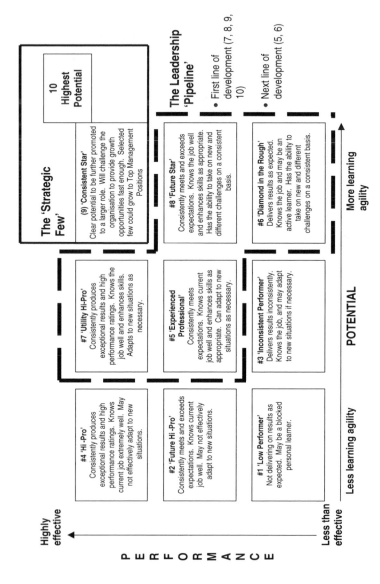

Figure 8.2 Definitions of future leaders.

The 'Strategic Few'

10 Highest Potential

(9) 'Consistent Star'
Clear potential to be further promoted to a larger role. Will challenge the organisation to provide growth opportunities fast enough. Selected few could grow to Top Management Positions

#7 'Utility Hi-Pro'
Consistently produces exceptional results and high performance ratings. Knows the job well and enhances skills. Adapts to new situations as necessary.

#4 'Hi-Pro'
Consistently produces exceptional results and high performance ratings. Knows current job extremely well. May not effectively adapt to new situations.

#8 'Future Star'
Consistently meets and exceeds expectations. Knows the job well and enhances skills as appropriate. Has the ability to take on new and different challenges on a consistent basis.

#5 'Experienced Professional'
Consistently meets expectations. Knows current job well and enhances skills as appropriate. Can adapt to new situations as necessary.

#2 'Future Hi-Pro'
Consistently meets and exceeds expectations. Knows current job well. May not effectively adapt to new situations.

#6 'Diamond in the Rough'
Delivers results as expected. Knows the job and may be an active learner. Has the ability to take on new and different challenges on a consistent basis.

#3 'Inconsistent Performer'
Delivers results inconsistently. Knows the job and may adapt to new situations if necessary.

#1 'Low Performer'
Not delivering on results as expected. May be a blocked personal learner.

The Leadership 'Pipeline'
- First line of development (7, 8, 9, 10)
- Next line of development (5, 6)

More learning agility

Less learning agility

POTENTIAL

Highly effective

Less than effective

P E R F O R M A N C E

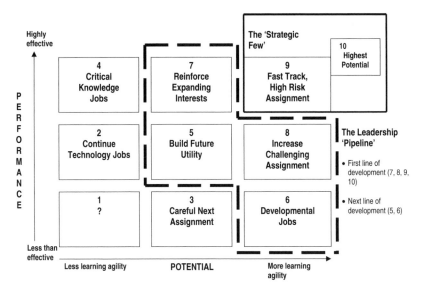

Figure 8.3   Development paths for future leaders.

take on significantly larger jobs. But we don't have a language to say what we mean by that potential. When analysing potential we should not focus on specific competencies but on more underlying capabilities that enable the person to develop the competencies that will be required in more senior positions. These underlying capabilities include intellectual factors, interpersonal factors, motivation and resilience and a generalised approach to business tasks. These underlying capabilities enable an executive, through a combination of self-awareness and through their ability to learn, to build the competencies that will be required at the next few levels above their current job.

Figure 8.4 presents a model (developed together with Brian Sullivan) which shows the relationship between underlying capabilities, competencies and job performance. In order to examine executive potential, however, we need to use this model and to focus on the difference between the performance required of the executive in today's job and the performance required at the next management level. The most useful approach for examining these

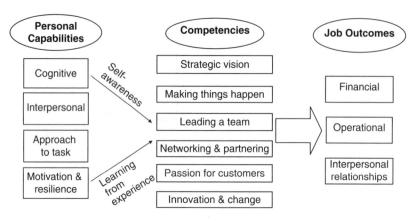

Figure 8.4 Model to assess individual executive capability.

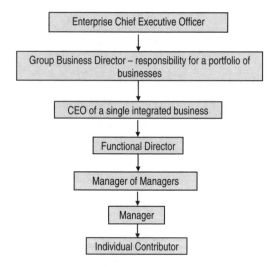

Figure 8.5 Key managerial transitions.

differences was developed by GE and is summarised in the book *The Leadership Pipeline* (a brief review is given in Appendix 2). Their concept states that management jobs in large organisations become more and more complex as the breadth of responsibility increases. As can be seen in Figure 8.5, the GE model describes seven key management transitions and for each transition it identifies what are the main differences that are required for succeeding at the next level.

In large businesses, each management level requires very different behaviours and, therefore, capabilities in order to be effective. As a result, when an executive performs very well at one level and is promoted to the next level of management, if he or she continues to exhibit the same behavioural patterns then they will not succeed. In their book *The Peter Principle* (William Marrow, 1969), L.J. Peter and R. Hull describe the situation where people are promoted to the level where they are no longer competent to perform effectively. This is a relatively static concept of potential where people are able to perform at a certain level and are not able to perform above that. Alternatively, according to the GE model, capability is much more flexible. We are able to perform at the next level but we simply do not understand how the performance at the next level is different from the performance at the current level where we have been so successful. In order to ensure effective career management processes so that executives who are within talent pools succeed in performing more senior jobs once they are appointed to them, we need to have systematic talent management processes that address the differences between jobs at different levels. This starts with the need to analyse the hierarchy of executive positions in your business by categorising them into five or six management levels that have significant qualitative differences in terms of their requirements. Once we understand the managerial hierarchy then, for each level, we need to identify key behaviours (in each competence area) that are required to be successful at that level. This will lead to assessment and development processes to ensure that people within the talent pool have what it takes in order to succeed at the next level. In addition to developing potential, we need to use different profiles for each management level as a basis for in-depth on-boarding processes that will help executives, before and during their initial entry into a new position, to understand what is different in the requirements of that position compared to what they were capable of and did effectively at the previous level.

Figure 8.5 identified six key management transitions that require significantly different kinds of behaviours in order to be successful. The reader is encouraged to read the book *The Leadership Pipeline*, that describes each of these transitions in detail and specifies the development activities that GE has put in place in order to ensure effective transitions. I will outline the key elements of transition since they are important for building effective talent management processes. Managerial levels are not directly parallel to the hierarchy from an organisational status point of view. In many cases people who occupy very senior positions are actually performing jobs that from a managerial point of view are not very complex (while still requiring a great deal of technical expertise). For example, a Head of Legal Services for a large international business is an important position. But a person in this position usually manages a small number of lawyers and uses some outsourced resources. Therefore, from a managerial point of view this is not a very senior position, whereas from an organisation hierarchy point of view and in terms of their rank within the business this person would be perceived to be a senior executive.

When describing key management transitions there are a number of characteristics that cut across the whole spectrum. First, as executives go up the hierarchy, each step requires very different behaviours in order for the individual to be effective. The flip-side is that when an individual executive continues to perform in a way that he or she used to perform at the previous stage (which made them so successful there), then they will fail in terms of the requirements of the next executive level. It is, therefore, important to understand the differences between each level and to use this information to develop people.

Second, as you go up the management hierarchy, you spend less time in doing your own work and more time in managing others – this increases at every transition. Therefore, people who continue to focus on what they themselves do and do not spend sufficient time on managing others will not be successful.

Third, as executives go further up the managerial hierarchy, there is an increased broadening of the thinking required at every transition. Managers need to begin to understand a much larger whole as a system of interdependencies between different business units as opposed to just understanding their own part of the puzzle and assuming that if they do their part well then everything else will work out.

The fourth general principle is that moving up requires a person to identify and realise a breadth of potential synergies between component parts of the businesses below them. It is not enough to ensure that every part of the business works well – the higher the degree of integration between business units below you the more effective the whole entity will become.

The fifth general principle suggests that as people progress, the complexity of management increases while the level of information decreases. As you progress up management transitions you will have a smaller proportion of the information you need for decision making. The organisation becomes more and more complex and there are too many layers involved in passing on information and making judgements about what is and what is not important. Therefore as executives go up the hierarchy they have to take more complex decisions with less information than would have been required in order to make those decisions at the levels below them. It is harder to take the true pulse of what is going on in the business.

Finally, as executives go up the management hierarchy, their timespan changes. People need to think more about the future and to try and balance that with the needs of today and next year. Middle managers need to think in terms of annual budgets and monthly performance reviews. As they become more senior, they have to take more strategic decisions where the time-frame for investment and for implementing change is much longer than a 1-year budget process.

In understanding the hierarchy of management positions, we need to compare line and functional jobs. As Table 8.1 shows, the levels are related but different. Heads of sub-functions report to heads of functions who then report to Group functions. It is important in understanding the managerial complexity of a role and in being able to compare various functional roles to various line roles.

Table 8.1 identifies only one line hierarchy and one functional hierarchy, but in all businesses there are a number of line hierarchies depending on the different Divisions and a number of functional hierarchies that include Finance, IT, Human Resources, Procurement etc. As a result, in order to develop a systematic talent management process (and as we will see in Chapter 9, to develop career paths) it is important to understand how these interrelate. A map of the different job families (including line and functional) compared according to the different managerial levels will provide the foundation for understanding potential and for career management.

Table 8.1 Key managerial transitions need to include both line and functional jobs

Line	Functional
Enterprise CEO	
Group Business Director	
(portfolio of companies)	
CEO of single business	Head of Group function
Division head	Head of function
Manager of managers	
Manager	Head of sub-function
Individual contributor	Individual contributor

In general, line jobs require more accountability and, therefore, a broader perspective than functional jobs since line jobs have a number of functions under them and an executive needs to integrate the different capabilities and types of understanding that are required across all of these functions. On the other hand, functional jobs also form a managerial hierarchy and more senior functional positions require a much broader perspective and increased partnering with other functions. Less senior functional jobs can be managed in isolation. For example, an executive can be effective as a treasurer without necessarily understanding the interrelationships between that and other functional areas.

When reviewing career paths and creating talent management processes, it is important to combine line and functional jobs. This enables high-potential executives to be prepared for truly senior positions by rotating between different types of functional and line jobs and thereby acquiring the depth and breadth of expertise that will be required for success at the top.

The following boxes describe, in more detail, the key requirements associated with each management transition and the danger signs when that transition is not made effectively. They are based on Brian Sullivan's work extrapolating from the GE experience described in *The Leadership Pipeline*.

Transition One: Becoming the 'Manager of others' or 'Team Leader'

- You now need to shift from doing work to getting work done through others.
- It is not that you just tolerate it, but must now view other-directed work as 'mission critical'. This is the most difficult thing to learn at this transition.

Continued

■ You have to learn not to be forever 'putting out fires', i.e. doing things yourself.

The danger signs of not succeeding through Transition One:

■ **Overpowering your subordinates** with your technical expertise. The hands-on, problem-solving crackerjack, technically smart engineer working out the engineering solution himself ends up competing with his own direct reports to whom he has given an assignment.

■ **Doing things yourself**: fixing other people's mistakes – sometimes to show off . . . or, more usually, through frustration with direct reports not doing the job your way/as well/as quickly.

■ **Not delegating** clearly and with regular follow-up review, monitoring 'how' things are being done and supporting – seeing it as abdication and being able to 'let go'.

■ **Not coaching**: not emphasising the value of coaching, as building problem-solving skills – rather than solving the problem or taking the decisions – and enabling people to grow.

■ **Hiring below-par people** who are either not capable of doing the job or who do not match the values and culture of the business – so that 'they don't fit'.

■ **Not taking pride in your team**: still taking ownership and pride in your own task delivery success and not in the success of your people. Distancing yourself from their problems and failures.

■ **Not being available**: not showing the value of simply being available, genuinely approachable, communicating accessibility.

Transition Two: On becoming a 'Manager of managers'

■ You cannot now manage managers as you would and did manage individual contributors: it is different.

■ The skills of 'managing managers' are deceptive, not obvious: hence this promotion is often seen as a stepping-stone rather than as a major career passage. Enthusiasm for this Transition Two promotion is more muted than for the promotion through Transition One.

■ And because the skills are not obvious, selection/promotion errors are often made and the training/development given is often insufficient.

■ You are now responsible for the greatest number of people who do the most 'hands-on' work (there is a big multiplier: you can go from managing 14 to managing 150 through 10 direct reports) – work that is directly related to the business's products and services. Hence, the impact of a 'managing manager's performance on QUALITY is critical.

■ You now have to focus on empowering/enabling the direct reports to manage!

The danger signs of Transition Two not succeeding:

■ **Having difficulty delegating**: just cannot get away with this now (at first level, yes) since simply cannot do everything yourself. Work gets delayed since centralised.

■ **Poor performance management**: not giving good direction, goal clarity, feedback and coaching to direct reports.

■ **Failure to build a strong team**: working with direct reports mainly one-to-one and not as a productive team – each learning from the others – instead, encouraging silo thinking, preventing the synergy from sharing.

Continued

■ **Disproportionate focus on getting the work done**: and not valuing your role as coach and developer and discounting strategic or cultural issues.

■ **Choosing clones over contributors**: people who are too similar to yourself and do not complement you, who may thus be unwilling to challenge you enough and less likely to bring different perspectives.

Transition Three: On becoming a Functional Director

■ This is a big promotion.
■ You are now the member of a business team and you report to a GM or Business/Managing Director.
■ Often former peers now report to you.
■ From now on, you are never sure you have all the information, or whether all the information you have is correct.
■ You now have to think about the function from multiple perspectives; to see the function supporting the overall business objectives.
■ You will be communicating collaboratively with multiple functions and multiple levels − and geographically. You can no longer be into blaming other functions − they are yours!

The danger signs of moving to Functional Director:

■ **Mainly operations and too little strategy**: not making the transition from an *operational* and/or project orientation to a *strategic* one that ties your functional activities to the business goals.

Continued

- Still predominantly **focused on the short-term**.
- **Not valuing** work that is unfamiliar or of relatively less interest.
- Not **'letting go'** of work in the areas of personal interest and abdicating (or not trusting the competence of people) in the areas of relatively less interest.
- **Over- or under-delegating**: too much with no control system: abdicating – or too little and trying to control everything: micro-managing.
- **Not becoming a 'Leader'**: still showing more interest in being a **hands-on Manager** of others or even an individual performer, than in being a Leader.

Transition Four: On becoming a CEO of a simple business

- Often the most satisfying transition – and most challenging – of an executive's career.
- It brings significant autonomy, which executives with leadership instincts find liberating.
- Now can see a clear link between their efforts and a marketplace result.
- In capability terms, it is not just becoming more strategic and more cross-functional – though it is important to continue developing those skills.
- Now they have to work with staff functions so they feel valued and deliver and do not drain energy.

The danger signs of Transition Four, to a CEO:

- **Needlessly devilling with the detail**: going into the detail to a degree that can no longer be justified.

Continued

- **Uninspired communication**: still talking from your functional perspective and not from that of the business.
- **Inability to assemble a strong team**: for example, favouring your old function in selection; not wanting the threat of real talent; not building a team spirit or making conflict creative.
- **Not really grasping the business model for how to make money**: becoming obsessed with one activity, e.g. number of customer calls; not seeing the entire profit chain; not wanting to show your ignorance about core basic work processes not involved with before.
- **Problems with time management**: trying to do too much; all is frenetic; not finding time for coaching or for the future.
- **Neglecting the 'soft' issues**: no time spent on reshaping and deepening your business's culture.

Transition Five: On becoming a Business Director for a group of businesses

- At first sight, it can be deceptive – and not appear too arduous – if you can run one, you can run four!
- A Group Business Director has now to value the success not just of one (maybe their former) business but the success of several – and all *other people's* – businesses. Very hard for hands-on executives, for results-oriented executives – or executives who just love receiving the lion's share of the credit!
- You are no longer running a business – the thing you liked most of all! For the first time you have now ceded just about all direct involvement in running a business. You have to 'let go' of the frustration arising from your conviction you could operate any of the businesses better than any of

Continued

the BD/GMs. Wishing you were doing so will lead you unconsciously to usurp the authority of the BD/GMs.

■ The skills are now more subtle and indirect. You should now be seeing issues in the broadest possible terms. It is much more complex and ambiguous than investing in just one business.

■ You have to think 'holistically', about the collection of businesses you run and their relation to the larger corporation.

■ Beware: if there is no real strategic entity to this collection/group of businesses then it is not a real transition. The job will feel more like a span-breaker, with you helping the CEO manage it all. In a smaller company there will not be a GBD at all – the next step is the CEO.

■ It can be a real and valuable managerial transition – despite some still seeing it as a non-job, and only as a necessary evil stepping-stone to a CEO job.

The danger signs of Transition Five, Business Director of a group of businesses:

■ **Acting like Business Directors** rather than Group Directors: usurping the functions of their Business Directors, thereby starting a chain reaction right down the line.

■ **Passing up Business Director developmental opportunities**: not 'growing' their direct reports as Business Leaders, not seeing it as a coaching, nurturing and hands-off role.

■ **Maintaining a distance from the corporate functional team**: still seeing them as the 'ivory tower' – and not actually spending time on essentially 'corporate' issues.

■ **Not prioritising the portfolio strategy over individual strategies** and not making decisions that differentiate businesses on the basis of likely results – and still focusing on individual business strategies.

Continued

> ■ Not contributing on the 'uncovered' challenges: new products, new developments, new markets, alliances, acquisitions – i.e. the future, rather than existing, businesses.

Transition Six: Meeting the key challenges for an Enterprise CEO

1. **Delivering consistent, predictable top and bottom line results**
   Value short-term and longer-term balancing, investing time to achieve that balance; anticipate long-term ramifications and adjust short-term tactics with the long-term in mind. Having the emotional fortitude to make unpleasant decisions.

2. **Building a vision and setting a forward strategic direction for the enterprise**
   Keeping the Company moving forward and steady; vision, strategic acumen, positioning know-how. Clarifying assumptions about the changing economy, industry, market, technology, the competitive patterns to heed and then the business models that will make money. Craft a vision statement that is not unfocused, but is concrete.

3. **Shaping the soft side of the enterprise**
   Managing the environment of relationships such that energy is released at *all levels* – real communicating 'down the line'. Monitoring good selection, feedback giving, ending job–person mismatches, retaining high performers through challenging opportunities and appropriate reward.

4. **Maintaining an edge in execution**
   Ensuring decisions are taken from the top down so that things get done. Hence 'knowing what is going on',

Continued

spending time diagnosing in depth, 'ensuring they hear the bad news', ensuring the Board is productive and decisive.

5. **Managing the Company in a broader, global context**

Paying attention to the shareholders, the environment (local, global), to the community, to Health & Safety.

The danger signs for an Enterprise CEO:

■ **Ignorance of the reality around how things get done**: this goes back to challenge 4 – either not interested in listening and learning or not aware how to impact on obstacles to get results.

■ **Spending the majority of your time on external relationships, particularly on investor relations**: not balancing their time to ensure someone is minding the store.

■ **Not seeing the need for a sequencing and over-lapping of strategies**: either focusing only on the immediate strategies, over-estimating their 'half-life'; or focusing only on the long-term strategy but not lasting to see it live.

■ **Not spending enough time on the 'soft side' of the business**: this goes back to challenge 3 – the sheer complexity of people issues can bias the CEO to financial, product and market issues – or, selecting past 'buddies' to key posts who don't tell it as it is.

■ **Board meetings are too focused on the past and on consensus**: Too much time on reporting results, discussing past decisions and events.

Given this analysis of the nature of managerial transitions and the potential that is required in order to succeed when executives move from one managerial job to the next, what should large businesses do in order to use this as a basis for talent development?

The process should start by mapping executive transitions through an analysis of the key jobs within your business. This analysis of jobs makes it possible to focus on transitions that executives will have to go through throughout their career. Identifying future executive talent needs to be built on an objective assessment process that makes it possible to validate line managers' nominations. As a line manager, when I review the people who work in my team I naturally think that I can identify a few of those who have long-term potential. However, my own assessment is limited by my own potential and breadth of experience which impacts my understanding of what is actually required to perform well at more senior executive levels. It is therefore critical to validate line managers' assessment of potential with more objective processes. The assessment process for middle managers who potentially may go up to senior executive positions tends to be done in the form of an assessment centre. Groups of managers spend a day or two going through a number of simulations that are used to ascertain their potential in the long term. In addition, it is customary to use psychometric test data and sometimes also 360° feedbacks from bosses, direct reports and colleagues in order to provide more in-depth input about current competencies and capabilities. All of these assessment techniques have their limitations and, therefore, the best format involves using multiple sources of data that are indicators of potential within specific areas of capability. Ideally you would expect to get data about intellectual capability, about interpersonal capability, about motivation and resilience and about approach to task as ways of assessing long-term potential. The more data sources you have that are keyed into these, the easier it will be to get a valid assessment of the person's potential.

But identifying promising executives is not sufficient since we need to develop people and enable them to build on the potential that they have within them. One of the most difficult decisions that organisations reach is the concept of transparency. Many organisations fear that if they say to 10% of their management population that they have long-term potential and they will help them to develop, then this will de-motivate the remaining 90% who will feel that they are being told that they have no future in the business and that this may push them to find work elsewhere and reduce their level of motivation to perform in their current jobs. As a result, in many businesses, while a lot of energy is spent on identifying people with high potential, sometimes these people themselves do not know that they have been identified and there is not a lot of focused attention on this population. From a talent management perspective, as described in Chapter 1, the concept is to invest disproportionately in people with the potential to have a very large impact on the performance of the business. Therefore, if we identify a small number of managers who have long-term potential, we must invest disproportionately in them so that they will build on their underlying potential and actually become successful in the long term. Regarding the question of transparency, organisations have taken a number of routes. The main approach is to say that the high-potential group is a fluid concept that changes from year to year. This means that when executives move into a 'box nine' rating in terms of performance on the job and perceived potential then they can enter into this group of high-potential executives. Similarly, when the performance of people who are already in this select group drops below the top levels, then they are taken out of this group. This message makes it possible to convey to the entire management population that anybody has the opportunity to enter this select group on the basis of their actions. Moreover, effective businesses are clear in communicating to all of their managers what specific capabilities are required in order to be in this select group. Therefore, as an executive, if I want to be selected, then my manager can tell me what I need to do in order to demonstrate my commitment and my long-term potential to succeed. In a number of businesses, the assessment centres are also open to self-nomination processes. Even if my manager and I have a personality clash and he does not want to nominate me as someone who has long-term potential, if I am ambitious enough, then I can raise my hand and nominate myself and prove that I do have the long-term potential to succeed. Therefore, this combination of being clear about the criteria for having long-term potential and being open in enabling executives to put themselves forward means that employees will feel that this is a fair game, as opposed to something that is discussed quietly behind closed doors. It is also important to recognise when discussing transparency that many executives do not really want to belong to this high-potential group because the investment required from the individual goes way beyond that which is demanded of them in their day-to-day job. Participating in seminars, contributing to cross-functional teams, taking an international assignment and engaging in further development activities requires a significant amount of extra effort from individuals and many people do not have the motivation and tenacity required. Therefore, as long as everyone is clear about the criteria for getting in and about the demands of participating with that group, then you will find that many executives would be comfortable in not belonging to that group because they do not really want to invest what is required.

Once selected to a high-potential talent pool, the success of the business in developing feeder populations depends on how much they invest in these executives. Just listing names in a box will not impact the leadership cadre and the day-to-day political reality means that managers, when they do have a senior executive opening, will either appoint people that they know or go externally and recruit people who have an impressive career path. Once the business develops a talent pool it is critical to ensure that both career management processes and individual development activities are focused on this high-potential pool. The data from the assessment will identify each individual's strengths and weaknesses and it is important that training programmes and individual coaching are focused on these. Individuals will then feel that they are actually helped to develop their capability in line with what is going to be expected of them if they are going to be selected for more senior executive positions. In addition, being part of the talent pool has to include a vague 'promise' that every 3 or 4 years the individual, if they continue to perform as expected, will be able to move to a more challenging job. There is nothing more frustrating than being told that you are a high-potential executive and that one day you will be part of the senior executives leading the business and then seeing job opportunities filled by others and you being left coasting in your current position for 4 or 5 years.

In order to ensure that the high-potential pool is actually used when internal resourcing decisions are made, it is critical that the organisation works systematically to open up critical jobs across the managerial hierarchy and to ensure that appointments into these jobs are done through the intervention of the centre, as opposed to leaving the choice for those appointments to the person who is recruiting. Managers will usually have a veto in case they do not feel that they can work well with somebody who comes from the high-potential talent pool, but otherwise these critical jobs should be left open so that exceptional individuals can go through them and can gradually develop the career breadth required to reach senior executive levels. From that perspective, the management of the talent pool, which is a key job for the Head of Human Resources at Group level in large international businesses, should have its own objectives, which are reviewed regularly by the executive team. Those objectives should include placing people in key jobs every 3 or 4 years so that it is clear that the executive talent is not only identified but is actually put into use effectively to improve the overall leadership cadre of the business.

SUMMARY

Most large businesses have systematic processes for identifying future executive talent. These start with the performance management process where managers review the individuals who work for them, not just in terms of their performance in their current job but also in terms of their potential for future jobs. People who are highlighted as having both high performance and high potential are considered to be candidates for the high-potential talent pool which is designed to provide leadership for the future of the organisation.

Most businesses that are sophisticated in this area will also employ objective assessment processes in order to validate the recommendations of line managers. A number of businesses will also enable individuals to self-appoint so that personality clashes with their managers do not prevent executives from moving forward. The key to building an effective talent pool is to open up career paths across the organisation and especially across Divisional boundaries which usually prevent talented executives from progressing. Systematic management from the Group centre enables talent pools to be used effectively to resource key executive positions at various management levels. It ensures that the most talented individuals do see their future within the business and do not seek opportunities elsewhere.

In addition to job moves which tend to happen no more frequently than every 3 or 4 years, it is important that every business has a series of development programmes that are tailored to the individual needs of executives that are sitting in talent pools. These programmes will usually include input from business schools around specific competence areas, as well as more in-depth personalised coaching that helps the individual to develop their strengths and limit the negative impact of their weaknesses. Mentoring programmes are also especially effective not only because they enable the young executive to learn from the experience of others but also because they enable the individual to build a network of senior contacts that will then minimise the risk associated with appointing them to a more senior position.

CHAPTER 9

CAREER PATHS

*I*n the past, large businesses had planned career moves for their executives and it was not uncommon to expect that individuals would spend their entire career in a single organisation moving from one position to the next every 3 to 5 years until they reached the highest level that they were perceived to be capable of. Those days have disappeared. Most businesses have delayered in the 1980s and 1990s and many managerial jobs were eliminated, creating large gaps between steps within the management hierarchy. There was also an ideology adopted by many organisations and Human Resource functions that assumed that it was a paternalistic approach for the business to take care of the careers of its executives. Individuals were expected to be responsible for managing their own career. As a result, it became fashionable in the 1990s to run career management workshops for managers within the organisation in order to help them to focus on their interests, identify the kinds of positions they were interested in, help them to work the system internally and develop their own careers within an internal marketplace.

These cultural processes created the current situation where many large businesses find that they do not have the management talent that they need in order to continue to expand. Similarly, talented people, once they reach junior executive levels, start to look outside their own business and feel that they do not have the best opportunities inside and should explore external opportunities. In many businesses, executives feel that the best way to get ahead within their own organisation is to first leave it and find a job outside and then come back. Sometimes when people come back from outside they are viewed as having better expertise than those people that have been developed in the same business throughout their career.

I have interviewed a number of very senior executives in various international businesses and the following quotes describe some of the ways that they feel about the management of their career:

> We don't get much support for our career at all. Where I am based you don't get much support. It is very hard to move around in this company. I worked for other companies that know how to move people. Here you have to fight for your personal solutions and there is no active involvement that is focused on your development.

> I don't feel that we get consistent help to manage our careers. It is hard to get consensus and you can't 'sheep dip' executives at my level but it would be good to have personally tailored things. The company has been passive in this area. No one sat with me to talk about where I am going and my development needs.

> There is not much value associated with the talent management process at all. I had an open position but there were no good candidates identified internally despite the talent management process and that is especially true for international positions since we don't handle these assignments well.

It is a good discipline for us but it is too over-engineered and too paper- and process-driven. Knowing the people and talking about them is key. Too much paper filing reduced effectiveness. But if you test the effort versus outcome, there is not much impact. Key people here have left since they were not clear about their future and no one did anything about it. Talent Development should be less paper and more stronger commitment to implement the changes that are needed.

Chapter 8 described the concept of managerial transitions and how pools of high-potential executives should be identified in order to enable individuals to bridge the capability requirements that are different from one level of management to the other. Identifying job families, such as functional and line jobs, and describing key managerial transitions between those provides the business with a broad career map that can be used to best utilise the talent that is available within high-potential executive pools. But career paths are something that needs to be clear to everyone in the organisation so that individuals will be able to think about the possibilities that are available to them in the broadest possible terms. If I am an ambitious young executive, it is important for me to see that there are many more opportunities open to me across the business rather than thinking that the only job that I can take over is that occupied by my boss, who may not be close to leaving. Sophisticated organisations develop, therefore, a simple career map and make it available to executives through development processes so that they will know what they can strive for. The difference between career management efforts today and those that were typical in the 1990s is in the degree of involvement from the centre. The original paternalistic approach was replaced for a long time with a self-management process in terms of careers. Today businesses realise that in order to have the required executive talent the organisation needs to manage the careers of a select group of executives, and maximise the possibilities that are available to them. This creates an interaction between the person's responsibility to put themselves forward and to continue to develop their capability and performance and the organisation's responsibility to enable high-potential executives to move into key positions in a systematic way rather than leave everything to the chance of an internal marketplace.

Once there is clarity across the management population about career paths and the hierarchy of managerial positions that cuts across Divisions, there is a need to put in place a systematic process for helping individuals to develop their careers. The first choice will be with the person's manager who has the main people management responsibility that translates into not only managing performance today, but also looking at future career possibilities. The advantages of the line manager are that he or she is there on the spot, knows the individual well and, therefore, can help them to become self-aware about their strengths and limitations and to think about what they need to do to develop their capability. Figure 9.1 has been designed to assist managers in this task.

On the other hand, a person's manager has some limitations as the career coach. First, from a psychological point of view, it is difficult for me to think that one of my direct reports has the potential to replace me today or, even more extreme, to become my boss within 2 or 3 years. That requires an exceptional level of openness and generosity on my part and we cannot expect every line manager to have it. Moreover, even if I am very open to the fact that the executives who work for me may be more capable than I am, I still have a limited perspective on what are the requirements for more senior jobs than those that I have ever done. I certainly don't know very much about senior jobs in other Divisions and functional areas across the business where I may have never worked. Therefore, in order to develop individuals' careers, it is important that assistance is provided by people other than their direct line managers.

Our business needs a pool of exceptional executives in order to continue to demonstrate exceptional business performance.
This can be achieved by implementing the following Talent Management initiatives:

IDENTIFYING TALENT

- During annual Performance Management sessions for each executive, rate their Performance as well as their Potential to take on significantly larger jobs within the next two years
- Identify the top 10% of executives who are high both on Performance and on Potential
- Create a forced distribution for ratings so that you will be clear who are the best and who are the least effective executives in each business unit team

FOCUS ON OPPORTUNITIES FOR THESE TOP 10% WITHIN YOUR TEAM, SINCE INVESTING IN YOUR BEST 'PLAYERS' WILL BRING THE BEST RETURNS

Opportunity to have a great start	• Tell them that they are the best executives in your team • Talk with them about expectations; what is really important to them in terms of career and personal development • Help them to think about the future. It will keep them motivated and reduce the chance that you will lose them to the competition
Opportunities to learn and grow	• Use 360° feedback to identify their strengths & areas for further development • Identify courses, coaches and/or work experiences that will help them to develop in the key areas identified through the feedback • Match them with an internal Mentor who can help them to think things through and to develop their capabilities
Opportunities to make a positive impact	• Ensure that your best players are in the jobs that have the potential for the highest impact on business performance • Organise them into a strategic task force (with a senior management sponsor) to work on key projects that move the business forward • Challenge them to 'think out of the box' and come up with truly innovative improvements in their business unit
Opportunities to share rewards	• Review their salary data and ensure that they are at the top of the range for their job (so that the competition will not offer them a better package) • Try to increase their bonus as a percent of salary. High-potential executives like the challenge of exceptional performance resulting in exceptional rewards • Ensure that they are included in a long-term incentive process (share options)
Opportunities for work/life balance	• Find out about their non-work situation. What is really important to them and how can you show that you care about them as a whole person? • Every job does not need to be done from 9 to 5. Can you give them some flexibility that will allow them to be more productive?
Opportunities to be in the know	• Keep them informed about key business issues by circulating important documents for their review. High-potential executives like to know that you value their involvement • Have a quarterly meeting of your best executives to present key performance indicators and keep them informed about plans
Opportunities to be recognised	• Performance should be rewarded in public and not just through a personal annual performance review. Give positive feedback on the spot when you see something that is done well • Use your monthly management meetings to highlight exceptional personal achievement. Other executives may be jealous but that will motivate them to do something exceptional as well • Create special recognition awards for best cost ratios, highest increase in revenue, most creative new ideas, highest productivity, etc. to create a challenging and competitive environment where the best players can shine
Opportunities to share great ideas	• Use quarterly meetings with your best executives to solicit their input on the business and what can be done to improve performance • Have individual meetings with your best executives. Build an open dialogue where they can come to you with bad news coupled with constructive ideas for a solution • Encourage your best executives to come in for a chat, send you ideas by e-mail or anything else that will create a free channel of communication

ENCOURAGE CROSS-FUNCTIONAL & CROSS-BUSINESS UNIT CAREER MOVES SO THAT YOUR BEST EXECUTIVES WILL DEVELOP A BROAD BASE OF EXPERIENCE & PROGRESS RAPIDLY. WORK IN A SYSTEMATIC WAY TO REPLACE AVERAGE PLAYERS WITH YOUR BEST TEAM.

Figure 9.1 Talent management guidance page.

From a talent management perspective, the focus is only on the career management of individuals who are considered to be in the high-potential pools. This concept of 'invest in the best' is the focus of all talent management efforts where we are trying to invest disproportionately in around 10% of the senior executives across a business. It does not mean that career management workshops that are available to all managers are not a good investment. It is always helpful to enable managers to see a future, to develop their capabilities for their current job and for the next job that may become available to them. But within the talent management agenda, the Human Resource function has to become a career adviser in addition to its role as responsible for the corporate planning aspects which involve the best utilisation of talent across the business. It is important that if there are separate Human Resource functions within each Division, then people at the Group level need to develop the skills required for becoming career advisers. This involves an understanding of the range of managerial jobs that are available across the business and how they fit into different levels in terms of managerial requirements as described in Chapter 8. To be a career adviser one also has to be able to help individual executives within the talent pool to understand what their own strengths and development needs are and what they would like to do since motivation is a very important component in a person's capability to actually take on senior executive roles.

In addition to the role of Human Resources, sophisticated organisations that want to be effective in managing the careers of a select group of highly talented executives embed the career coaching concept within their line-management hierarchy. A number of my clients have provided career coaching workshops to their senior executives to enable them to build effective mentoring relationships. The head of one Division would mentor two or three highly talented executives from other Divisions. That not only helped the person being mentored to handle issues within their current jobs. It also helped them to gain a perspective about other jobs that may be open to them at the next level and broadened their perspective and enabled them to focus on what they need to do to become realistic candidates for higher-level jobs. Helping senior executives to become career coaches also opens them up psychologically to understand the importance of creating feeder talent and utilising exceptionally high-potential executives from other Divisions to fill critical job openings. This becomes a more effective path than their continued commitment to existing executives whom they are comfortable with but who do not have the capability to contribute as much to the overall performance of the business.

We have seen that managing careers requires first of all understanding jobs and career paths as a hierarchy of positions and then enabling Group Human Resources and senior executives to focus on the high-potential executives within a talent pool and to help them to stretch into higher-level jobs across the business. There is an obvious risk that is taken by both the executive and by the individual in every internal move. Taking my direct manager's job is a relatively small stretch as I am already very familiar with what he or she is doing and, therefore, I can prepare myself for that requirement. Taking a job at a higher level in another Division means that I know very little about the requirements for doing that job effectively and I may also not be prepared culturally for the way that part of the business functions on a day-to-day basis. Also, that management team may be resistant to accepting 'strangers' like me. There is also a risk for the recruiting manager to take on an executive who is labelled as high-potential regardless of their credentials. How do I know that they will be able to do an exceptional job for me as one of my direct reports?

In order to facilitate career development, it is important not only to enable individuals to have a broad view of what is available but also to provide support to the recruiting manager and to the individual who is taking on a new opportunity. This will create a balance between stretch and support – the stretch that will challenge me to take on new responsibilities and, therefore, develop my capabilities to the utmost; the support that I will get in order to ensure that I do not make too many mistakes or that I learn how to do the things before I actually need to do them. It is important to encourage an individual's ambition but change is always hard and we need to provide sufficient support so that people will not stretch themselves too much and fail. It is also important to encourage recruiting managers to take risks with high-potential individuals that they do not know personally. We have to help them to be relatively sure that the process will have sufficient support around it so individuals will have the opportunity to become successful in the new job rather than be expected to sink or swim.

If we start from the perspective of the recruiting manager, support should focus on helping them to meet potential candidates and choose from among the high-potential pool those that will be able to make the adjustment that is required by moving from one part of the business to another or from one job level to another. As stated earlier, mentoring relationships between senior executives from one part of the business and high-potential executives from other parts are one way to get to know people in-depth. Some businesses have enabled high-potential executives to take on assignments on cross-functional and cross-Divisional strategic projects that expose them to senior executives from other sides of the business. Projects have to be limited in their scope so that high-potential managers will still be able to remain exceptional in terms of their performance in their current jobs. But exposure to different areas opens their minds and enables them to present themselves and their capabilities to people who otherwise would not have the opportunity to get to know them. Research by the Conference Board suggested that in terms of international talent management, international assignments are one of the best methods that corporations use to build the capabilities of individuals, to work across cultural boundaries and, therefore, to demonstrate that they can become responsible for operations in different cultural environments from those that they have been used to (see Appendix 2). In addition, as described earlier, on-boarding processes are fundamental to support executives who move from one management level to another. This is even more important when moving from one Division to another because cultural adaptation becomes a fundamental criterion for success. As a recruiting manager it gives me comfort to think that the Human Resource function will provide in-depth on-boarding assistance to the candidates that I am recruiting. That will ensure that difficulties are identified early and that assistance in adapting to the new environment will be provided in order to facilitate a smooth landing in the new position.

Support, as described earlier, is required not only for the recruiting manager to overcome the risks associated with recruiting people internally. The individual executive needs support when they move from one job to another. Even if an individual has very high potential and is in the talent pool, there are risks for them individually in moving into unfamiliar territory. The probability of failure is much greater than in the kind of jobs that the individual has been used to performing so far. Individualised support in advance of moving from one position to the next will focus on understanding the new environment that the person is moving into, meeting with key people who work there and getting their input and emotional support as welcoming to the new executive and thinking through a plan for a gradual entry into the new position. These kinds of systematic on-boarding processes need to be the responsibility of Human Resources so that there is somebody who knows how to do them well and can ensure that transitions of high-potential managers are acted upon smoothly. When an executive who sits in a high-potential talent pool fails a new assignment, this information will travel around the business. Future recruiting managers will be much more hesitant to take on candidates from the pool because they will feel that the risk associated with this internal recruitment may not be worth its benefits. Therefore, whoever manages the talent pool must invest, not only in identifying talent and developing talent, but also in ensuring that on-boarding processes are carried out effectively to reduce the possibility of failure and facilitate entry into a new position.

The final issue around career paths for high-potential executives involves the frequency of moves. There is always a danger that, when individuals are labelled as high-potential and a great deal of resource and attention is focused around them, there will be a tendency to start to move them to another job very rapidly. A number of executives that I have worked with describe two or three individuals who have moved from one position to the next every 2 years or so and are, therefore, viewed as lacking any real accountability – butterflies that move from one flower to the next, pretending to be exceptional but actually never staying long enough to prove their capability in terms of real bottom-line results. The credibility of the entire talent management scheme can be put in question if a number of high-potential executives acquire a 'lightweight' brand. It is, therefore, critical to ensure that when high-potential executives are put into a new position they sit there for at least the 3-year period that is usually required in order to have real accountability for results and to produce real business impact that others can assess reliably. Ideally, a 3- to 5-year period at each management level is the best route. Exceptional executives may sometimes jump from one level to another, skipping over some interim jobs. It is better, however, to take the risk of enabling people to jump to significantly bigger jobs but stay there for 3 to 5 years in order to prove that the jump was worth the risk and that the individual did produce real business impact.

SUMMARY

This chapter has discussed the need to develop systematic career paths to ensure that talent management processes actually move individuals across the business, both in terms of management levels and in terms of Divisions and functional silos that usually prevent talent development. The key step for building career paths is to understand managerial transitions and create a simple career map that executives across the business become familiar with. In addition, there is a need to develop the coaching capabilities of senior executives so that they can mentor high-potential individuals from other parts of the business, get to know them and help them to move from one part of the organisation to another, as they continue to progress in their career. The chapter has also focused on the limited perspective that line-managers have about their direct reports. This increases the need for members of the senior executive team to take on a major responsibility in managing the careers of a very small group of exceptionally talented individuals. Group Human Resources also has a critical role in managing careers from a talent management planning perspective and as a career adviser to individuals, helping them to get the support that they will require to succeed. Finally, in-depth on-boarding processes are critical because, when high-potential executives take on significantly larger jobs, especially in other parts of the business, it is important to ensure that this transition is done effectively. Failure for a high-potential executive at that level will create a bad name for the whole talent-pool concept and recruiting managers will not be willing to take the risk associated with candidates that they are not familiar with.

CHAPTER 10

DEVELOPING EXECUTIVE CAPABILITY

*T*he problem with many talent management processes is that most of the energy is spent in planning and debates among senior executives. Very little time and resources proportionately are spent on actually developing the talent once it is identified. Line managers are asked to highlight the executives with the highest potential and performance within their organisations. This data is summarised across Divisions and debated at senior management levels. Many businesses also invest significant resources in validating data presented by line managers through systematic external assessment of capability, in order to be more secure that the people who have been identified actually do have the potential to take on significantly larger jobs. In a number of businesses, it is common to create talent pools that have high-potential executives and to use members of these pools as internal candidates when senior executive positions become open. This chapter is focused on the next steps in the process which is talent development.

High-potential executives have a profile of strengths and weaknesses and in order to develop the talent pool you need to invest in development so that when the time comes to take on broader executive positions they have been prepared for the challenges ahead. Many large businesses send high-potential executives to development programmes run by one or other of the major business schools. These programmes, while in most cases contributing to the development of participants, tend to be one-off investments that are not tailored to the individual requirements of any given executive, nor do they provide a systematic process for developing executive capabilities over time. In my conversations with senior executives who have participated in such business school programmes, they are usually complimentary about the content and the networking opportunities provided. They feel that going to a business school programme every five years is useful. It does not, however, provide them with the depth of input that would enable them to maximise their potential and, thereby, maximise their contribution in their current jobs and be prepared for the challenges ahead. This chapter presents a range of input possibilities that are used by businesses to develop the capabilities of their high-potential executives. This does not mean that input processes such as those described here cannot be made available to all managers within a business. The focus of this book is on talent management and, therefore, on a disproportionate investment in a select group of high-potential executives who can have a disproportionate impact on the performance of the business in the medium-term.

The first and maybe best approach to developing executive capability is to provide them with insight. The acquisition of managerial competence depends on a number of underlying capabilities that are then translated through insight about one's own strengths and weaknesses and through one's learning ability into the acquisition of new levels of competence. Focusing on insight, therefore, enables high-potential executives to seek their own development opportunities. In the best examples, businesses provide

intense input on an individual basis to their high-potential executives that is based on a combination of feedback from their manager,
direct reports and colleagues on examples of strengths and weaknesses, and in-depth psychological assessment of strengths and
development needs. Through Positive Psychology (see Appendix
2 for relevant references), we know that the best way for executives
to develop their capabilities is to avoid the trap of focusing on
weaknesses and trying to smooth them out and to focus on building their strengths. An executive's strengths are his or her competitive advantage. At best I can translate my weaknesses into something
that I can be a little better in. While, if I build on my strengths,
then I can become exceptional in these areas and provide a disproportionate impact on the business as a whole. Insight is an
individualised process where an executive, through a series of
meetings with an external coach or business psychologist, intern-
alises what he or she needs to do in order to understand their
strengths and build on them to make themselves exceptional in
these areas. In terms of weaknesses, it is important to understand
them and to prevent them from interfering with the way you
manage your strengths. It is not important to become significantly
better in these areas but rather to put in place support mechanisms
that will prevent your weaknesses from becoming critical stumbling blocks.

Providing in-depth insight to a high-potential executive is a
very effective process to enable them to utilise their ambition and
tenacity by finding alternative sources of input that will enable
them to build on this insight. The key is to ensure continuity. It
is important to enable the executive to gain insight through an
in-depth process at one point in time when he or she becomes a
member of the high-potential talent pool – but then, once a year
to go back to the external coach or business psychologist who
provided that insight and solicit external input. This is then followed by in-depth discussions about what has been achieved in
building on the person's strengths last year and what are the new

challenges that lie ahead. Insight is an exceptionally useful tool for high-potential executives since they have the internal motivation and drive that will enable them to seek whatever input they need without the organisation having to be more active in supporting their development in these areas.

As described at the beginning of this chapter, corporate training programmes are also effective as sources of input for high-potential executives. The key in planning these programmes is to ensure that they focus on the changing requirements around key job transitions in the managerial hierarchy. Businesses that have effective training programmes will usually start with a focus on the first transition into management, then focus on the transition to managing other managers, then focus on being the head of a business function, and finally provide input to executives prior to their becoming a Chief Executive of even a small business where he or she has broad profit and loss responsibility and oversees a whole array of functions. These programmes will attract not only high-potential executives that sit in various talent pools, but also other executives that are preparing to take on a new job at a new level of management as part of their normal career progression.

Another type of corporate training programme is focused around a modular format as opposed to the general management programmes that are typical of business school inputs. These short modular programmes focus on such topics as business strategy, finance for non-financial managers, presentation skills, customer service, and other topics that are perceived to be relevant to senior executives within the business. Typically, these modules tend to be targeted at junior managers. In some businesses there is, however, a growing awareness that senior executives face competence requirements at later career stages when they suddenly need input in a specific area in order to perform effectively. A short, tailored training module can provide that input and, therefore, enable the individual to develop their capability in a very specific area. Businesses that use tailored programmes for senior executives find it best to describe them in terms of the competence framework that is used to describe management jobs. Then, as part of the performance management process, when individuals identify a need for developing competence in a specific area, it is easy to select the appropriate content that will fit their needs. In a number of businesses there is also an individualised input format. Senior executives who need input can get it through individualised content-based coaching. This is similar to language coaching that is provided for executives who take on a job abroad in a country where they do not speak the language. Individualised content-based coaching is very effective in deepening financial understanding, improving personal presentation, etc. It is useful to have a map of the content areas where programmes are available, ideally with both a basic input module that provides the key concepts and an advanced programme that provides more in-depth expertise in a specific sub-area. This content map can be made available to all executives as part of the performance management process so that they can help their direct reports to select the approach that best fits their needs. As part of talent management processes, however, when high-potential individuals are involved, the discussion of strengths and development needs should be done much more in-depth and, therefore, focused content programmes become exceptionally helpful.

Coaching is probably the most prevalent form of input for senior executives and for high-potential executives in talent pools. In the USA and the UK coaching has acquired a positive branding and, therefore, it is not perceived as something that you prescribe to weak executives that need 'propping up'. On the contrary, coaching is an activity that successful senior executives take on as a regular support process for the challenges associated with complex senior roles. The problem with coaching, though, is that many businesses do not have a systematic process for understanding the specific needs that an executive has or for assessing the capability of external coaches to address these needs. Many businesses simply pay the coaching bills and it is up to the individual to meet a coach in his local club or to hear about a coach from a friend and to take them on without any understanding of the qualifications of the coach or the appropriateness of this type of coaching to the specific needs of this individual executive.

When dealing with senior executive talent pools, therefore, it is essential to be much more systematic in the use of coaching. The use of a coach should follow an in-depth diagnostic process where the individual gains insight into his or her specific development needs based on an in-depth analysis of strengths and weaknesses in line with current and future job demands. Once I am clear about the areas where I want to develop my capability, I need to have access to a recommended list of coaches that are able to provide me with the required input. It is best to classify coaches and their expertise according to managerial competence areas. The recommended list should, therefore, include coaches who focus on the area of business strategy, those who focus on effective management of operations, those who focus on managing people effectively, those who focus on building interpersonal relationships, those who focus on working effectively with clients, and those who focus on innovation and change. The competence profile that is used to diagnose senior executives' strengths and weaknesses in your business should be the basis for having a preferred supplier list that identifies external coaches and their area of expertise. I would be very suspicious if a coach claimed to be capable of providing coaching across all areas of management competence, since no one has that breadth with the depth of expertise required to provide coaching input. It is not simple to assess coaches and ideally it is up to the Human Resource function to define the criteria for coaches within each competence area. This needs to be followed by a process for interviewing potential coaches and taking references. That will enable the business to gradually accumulate a list of effective coaches who have received good feedback from their executive clients. In defining coaching it is obviously important to focus also on the expected output. Human Resources and line managers who pay for coaching should also be involved with the coach and the 'coachee' to ensure that a long-term relationship does not just become mutual 'back-scratching' but actually provides effective input that leads to competence development within a predefined timeline. Taking coaching seriously in terms of classifying areas of expertise for the coach and helping the individual executive to assess progress will enable the business to get significant benefits from the development resources that are applied to this area.

In addition to external coaching, sophisticated organisations that invest significant time and resources in their talent management use internal mentors so that executives across the business take on support roles for others and help them to develop. Research indicates that the process of mentoring others actually helps the mentor to crystallise his or her own expertise and, therefore, contributes to both sides. In identifying internal mentors, it is important to classify their potential contribution according to the competence framework that is used for understanding senior executive performance. Therefore, an individual can expect to have a mentor that can help in developing a vision and strategy. That person would be different than the mentor that can help them to build a network of contacts across the business or to manage their people effectively. In identifying internal mentors, the key is not only to find people who have the expertise in a specific competence area but also to use senior executives who are key decision makers in internal recruitment processes. As we saw in Chapter 9, the biggest barrier to the success of talent management processes is the lack of familiarity of recruiting managers with high-potential executives that come from other parts of the business. Mentoring processes that are conducted by senior executives for others who work in different areas of the business enable them to become familiar with each other and, therefore, to open up career paths. In the case of internal mentoring, it is key not only to identify people who are perceived to have the expertise and willingness to take on this task but also to provide input on how to do it effectively. Executives need to understand what it means to mentor others and not end up telling their own life stories and assuming that this will enable a 'mentee' to develop their capability. While there is a plethora of training organisations that would be happy to train your senior executives in mentoring skills, in my experience it is usually more important to provide modularised brief inputs on how to mentor effectively, to 'hold the hands' of the mentor as he or she goes through initial sessions with their 'mentee' and gradually help them to learn from their experience and to refine their mentoring capabilities. This approach will enable senior executives to participate in the process, since they will not be able to take off a few days and participate in an external training programme. Moreover, this gradual guidance will also enable the mentor to build their skills on the basis of experience and feel more secure in what they are doing.

Strategic forums are also a very successful format for developing the capabilities of high-potential executives in talent pools. One of the key needs for successful executives, who have the potential to take on more senior roles, is to help them to develop a broad perspective across the business, since they may have come to their current job by going through a single, relatively narrow management path. Involvement with other executives, from diverse parts of the business, in thinking through key strategic issues, will help executives to understand the business as a whole and to think about issues that they have never been exposed to before. Strategic forums tend to focus on issues such as branding, on sharing clients across Divisions within the business, on international expansion opportunities, on an analysis of competitive advantages and disadvantages, etc. The best forums are those led by members of the senior executive team since they ensure that executives will take their participation seriously. It will also provide members of the executive team with a direct insight into the capabilities and contribution of high-potential executives who participate in their forum. This will enable senior executives to take recruitment risks that are associated with future appointments of those high-potential people to job openings within their area of accountability. Some strategic forums take an Action Learning format, where individuals have periodic meetings and, in between, are expected to work in small teams on specific proposals or on testing initial ideas. One of the dangers of strategic forums is that they require participants to do an immense amount of work which is unrealistic in conjunction with their normal day job. There is no point in having a strategic forum that will require participants to put in more work than they are capable of doing. Therefore, the best forums are those where most of the work is done during off-site meetings. It is better to have a two-day meeting every three months where something is achieved than to have short meetings that require a great deal of homework that will be frustrating for busy executives.

When talking to senior executives in a number of client businesses I found that the concept of involvement is absolutely fundamental. High-potential executives in very senior positions are motivated by career development and by personal growth considerations. Therefore, having the opportunity to be involved in issues that go beyond their specific job accountabilities is a key motivator. They enjoy the opportunity to learn and to contribute while also appreciating the recognition involved in being invited to participate:

> There is a lot to gain by involvement and sharing ideas. Successful organisations are less hierarchical and have a process for involving a wider group of people; I am not clear how we can do it here in such a large organisation.

> We should have more opportunity for involvement. People who play a part in setting the agenda feel personally committed to it and

play a stronger role in cascading it. Setting the agenda is a core part of leadership and we are not good at it.

Organisationally, there could be more opportunities in the calendar for the senior management in addition to the once-a-year conference. This would be good for the Group since if people participate beyond their functional position it would create more discussion, broader contribution, and the ability to learn from each other.

On some issues I would like to be more involved but not as a superficial exercise, which will just be a waste of time. Maybe we could look at key issues that are important to the Group Executive and then contribute some work that can then be useful. But only if it will be used. If you want to get meaningful engagement across the Group, there are similarities across our business and maybe we should have more people from across the Group sitting on operating Boards, almost as non-executives, and call this 'learn and contribute'. It will take time but it will help share information and develop people in a real way.

Another development opportunity is short assignments, as described in the Conference Board report (see Appendix 2).

A majority of companies want to accelerate the development of their global talent.

Seventy-seven percent of the 81 companies surveyed by the Conference Board on global leadership development report that they are seeking a variety of approaches to improve their global talent development.

Providing targeted feedback on performance and potential was cited by 47% of the survey participants as being the most effective tactic in accelerating the nurturing of global talent. The most effective practices to develop global business leaders are longer-term international assignments (cited by 33%) and international cross-functional team participation (18%).

Well-managed firms (firms with a return on investment equal to or higher than their respective industry averages) are more likely to accelerate global leadership development by giving global leadership talent access to a few, targeted, developmentally rich positions, providing greater opportunities for global networking, using assignments in foreign client or supplier organisations.

The advantages of short assignments are that individuals can in a few months begin to understand the issues in a different part of the business and to acquire some of the skill that will expand their horizon and, therefore, to develop broader awareness. The problem with many assignments, though, is that it is very hard for exceptional executives to take off a few months from their current jobs without being left in limbo. As a result, their career, instead of being helped, is being hindered. Also, many short assignments are not real and become Human Resource 'fantasies' about development opportunities, rather than enabling senior executives to truly contribute to a corporate goal. There are rare opportunities where short assignments are the most appropriate avenue and that is usually when there are natural breaks in the careers of high-potential executives and a short assignment is helpful without creating a block to further progression. But in my experience, it is always very important to ensure that the follow-up career plan is put in place to ensure what happens once the assignment is completed, as opposed to assuming that something will come up, which does not usually happen in an effective way.

A number of businesses invest heavily in on-line management resources that are designed to provide executives with input about various areas of management and skills development exercises that can be used as part of executive self-development processes. In my experience, on-line materials tend to be used by junior managers, especially when they are embedded as part of a face-to-face training programme where assignments are completed between group meetings through on-line modules. It is rare that senior executives go to on-line resources in order to develop their management capabilities, since this input is usually best provided through face-to-face contact. A number of businesses have, however, built effective on-line libraries where executives can find input around specific content that they encounter as part of their job (changes in the law, technological developments, etc.). On-line resources tend to be effective when they provide the content that the executive needs to acquire in a quick way and can be accessed as and when they need it. On-line input tends to be less useful when it is focused on general executive development to match broad competence requirements.

When talking about personal development, many senior executives tell me that they read management books on a regular basis, usually when they are on business trips. Books provide relevant input that can help to broaden the horizons of senior executives. A number of businesses who take executive development seriously have started to provide recommended readings. Every 3 or 4 months, a book or an article that focuses on a new business concept is suggested to executives in senior positions and those in the talent pool. A list of 25 books serves no purpose, but if I get a recommended book once a quarter then there is a high probability that I will take the time to read it. A common set of books that senior executives across the business read does facilitate a shared language across the business so that a number of fundamental concepts around strategy, culture, logistics, finance, etc. begin to be discussed by the executive team. This facilitates the development of a more in-depth thinking group that can apply those concepts to a broad range of strategic issues. The focus of talent management efforts is on a select group of high-potential executives and they will be highly motivated for their own personal development. If we provide them with a very restricted reading list and forums where they can discuss the meaning and application of business concepts, then they will find that intellectual challenge useful.

SUMMARY

In this chapter we have seen that developing executive capability is one of the most fundamental components of an effective talent management strategy. A number of businesses invest a great deal of time and resources in identifying executive talent and in validating those choices but then neglect to develop executives' capabilities. Therefore, they do not facilitate the growth of the talent that they have identified.

This chapter has presented a number of input modalities that have proven to be effective in large international organisations that invest in their talent management processes. The key is to ensure that input is matched to an in-depth diagnosis of the individual needs of a high-potential executive, rather than implementing 'sheep dipping', processes where groups of people are provided with the same input that is deemed appropriate for everyone. Individuals vary in their capabilities, job requirements and interests. Developmental input is most effective when I perceive that it suits my specific needs and that it enables me to build on my strengths and to limit the negative impact of my weaknesses.

CHAPTER 11

BREAKING DOWN SILOS
THAT ARE BARRIERS TO
EFFECTIVE TALENT
MANAGEMENT

*O*rganisational silos are the main barriers to effective talent management. All large businesses have Divisions that focus on different products or services. In addition, the organisation has functional areas such as Finance, IT, Human Resources, Marketing etc. that provide specialist input to the Group and the Divisions. There are frequent interactions between the functional areas and the Divisions and there is usually less interaction on a day-to-day basis between the Divisions within a large business. Organisations conduct their talent management process through a bottom-up approach. Managers within business units review the people, who work for them, pass on recommendations to the next level up and the data get crystallised at the Head of Division or Function level. These summary talent management reports are then brought to the Group executive team level. At that point, however, most of the recommendations and conclusions have already been worked out within each separate part of the business. As a result, while the talent review at the Group level does look across the business, that discussion is really focused on the activities that each Division and Function has already decided to take forward.

In order to understand talent management efforts we need to consider that most executives are motivated to keep their best people. The executives who work for me help me to be successful. I will, therefore, reward and coach my best people and I will try to keep them as long as possible to enable me and my business unit to perform at its best. As a result, talent management efforts that attempt to take some of my best people and transfer them to jobs outside of my area of accountability will naturally encounter my resistance. Similarly, day-to-day management processes mean that executives de facto operate in relatively small entities even though their business unit is a part of a much larger corporate entity. On a day-to-day basis, I will be familiar only with executives who work in my business unit. Also, when these executives think about their own careers they will think in terms of the jobs that are available around them and that they see as realistic possibilities to step up into once there is change at the next layer up. Moreover, business units think of themselves as very different from other units within the same organisation. Within banking, for example, the retail people think of themselves as very different from those who deal with businesses or those who deal with wholesale financial transactions. In energy companies, the upstream people are thought of as being very different to the downstream people. In large retail conglomerates, people who work with electronic goods are perceived to be very different to people who deal with clothing or food. There are real differences in content between one Division and another even in relatively similar organisations. High-tech manufacturers would claim that people who work on aircraft have very different expertise to people who work on ground vehicles. But even in very similar business environments, each Division develops its own culture. Even clothes retailers will have multiple brands and the culture that each brand develops tends to focus on the kind of clientele that they are trying to attract. Therefore, the culture of the youth-orientated retail Division would be different to the culture of the Division that is focused on older consumers.

The fact that there are different cultures within each Division may be useful for building internal solidarity but it hampers talent management efforts. When looking for internal candidates to fill an executive position, the natural tendency of the recruiting manager is to look for people who come from their own Division since they assume that it will be difficult for an executive who comes from another Division to adapt to the different culture and content of the work. This is also true for candidates. When high-potential executives look at jobs they will be hesitant to pursue opportunities in other Divisions that are less familiar to them and that are perceived to have a different organisational culture. Realistically culture does have an impact on behaviour and the content of jobs in terms of the expertise required, varies from one Division to another given the nature of their products and services. But as managers progress up the hierarchy, their success starts to depend more on common capabilities around strategic vision, leading large-scale operations, managing large teams with a number of management layers across wide geographical and functional boundaries and interacting with a broad range of other functions effectively. Therefore, senior executive roles tend to be quite similar in the elements that determine success. Differences in content and differences in culture tend to be exaggerated when focusing on internal recruitment processes. That is based on the perceived risk in bringing somebody new to an existing position. It is easy for me as a recruiting manager to assume that someone who has done the same job in the exact same culture will be much more successful than someone who has done a somewhat different job in a somewhat different organisational setting. But in reality, the capability profile and job performance may actually be the opposite. Executives who come from different business environments and have worked in different content areas may have more expertise and bring with them a fresh perspective, which will foster creativity and innovation. But organisational silos tend to act as a barrier to effective talent management because they restrict the movement of high-potential executives and keep them within their existing areas of operations. An opening for a key executive position will not necessarily draw the best candidates from across the whole business but will tend to draw from a very small pool of candidates from within that same Division or functional area.

The following quotes from my interviews with senior executives in a number of different international businesses illustrate their perception about career opportunities across the business:

> Future career opportunities would be a good topic for discussion. It would be good to know what future I have here. That is how we lost some good people since good people may leave if they are not sure that they have a future here. The risk is that we 'box' people and don't give them broad opportunities, so it would be encouraging to talk about a breadth of opportunities.

> I have created and taken a lot of the opportunities myself. I became a candidate for diverse roles and that gave me a lot of opportunities. It is rare though to have meaningful conversations about my skills or possible future roles. But in practice, when things become available, I got them and that was excellent. The roles were good but the communication process was badly managed; things just come out of the blue. The way in which transitions were handled was de-motivating even though I loved the job opportunities. It really makes you feel under-appreciated when you should really be happy about the opportunity.

> We are poor in stretching people into diverse positions where people really learn. It is a passive process to fill positions when they become available. But there is no dialogue with individuals about where they are going. Assuming that I am successful now, what is the future and what should I do to prepare for that? When you get a call from our competitors the key is to know that my current

organisation is willing to make a commitment to me. We lost good people because we did not make a commitment to them. This makes it possible for a person to plan their future and the really excellent organisations do this much better than we do. Also we are very narrow in our thinking without considering cross-functional teams so we are not developing global leaders. That impacts people to align themselves too much with their silos. Also, there are no significant conversations at Group level about the executives doing that. We are not really developing people in terms of functional and geographical stretch.

Since business silos form natural barriers to talent management, it is critical for the senior executive team to focus on the need to move high-potential executives from one part of the business to another. They should discuss the advantages and disadvantages of such moves and make an overt commitment to increase internal diversity and to develop a cadre of high-potential executives with a broad base of expertise. As a result, businesses that are highly focused on effective talent management practices target themselves in terms of movement across organisational silos by specifying a percentage, usually around 20%, of all internal resourcing activities at senior executive levels to involve candidates that come from other Divisions or Functions. This is matched with a similar targeting on external recruitment, thereby ensuring that more than a third of all internal executive appointments at senior levels come either from outside the business or from a different Division or Function. This diversity fosters innovation and creativity by resisting the natural temptation for each part of the business unit to remain with its own talent pool. The senior executive team needs to make a commitment to these targets and then to review them quarterly as part of their ongoing talent review process. This will enable Human Resource executives within each business unit to encourage their clients to recruit from a diverse background because they are aware that the senior executive team will scrutinise recruitment decisions, and problems with restricting talent movement will be addressed at the most senior level within the business.

It is not sufficient, however, to set targets and monitor actual resourcing activities. In order to enable effective movement of high-potential executives across organisational silos, it is critical to initiate proactive activities that will facilitate such movement. A retail bank, which is one of my clients, has a very effective programme where the top 30 executives in their most senior talent pool spend a day with two of the members of the senior executive team. These high-potential executives present their experience base, discuss their strengths and weaknesses, and highlight their career ambitions and what they think they need to further develop their capabilities. The presentation is prepared with support from the Head of Talent Management in order to enable the executives to 'market' themselves effectively. By spending a day focusing on a high-potential individual senior executive from another Division in the bank, members of the senior executive team gradually get to know a broad array of exceptional people from other parts of the business and, thereby, become open to alternative resourcing possibilities from other business units. This retail bank also has identified four or five external high-flying executives who work for their competitors and who have had a very diverse path into senior executive positions. They include, for example, marketers from FMCG companies who have moved into banking and financial specialists who have moved into general management positions. The executive team met with them informally to talk about their career path and what they thought that they brought to a business by coming from a very different background compared to most of the executives who were already there. These periodic discussions create a culture of curiosity where the executive team gradually open to the benefits of bringing external and internal resources from very different backgrounds than they themselves have grown up with. Otherwise, our natural tendency is to assume that our career path is the usual one and that anyone who has a very different career pattern will not fit the requirements.

In addition to working with the executive team to open their minds to the advantages of breaking down business silos it is important to ensure that the head of each Division and his or her management team focus on this issue and discuss it openly. Recruitment decisions within a Division are made by local executives with a limited horizon. The discussions within each Division management team are best facilitated by the Head of the Division and the Head of Human Resources. They need to look at high-potential candidates from other Divisions and discuss their advantages and disadvantages compared to existing executives within the Division. The key is in exposure. When we meet high-potential executives from other areas it opens our mind to a different kind of individual that may bring the expertise that we do not possess at the moment. It is comfortable to work with a team that is very similar to us. But the more similar an executive team is in terms of their background and experience, the less creative it will be in monitoring its competitors, understanding market trends and thinking outside the box when trying to address a competitive question. As a result, it is important that each Divisional management team thinks about the advantages of diversity and how it can gradually increase its own diversity and the diversity within each of the sub-teams that report to it. Diverse executives bring internal challenges to thinking and those challenges improve long-term business performance. From a talent management perspective, it is important to facilitate those discussions early so that when a position becomes open then the recruiting executive would look at it as an opportunity to bring in a very different type of executive, with different areas of expertise, in order to augment the existing team and broaden its experience and capability base.

The risks associated with change are hard to counteract. As a result, it is important for the Human Resource function to create a number of success stories that demonstrate the advantages from recruiting different types of candidates. It is enough that one executive from a different Division or Function joins a team and proves to be successful, for that team to be more open to take on another executive and gradually expand its breadth. The reverse is also true. When someone from outside the organisation comes in and fails, then the natural tendency is for the team to think that external recruitments do not succeed and to go back to recruiting the same type of people from within their own organisational silo. Human Resources needs, therefore, to provide support to the initial cases where high-potential executives are enabled to move from one part of the business to another in order to ensure that these internal movements become a success. This includes on-boarding activities that are described in Chapter 7 of this book. Working with the recruiting manager before the process has commenced and during the initial period when a new executive enters the team will be very helpful in easing that transition.

The initial steps towards breaking down organisational silos are very difficult. Gradually, as success stories start to permeate senior executive levels, then parts of the business become more open to experimenting with diverse talent pools. The key, therefore, is to build on success rather than try to confront the most difficult areas of resistance. Ideally, the Human Resource function should find one or two Divisions or Functions where the leader is open to getting to know talented individuals. By meeting exceptionally capable executives from other parts of the business on an informal basis, you can gradually open your mind. Planting the seeds early about highly talented executives in other parts of the business is the key. Human Resources can help Division heads to be attracted to two or three individuals that they find especially appealing and that will start the ball rolling. Then when a senior position becomes open it will be a natural step for the Head of the Division to seek the candidate that he or she has already been attracted to and to bring them in, using that recruitment opportunity. By focusing on two or three Divisions or functions and providing very intensive on-boarding support for the people who make the changes, Human Resources can create a small number of visible success stories. Informal and formal internal communication processes can then be used to provide a stage for the high-potential executive who has made the unusual move from one part of the business to another to tell his or her 'story'. When an executive who comes from a clothing retailer moves into a marketing position in an insurance company, it is interesting to hear her story and to understand what she brings to the new business setting. If that story is then accompanied by her boss describing what she added to the mix of the team then this starts to raise curiosity among recruiting executives in other parts of the business. They will think that it may be good for them to bring in executives who have different types of experience and, thereby, to increase the sharpness of their own management teams.

In general, breaking down organisational silos is not a simple organisational change process and it relates not just to talent management. In many cases large businesses encourage a diversity of cultures between Divisions in order to facilitate internal competitiveness, creativity and innovation. From a talent management perspective, this is always a negative factor. There is a very limited number of exceptionally capable executives, even in very large businesses, and it is important for the leadership of the business to use the available talent effectively, rather than to enable people to be buried within one part of the business and not to explore the breadth of opportunities that are available.

SUMMARY

This chapter has focused on the fact that organisational silos are the main barriers to effective talent management. Businesses invest a great deal of time and resources in asking executives to rate the potential of the people that work for them, in assessing the capability of high-potential individuals and in providing in-depth development input through business school programmes, coaching and individually tailored support. All this is done in order to develop the executive talent that will be able to improve the leadership of the business. These systematic talent management efforts will fail, however, if there are strong boundaries between Divisions and Functions. Even highly talented executives will not develop to their full potential within a limited area of the business and the organisation as a whole will not benefit from the diverse mix of capability and experience that exists across its various units. There are a number of activities that can be implemented to open the minds of recruiting executives so that they will be active in seeking out executive talent that has a different background to the typical career path that they have come to expect. We have also seen that it is important to create case study examples so that high-potential individuals will see the opportunities associated with taking the risk of moving from familiar areas and take on executive positions in very different parts of the business.

CHAPTER 12

TALENT MANAGEMENT
AND DIVERSITY

*D*iversity is not just a politically correct approach to developing senior executives. It is a requirement if we want to get the best executive talent into the organisation. If you assume that there is an equal distribution of capability between men and women, for example, then the fact that a senior executive team includes only men means that we have lost all of the top talent from the female population and may have recruited senior executives who are less capable just because they are men. It is also important for the business to match its executive profile to its client base. To the degree that the senior executive team is similar to the types of clients, then it will be easier for the leadership of the business to identify with potential client needs and to create a more competitive business proposition. One of my clients, who is a very large builder of family homes, found out through market research that the major decisions involved in buying a home are made by women. Most of their houses are bought by families and while the financial decisions involved may be influenced by the men, they found that there is a tendency in a lot of families for the women to be the ones that will focus on the selection of the location and on the facilities that they would expect to find in a house before a buying decision is reached. As a result of this analysis, my client changed the composition of its sales force, who are now mostly women. They found that women were better at communicating with both male and female clients around the selection of their home. Their sales force is trained to focus on the perceived benefits of the acquiring family rather than to focus on technical details that builders tend to appreciate. While changing the profile of its sales force, it is still a challenge for this client to change the profile of its senior executive team. Even in the top three layers, most of the executives are men who come from a building background. This executive team profile prevented my client from having the breadth of leadership that would provide them with competitive advantage since there was a large cultural gap between the senior team, its sales force and clients. As a result, in the last year, they have put in a great deal of effort to bring women from marketing back-grounds into senior executive positions across the business.

In my interviews with Heads of Human Resources from large businesses, I also found that while there is a great deal of concern about the issue of diversity as influencing talent management, there is still a long way to go in this area.

The issue of diversity was a difficult one for most of my inter-viewees. Some businesses are just thinking about it, while others have already invested a great deal of time and resources. However, as you will see from their responses, very few seem to be satisfied with the current state of play. The key in most people's mind is that we have a 'war for talent' to gain a competitive edge and we risk losing significant opportunities if we do not develop enough talented women and ethnic minorities who can rise through the executive ranks and contribute to leadership talent at the highest levels. The problem seems to be less in identifying the need and more in finding ways to address it effectively.

The first set of responses represents the businesses that are more active in this area:

Diversity and talent are the same issue – otherwise diversity doesn't work. Through diversity you build the talent pool and that is what we are focused on. You need to be creative in building the best talent pool and we are trying to put the two together, and we are doing some practical things: working with more search companies to understand why certain types of people are not coming to us or are leaving disproportionately. Also we are broadening the industries we go to. Initially we understood that we had to undo certain senior executive beliefs about the kind of experience that is needed to get to a senior level in the business. We brought some external speakers to the Board to talk to them and to open their minds at an emotional level and that opened up the process of looking at diverse talent. (Retail bank)

We started to talk about diversity of thinking. We don't want to close the culture so there is a question about how to include people who are talented though different. That is why we introduced a self-nomination process so people can come forward even if their boss isn't appreciative. These people then go through a systematic assessment process. We definitely have a gender issue at senior levels. We have diversity policies and do lots of fantastic initiatives. We do see ethnic diversity beginning to flow through even to our talent pool, but in an engineering-led organisation we have gender issues despite having been focused on this for a long time.

The emerging talent pools are OK – we are bringing in 50/50 graduates – but the numbers at the top are not right. We don't know why and are commissioning a study of that. We don't know why senior women seem to be leaving. Are there organisational biases that contribute to that? Also, on an individual level, women need to understand what needs to be done to participate. There is probably something about the nature of the work and the kind of environment where people can stop-start their career and other trends in a modern business. That won't go away so we need to think of what is required to keep women in senior roles. It's a huge problem for us. (Public utility)

We are not very good at this. We did a lot on disability but not enough on gender or ethnicity. We have now set up a senior steering group and that is raising the profile of the issue. We have also put diversity as a criterion for search consultants so that we can start to see more diverse candidates for senior jobs. We have a very mixed work force ethnically and gender-wise, but we need even more to be able to face our customers well. The key is that we do not have a good story at senior levels: in the top 60 we have eight women and two from ethnic minorities, and that is not what we need or want. (Energy business)

The responses from other businesses in my interviews demonstrate a much less active position. Is diversity an ethical/cultural/politically correct issue, or do we really need to tap into a diverse pool in order to have the breadth of talent required for gaining real competitive advantage in the marketplace? The following quotes represent a more ambivalent position:

We are not very good here and I assume that reflects the industry sector in which we work. There are many women in customer-facing positions since many of the key buying decisions are made by women, but the situation at our senior management levels does not reflect that. (Construction company)

It's not an overt point but it's a nagging agenda that goes on. We have a male/female issue and issues on ethnic origin and linguistic ability and mobility. The higher you go, the fewer women, ethnic minorities etc. People see this issue but are not clear what we should do about it. (Financial services company)

Interesting question. Ideally talent and diversity should happen together but in reality we are terrible at it. On average our senior managers are right-wing, white, and middle-aged. In the US we have a Diversity Council, but no real impact, not for bad reasons just because people recruit people they know. In the global perspective the focus is on recruiting local talent so that introduces some diversity, which will still take time to get to the really senior levels. (International energy business)

We struggle to get females into important positions. We don't even have any women in this year's graduates. I don't know how much that relates to the external image of the business or to what our managers are looking for. We are OK in terms of ethnic backgrounds but don't have any measurements or targets on that. The management is concerned and interested in getting more women in but we are not clear how. (Financial services business)

The problems associated with creating a diverse pool as part of talent management efforts come from a variety of sources. First, recruiting executives do not always see the added value in bringing in candidates from a different background than what they are used to. It is natural for men to seek to work with other men and for men from one ethnic background to assume that people from other ethnicities are very different and will not necessarily work well as members of their team. Also, executive teams want to create a highly cohesive culture because their assumption is that the more cohesive the team, the easier it will be for them to perform effectively together. While cohesion is a positive force, it is much less effective when it results from similarity than when cohesion is based on diversity. Management teams where everyone is similar, in terms of their technical expertise, career background, the business culture that they have worked in and their perspective on life, will generate a very restricted range of solutions to competitive issues. They will, therefore, be less effective in addressing the needs associated with a diverse client population or in handling competitive challenges effectively. Individuals also have a restricted perception of recruitment options. They assume certain kinds of jobs fit people with specific backgrounds. It is not surprising, for example, that most Human Resources employees tend to be women and that the Finance function tends to be populated mostly with men. Similar perceptions exist around working in financial institutions or in engineering businesses. Some restrictions come from the nature of resourcing decisions that are made by recruiting managers, but many are due to candidates' self-perceptions. Women are influenced by other women in thinking about appropriate career paths and it is unusual for them to think of jobs where they have never seen a woman perform before. Also, restricting work practices reduce flexibility within an organisation in ways that may impact one group more than another. Flexible work arrangements can address different employee needs and, therefore, make jobs more attractive to different candidates.

In thinking through the solutions to increase the diversity of your executive talent pool you need to focus on approaches that relate to the recruiting manager, the culture of the recruiting organisations and to the candidates and what will help them to identify with certain career paths and to take on risks associated with unconventional job opportunities. Some of these solutions are similar to what I have discussed in the previous chapter around breaking down organisational silos, but in this case, they do not relate to corporate entities but to mental silos that recruiting managers and executive candidates have in their minds.

The first topic to be addressed in expanding the diversity of an executive talent pool has to do with the senior executive team. It is critical to open their minds to the importance of diversity and how that can be translated into specific targets when looking at the resourcing patterns across the business. Opening a person's mind is achieved gradually by familiarising them with the unknown. This is how we learn to like unusual foods or unfamiliar music. Executives can meet successful individuals who came from different backgrounds and are very successful. Meeting a woman marketer working in an engineering team and realising how she can add a whole other dimension to the competitive thinking within that team will open people's minds to the advantages of recruiting women. Meeting a senior financial executive from a different ethnic background who understands the diverse requirements of the bank's clients who come from that background will facilitate a discussion in the senior team about the importance of creating internal diversity that relates to the external marketplace diversity of their potential consumers. Meeting with individual executives who have themselves overcome difficulties and contributed disproportionately, will enable the senior team to set realistic targets for improvement in this area. The house-builder discussed at the beginning of this chapter has ensured that, over an 18-month period, the number of women in senior executive positions grew from zero to 20%, and they have specific targets for the next 18 months.

Talent management review processes in most businesses are conducted from a bottom-up perspective where each business unit identifies its high-potential executives and brings these names up for aggregation, first at the Divisional level and finally at Group level. Highlighting diverse candidates in Divisional talent reviews will begin to bring this issue to the forefront if it relates to a targeting directive that came from the Group executive. It is critical to assess high-potential candidates in an objective fashion, regardless of their background. This will ensure that candidates from ethnic minority backgrounds or female candidates are not less capable than other candidates. We need to avoid a positive discrimination process. That will backfire and create self-fulfilling prophecies where diversity is initially encouraged and then dismissed as a process that will actually reduce the leadership capability of the organisation as a whole. The focus in talent management needs to be on identifying a very small number of exceptionally capable women and candidates from ethnic minority backgrounds, assessing their capability objectively and, thereby, ensuring that they are at least as capable, when compared to the other executives that are sitting in the talent pool. Highlighting those candidates within talent management discussions in different Divisions will open people's minds to the fact that they can use diversity to 'spice up' the composition of their management teams and ensure more creativity and innovation in the leadership of the Division. This cannot be done just by talking about names and assessment results on paper. It is important that the top management teams within each Division and across the business as a whole actually meet these candidates and begin to form a personal impression of their depth of capability.

The focus of efforts to bring diversity to talent management has to do with breaking the psychological mould that is ingrained in people's minds. This can be achieved by one successful case study. One female senior executive who is very effective in a team will change everyone's perception in the most fundamental way and will encourage recruiting managers to bring in more and more women from more diverse business backgrounds.

> We don't believe in promoting diversity through specific targets. We have a very strong performance culture driven by our CEO. Our senior appointments show an unusually high proportion of women, age distribution and ethnic executives in director positions. So we have a decent record but that has not been conscious – just a reflection of a focus on performance. We don't seem to encounter blocks to bringing in women and people from ethnic backgrounds in this sector. We don't really think about it and it just happens. Maybe that is because we have a woman CEO? Who knows? A lot of this is about successful role models. So it's key not to push people who are not good role models or to have positive discrimination that doesn't work since you will start to lose your best people. When you make a good appointment based on competence then you create a great role model. (Large retailer)

The key for Human Resources is to identify a very small number of exceptional candidates from a diverse background and to ensure that when they go into a new executive position they become successful. Better one shining success than a large number of mediocre resourcing decisions.

The key to working with high-potential candidates who come from a diverse background is to understand that the problem is not only with the recruiting managers but also in the perception of the high-potential candidates themselves. It is important to talk to female executives and to candidates from minority populations in order to understand their perceptions, what they think are appro-priate jobs that will enable them to utilise their talent and to understand why they think in certain ways. One of my clients used external consultants to interview young female executives. This helped them to understand why they were successful in recruiting a significant number of women engineers for entry-level jobs, while many of these women did not rise beyond middle-management levels. They found through that research that many female executives perceived that senior executive positions did not have the flexibility that would enable them to have children, enjoy their family lives and be successful in line with the requirements of the job. Also, a number of female executives had certain assump-tions built in about the nature of engineering tasks that they were good at and those that they perceived were much more appropriate for male engineers. The need to understand these self-perceptions was not about their degree of truth or falsity but about understand-ing the emotional perspective that high-potential executives had about what were appropriate career choices and where they were likely to be successful. Talented executives will only go for jobs where they think that they have a realistic chance of becoming successful, since their work is very important for their perception of themselves. By understanding the beliefs that potential candi-dates have, it is possible to begin to create resourcing materials that enable the recruiting manager and Human Resource depart-ments to convince high-potential women and minority executives to come forward and take on potential job opportunities across the business that usually they would not consider to be realistic or advisable.

A number of businesses have also carried out research exter-nally to identify key candidates in other business environments that may be appropriate for them (see Chapter 7 for a discussion of talent scouting). By using executive search firms who have a broad perspective on the market it is possible to identify business sectors where there are a significant number of senior women executives or senior executives who come from specific minority backgrounds. Interviewing successful candidates in those organisations will help you to understand their perspective about appropriate careers and why they would not come to work for you. These interviews also raise candidate curiosity about moving into a business sector that they would not have considered before. One of my clients is an international financial services company and they found that women marketers thought that the business was a boring, male-dominated group who were extremely risk-averse. It never occurred to these female interviewees that they could find fulfilling, creative and exciting careers within that business environment. Focusing specific recruitment activities on bringing in female marketers from FMCG and female retailers into the retail financial market helped this client to start to create a much more diverse senior executive team that was able to think about more appealing products and market them effectively to their client population where a lot of the buying decisions are made by women.

In addition to understanding the perceptions of recruiting managers and the perceptions of high-potential executives from diverse backgrounds, it is also important for businesses that want to create effective talent pools to focus on the executive search firms that they use. A number of my clients who are very assertive in their talent management processes have now briefed their executive search suppliers to ensure that they understand the importance of diversity and that they introduce a candidate shortlist that includes executives from diverse backgrounds. The key is not just to say: 'We always want to see a woman and a person from certain ethnic backgrounds on the shortlist', because that will tend to actually reduce the quality of candidates put forward. The key in briefing executive search firms is to say that, in order to introduce highly talented diverse executives, they are encouraged to bring in potential candidates for the position that come from very different business backgrounds. Advertising companies, marketing departments, and Human Resource functions tend to have many highly talented women. With encouragement, some of those candidates may be interested in pursuing careers in businesses that operate in environments which tend to be highly dominated by men.

The key for effective talent management of diverse pools of executives is to ensure that job moves, either from outside the organisation or from one Division to another, are well supported. Chapter 7 described what is involved in effective on-boarding processes. We need to prepare a recruiting executive and a newly appointed executive so that they will be able to be successful in integrating into a new business environment. These on-boarding processes are even more important when bringing diverse candidates, since there may be an initial clash of perceptions between the individual, the recruiting manager and other members of the management team. Everyone involved needs to become aware of their perceptions and how the reality may be very different. People have their own belief systems and a management team that has worked well together for a number of years will be resistant to bringing in a new person who may seem odd. Some of us remember what it feels like to be a child entering a new classroom where all the other kids have already formed their own cliques and are not open to help a newcomer to become an integrated member of the team. Similar processes exist with senior executives and it is important to prepare the team to integrate a new member effectively. This is true for any recruitment but when the new candidate comes from a different business culture, a different functional area, and a different personal background (being a woman or from a minority group) it is even more important to initiate processes that will facilitate effective integration. It is useful to talk about the issues openly and enable the team to understand why diversity is not only a politically correct topic. Why is diversity a critical requirement to ensure creativity and innovation and to understand clients/consumer requirements and how to approach them in a competitive manner? It is important to help the management team to value diverse reactions to existing problems and situations rather than to assume that it is only when we are all in agreement from the beginning that we are a really good team.

SUMMARY

This chapter has focused on talent management and diversity to ensure that a broad talent pool is used to select the most capable senior executives to lead the business. Cultural diversity that relates to gender and ethnic origin can become a true competitive advantage by enabling the business to understand the variety of consumer needs and to generate more creative and innovative approaches. Building a culture of diversity within each management team will ensure that members are not only paying lip-service to having a woman or somebody from a different ethnic background in order to feel good about who has been included. Facilitating real diversity in belief systems, backgrounds, ages and technical expertise will come with the understanding that a wide range of inputs will improve the overall performance of the team and, thereby, the performance of the business.

Increasing diversity depends on concerted internal communication efforts, both with the senior executive team and with Divisional leadership teams about the importance of this topic for their success as a business. Moreover, efforts at recruitment will be successful only if the perceptions of potential senior executives are also influenced. Candidates from diverse backgrounds need to be encouraged to open their minds to alternative career paths that may bring them different opportunities than they have seen in the past and had assumed would be appropriate for them.

Finally, as we have seen with other elements of talent management, in-depth on-boarding processes are key to ensure that new candidates are integrated well within their new business environment. In diversity, it is especially critical to have one successful candidate as a means of opening everyone's mind to the benefits of different kinds of people and, therefore, intense on-boarding processes will ensure that this process of integration works well.

CHAPTER 13

EMPLOYER BRANDING AND TALENT MANAGEMENT

*T*alent management processes are focused not only on systematic planning to identify the right people and manage their careers and on development work that enables people to build their potential. There is also a significant communication process involved when trying to attract the best talent internally and facilitate transitions from one part of the business to another. It is even more so when trying to attract the best talent in the marketplace to come to your business and leave behind other opportunities that may be very attractive as well. It is important, therefore, to initiate talent management activities to create an effective brand and communicate that within the business.

The concept of employer branding has become popular in recent years. Businesses have spent a great deal of effort understanding how they are perceived in the employment marketplace and initiating significant communication exercises to improve their brand. Attracting the best candidates is a key component of providing competitive advantage and, therefore, employers focus a great deal of energy in this area. Employer branding is a process that has adopted marketing techniques used by businesses to produce effective consumer brands and translated those into internal organisational processes that focus on creating a recruitment brand. A recent book, *The Employer Brand*, by Simon Barrow and Richard Mosley on the concept of employer branding states the case as follows (see Appendix 2):

> Your most important Brand relationship is unlikely to be your choice of breakfast cereal, your car or even your football team, but the Brand you work for – your Employer Brand. How people feel about their Employer Brand is increasingly critical to business success or failure. Leading companies realise its importance in attracting and engaging the people they need to deliver profitable growth. They are also beginning to recognise that a positive Brand experience for employees requires the same degree of focus, care and coherence that has long characterised effective management of the customer Brand experience.

Most employer branding efforts, however, focus on attracting junior staff – marketing the organisation to fresh recruits, either in the university graduate recruitment rounds or aimed at bringing in front-line staff to deal with clients in hotels, restaurants and other settings. Just like branding exercises that focus on consumer products, it is important to extend the concept of employer branding and introduce the notion of segmentation. We need to ensure that when we market a product or service we are clear what consumer segment we are trying to attract and how our branding efforts will focus on the perceived needs of those consumers. When dealing with employer brands, we similarly need to become more sophisticated and create special messages that focus on the executive population, which may be very different from the messages that will attract graduating students or front-line employees. A senior executive leaving one part of the business and moving to another Division is taking a significant risk, since his or her past success may not be enough to overcome the difficulties of performing in what may be perceived to be a very different business environment. Effective branding will help to attract executives to aspire to diverse roles. Similarly, when executive search firms try to attract a variety of candidates from different competitive organisations, one of the main things that is important is the perceived brand of the recruiting organisation. A commodity is differentiated in terms of pricing. It is important in the recruitment sphere that executives are not attracted by a bigger financial package but are attracted by the opportunities of joining an employer that they perceive to have a stronger brand than their current employer. Executive mobility has become commonplace and most would expect to move, on average, every 3 to 6 years in order to develop a breadth of experience. It is expected that an executive's résumé would reflect the brands that a very talented person would like to associate with. We buy branded clothes, drive a branded car, send our children to well-recognised (branded) schools and spend our holiday in fashionable locations. This is much more important with a person's career. When you think of a potential candidate, you tend to be impressed by the organisations that he or she has worked with in the past since you assume that their quality reflects the quality of the candidate in front of you. Therefore, when a high-potential executive is looking at alternative job opportunities they will be drawn to an employing organisation by the salary and the title involved but, more important, they will be drawn by an employer whose name on their résumé would increase their marketability in the future.

When I interviewed Heads of Human Resources from a sample of large businesses I also asked them about the nature of their efforts to establish an executive brand for their talent management processes. There was a wide range of responses to this question and it was clear that having a general employment brand did not really address the issue of branding at the executive level. Most respondents said that they had an image of the type of executive that succeeds in their business but it was not used on a formal basis, nor was it typically used to guide external recruitment or internal promotion processes.

Some respondents pointed out that they did not want to clone executives and that, in fact, they were trying to move away from an old image of the type of person that succeeded in their business environment. More variety was viewed as a positive change. The concept of an executive brand in these cases focuses on what the business could offer talented executives in order to encourage external and internal recruitment.

The following quotes illustrate the ambivalent state that characterises our respondents' businesses in terms of the need for an executive brand:

> Increasingly, we want to build on our success by saying that you are joining a Group with a diversity of businesses that will open more career opportunities. We are consistent about the type of people who are successful here. We need to be careful not to have Stepford wives and husbands. The key people have shown common features but also differences. We need to accommodate people who are different. Not everyone will meet all our criteria, but some have other key characteristics. At senior levels we focus on how people fit into the organisation. The way they go about the job is key to success here. We have created a brand in one of our businesses but not at senior levels. We haven't done work on this in the other businesses and are just beginning to think about what the Group means. (Large retailer)

> We do understand what people seek at senior levels but we don't really know how we are perceived by senior execs, other than the fact that our brand has improved. We want to move from being perceived as 'hairy-arsed' retailers towards being seen as professional managers but with the capacity to get stuff done. In our business we don't have a lot of structure around people so to be successful you need to do a lot of things on your own. There is a big workload without much support. We are becoming more

tolerant of executives from other businesses while in the past you had to come from a tough retail background. Also, we are starting to develop a reputation within functional areas but the challenge is to change the image of the business. We are at a transition point now because we have to grow up and implement more classic general management requirements, while not losing the essence of our success. Once we have that brand in a clear way then we can use it for all of our activities with executives especially assessment and development. We can also use it for our recruitment suppliers so that they know what we are looking for. (Large retailer)

We have done this to some extent by default. We asked external recruiters to do research and ask what candidates for executive positions thought about the company – especially what women candidates thought. So that gives us a beginning even though we still need to do something with this data. We have done things about a mass attraction strategy since we need to recruit a lot of people regularly, but that is different from what we are talking about here. (Retail bank)

We have a lot of work being done internationally on the employer brand. The idea is something like an 'expert friend', but there is something confusing in this. In reality, things are more complex. At Group level we are looking for values and behaviours. That goes on top of specialist knowledge, delivery and process focus, but people who move around the world have to have the values and behaviours bit. It is confusing. We should be clear of what we want from the Top 200 and use that. However, you never want to limit yourself and need to be open to new ways of thinking around values and behaviours. Consequently there is no sense of brand. People are not really loyal to the business but are to their boss or function. We need to change that so that people become loyal and committed to the brand. Organisational loyalty enables you to get much more out of people. The brand has to open up a world of opportunities to people instead of keeping them in silos. At the moment the pool of people below the Top 200 are process, tick-the-box people, rather than being outcome- and change-focused. (Financial services company)

Some organisations talked about branding in a different way. Instead of thinking about what they wanted from their talented executives, they thought in terms of what they could offer their most talented executives. Their concept is that of the brand as a vehicle that will make the business attractive to internal and external high-potential managers.

> We have just developed an employer brand based on a lot of research about what made us an attractive employer at all levels. The higher you go, the more important career opportunity becomes – offering real opportunity does differentiate us. We are looking to refresh our competencies in light of our vision and brand. That is based on our strategic belief that our success as a service company is focused on the idea that effective people create effective service, which then creates effective business performance. This is why we are so focused on ensuring that our people are effective and being happy is part of that. Now that we have moved from a focus on acquisition to focus on organic growth, the people development and performance that are associated with that are even more critical. We want to communicate opportunity to our people and our talent management brand therefore has to have a big element of that, not what kind of a person we are looking for but what we will give to the successful executive. That is what will attract and retain the kind of executives we want, but we have to make it real. (Consumer services business)

How does an organisation develop a brand that will help it to recruit the most talented executives externally and also to move around its most talented internal resources to create a breadth of experience for them and to increase the diversity of talent within its executive teams?

The first step in building an executive brand is to conduct in-depth research to understand how you, as an employer, are perceived by your executive population internally and by executives who may be potential candidates for joining you in the future from outside the organisation. Second, in order to understand how you are perceived, it is important to do some research with executives internally and externally about what is important to them in determining the effectiveness of an organisation as a strong brand to work for. One of my clients commissioned an executive search company to interview a targeted group of external candidates and asked them to describe what was important to them in choosing a place of work and how they perceived that business in light of their criteria. They found that the first requirement had to do with the success of the business. Executives would like to associate themselves with success and, therefore, candidates want to join businesses that are perceived to have strong financial performance and credibility in the marketplace. Second was the concept of career opportunities. High-potential individuals see themselves as moving up business ladders every 3 to 6 years and like to feel that by joining your business they will be able to make two or three management steps within it as part of building their own career. Ambitious people want to feel that the business that they are thinking of joining has systematic processes that will open up opportunities as part of internal succession planning processes or otherwise help them to build their career. Related to this desire to focus on careers, they found that high-potential interviewees were interested in their personal development. Businesses that were perceived to have systematic development processes that invest in identifying their strengths and weaknesses and helping them to maximise their potential were perceived to be desirable workplaces that ambitious senior executives gravitate to. Some of these desirable development opportunities had to do with engaging in a diverse range of activities so that executives could be exposed to international markets, could interact in cross-functional teams around a variety of strategic topics and could take up other opportunities that would broaden their capability. Finally, executives were interested in the culture of the business and issues around openness, receptivity and flexibility tended to be high on the agenda of high-potential, ambitious executives. Considerations around remuneration and long-term security were also important, but tended to be perceived as a symptom of the investment that a company was putting into its senior executives. Ambitious people were focused on their own capability to demonstrate exceptional levels of performance. Therefore, the opportunity to earn significant bonuses or to move up the pay scale was more important than necessarily what they would get upon joining or long-term security concerns.

This profile of needs from external candidates enables you to ask people about how they perceived your business in light of these criteria. You can also ask executives internally by interviewing those who are already identified as having a high level of potential and, therefore, are possible candidates for senior executive positions across the business. The focus would be on what are the most important criteria that would draw them to one senior executive position versus another and what are their perceptions about different parts of the business and the degree to which they provide the desired environment. In my experience, when interviewing senior executives about internal career opportunities, they are consistent in identifying characteristics of different Divisions. Executives tend to be drawn to Divisions that are seen to invest heavily in the development of their senior executives, to allow flexibility in decision making and creativity, to facilitate co-operation and to provide opportunities for learning and expansion. They are much more reluctant to join Divisions that are perceived to be rigid, closed and hierarchical and, thereby, have an autocratic leadership style. Poor marks are also received by Divisions that lack strong leadership, where people drift and there is a poor record of performance that prevents highly talented individuals from maximising their potential.

This information from external and internal interviews with high-potential executives will enable the Group Human Resource function to provide the executive team with a map of the attractiveness of various parts of the business and the impact of that on the ability to create the leadership that the business needs for the future.

In addition to understanding what is important to candidates and how they perceive your business, it is also essential for effective talent management to be clear about the type of executive talent that your business needs in order to gain and sustain competitive advantage in the marketplace. This information usually comes from in-depth discussions with members of the senior executive team in order to understand the kind of expertise, background, capabilities, personal characteristics and mobility levels that future executives should have in order to continue to provide the leadership required. Issues around exposure to international markets, in-depth consumer marketing experience, familiarity with technology and similar concerns would typically describe the kind of executive that will be required in the future. In my experience of interviewing senior executives, the background of the current top team is not necessarily what they would like to see in their successors. The current team may be composed of executives who spend their entire career in one organisation or in one Division or Function. But for the future, a Chief Executive and his or her senior team may be very clear that the leadership required will be much more diverse in order to build the creativity and innovation that create competitive advantage.

Clarifying the type of people that are required will make it possible to build a clear executive brand that combines what the business is looking for and what potential candidates are looking for in joining a business. The definition of the brand should focus not only on who the people are that 'we want', but also on what we can give to the best people to attract the type of executives that we want.

This concept of executive branding can, in some cases, be further segmented. Research may identify some commonality across all populations of high-potential candidates, but also some differences between candidates who come from different backgrounds. That may include gender and ethnic origin, but also background in terms of market segment. If your organisation is trying to attract marketing-orientated people it is important to understand what would bring a senior executive from an advertising agency or an FMCG business, or from a fast retailer to agree to come to an organisation that they may perceive to be extremely conservative and unattractive. The more you understand what you are looking for and what they are looking for, the more you will be able to create highly targeted marketing materials that address these mutual needs.

Developing marketing materials will clarify what it is that you are looking for and what you are offering to the executive candidates that you want within your talent pools. These materials can then be used as part of internal performance management processes, on intranet sites, and as part of internal job interviews when positions become available. They will create the buzz that will encourage ambitious executives to step forward and apply for positions that they would naturally hesitate to look at. This marketing approach is especially important when you are trying to convince exceptional candidates to move from one Division to another and to cross boundaries where they may start to feel insecure. Clarifying with the recruiting manager how the new position can become attractive will enable you to relieve candidates' fears and to create an excitement about enabling them to broaden their experience base and, therefore, become more attractive executives in the future.

Exceptional candidates are aware that their market value increases the more they can demonstrate that they have been successful in a broad array of situations. Therefore, by convincing internal candidates to make courageous moves from one sector to another you can also show them that their marketability will increase. A marketer who has worked in a retailer and a financial institution will have much more value in terms of future employment opportunities than one who has worked only in one sector throughout their career. The same processes apply internally when people only work in one side of the business and, therefore, gradually limit future employment possibilities for themselves. Exceptional executives, who will sit in your talent pools, will be motivated to achieve significant long-term career progression. They would, therefore, be willing to take on risks in moving from one job to the next, as long as they understand that the movement will be in their interest and that the business will support them both in moving and in coming back from one position to another.

Businesses encourage senior executives who are exceptionally talented to take on international assignments as a way of broadening their capabilities, awareness of cultural issues and ability to manage global processes. These transitions are very important in building a person's career, but only if the business sets out systematic processes to enable people and their families to succeed while being abroad and to bring them back to desirable and influential positions. It is very easy for the business to send people abroad and forget about them. When the time comes to end an assignment, the executive finds that he or she has been forgotten, since all of the new opportunities tend to be based on individual networking that is much easier when you are sitting at the headquarters than if you are in an outlying country. When one or two foreign assignments leave a senior executive stranded, everyone hears about it. Future top-level candidates will then hesitate to take on such assignments because they know that the risks involved would not be backed up by intensive support from the headquarters business.

Developing branding to facilitate moves across organisational silos needs to be backed up with external marketing materials that highlight the type of executives that you are looking for and how what you are offering will attract exceptional candidates. These materials need to be used for in-depth briefing of executive search companies. Otherwise they have their own perceptions of your business and will focus on the type of candidates that they think would fit your culture. This is especially important in organisations that have a very traditional image such as insurance or engineering companies. If the business wants to change and become more competitive in its approach it needs to create a different image. This image is transferred not only through the financial press but also through executive recruiters that represent the image when trying to attract potential candidates.

Some of my clients have invested not only in creating 'fancy' brochures for recruiting graduate students, but also in educating their search businesses and providing them with well-packaged materials that illustrate how the business is different from what it is stereotyped to be. By making it easier for your executive recruiter to 'sell' your business as an attractive place of work, you are increasing the probability of attracting top-level executive candidates who will provide the leadership that you are searching for.

As with all branding exercises, it is important to ensure that the concepts reflect reality rather than a fantasy that the consumer will find to deviate from the real product once they sample it. In terms of recruiting executive talent, it is easy to talk about flexibility, openness, diversity, development and other buzz words, but it is much harder to make these things happen. It is, therefore, critical to ensure that branding efforts are going hand-in-hand with the actual implementation of your talent management strategy. The business needs to actually provide candidates with the on-boarding support, the personal development and the long-term career progression opportunities that you have promised in order to attract them. Candidates talk to their executive search recruiters and to others in the marketplace. It is easy to destroy your efforts when an executive entering a new business has a bad experience, feels that the existing team rejects the newcomer because they are very comfortable with their old culture and all the words about innovation have not really permeated the culture of a Divisional management team. As a result, it is important to collect ongoing feedback from candidates once they are already settled inside the business, both those who come from outside and those that have made significant moves internally. Members of your executive talent pool should be interviewed annually in order to see what they feel about the place that they are working in and how their experience matches their expectations. Feedback from these executives should be presented annually to your senior executive team as a reflection of the environment that highly talented executives actually encounter in their day-to-day work. In my experience, the senior executive team wants to find out what the perception of the top 50 most talented executives is about the work environment that they encounter and how they think that environment could become more effective.

This feedback loop between executives in the talent pool and the senior executives leading the business can provide reinforcement for culture change across management teams in different Divisions. This will gradually match the existing real culture to the aspirations of the executive team in terms of the kind of leadership culture that they would like to see across the business. Moreover, executives in your high-potential talent pool will understand that the business is on a journey and that things are not as yet perfect. In fact, this population of executives tends to be drawn to challenges and is interested in impacting the business in the medium term and being part of the change, rather than stepping into a perfect environment. The key is in being listened to.

If you want to create a strong brand and a feeling among your high-potential executives that this is the right place to be, it is important that they feel that they have the ear of the senior executive team, that their feedback is solicited regularly and that actions follow in terms of helping them to maximise their potential wherever they are. Executives of this calibre are happy to continue to confront very difficult internal and external situations as long as they feel that there is a chance for them to win. That chance tends to be represented by direct contact with more senior executives who encourage them to work together on the organisational challenges that lie ahead.

SUMMARY

This chapter has presented the concept of branding, which has been applied in many businesses to the process of recruiting junior talent and can now be expanded through market segmentation concepts. Creating systematic branding efforts that focus on exceptionally talented senior executives, on how to attract them from outside the organisation and on how to encourage them to move from one part of the business to another will help the business to ensure that its talent management efforts are attracting the best leadership potential.

Building effective executive brands is based on a deep understanding of what highly talented executives need and want for their own careers and how they perceive your business and each of its Divisions in relation to their own personal requirements. Creating focused internal marketing materials and using them as part of career moves for talented executives in your talent pool will encourage executives to take on greater risks and to move from one side of the business to another. Using these marketing materials with executive search firms will enable them to create the attraction that will draw the best candidates to come to work in your business.

All of these efforts require continuous feedback loops because the internal working environment in all large businesses is mixed and there is always room for improving the challenges, flexibility and growth opportunities that are the main drawing attractions for highly talented executives. The key, as seen in this chapter, is not only to create effective working environments, but also to facilitate direct communication between the executives in your talent pools and the senior executive team. This will enable them to believe that the leadership of the business wants to work together with them to create the kind of future environment that they are seeking.

CHAPTER 14

INTEGRATING TALENT MANAGEMENT WITH OTHER HUMAN RESOURCE PROCESSES

*I*n building an effective talent management process it is important not only to have all of the relevant components in place but also to ensure that these activities are integrated with other Human Resource services provided to internal clients. Otherwise, we face the risk that managers will be confused. Every few months they will be asked to participate in another Human Resource process without understanding how one activity supports the other and how all of them contribute to the effectiveness of the business.

In many businesses, however, talent management processes are relatively stand-alone. While the senior executive group engage in them once or twice a year, from the perspective of an individual manager it is hard to see how they relate to other Human Resource processes. For example, in many businesses there will be a competence framework that is used for talent management, another competence framework that is used for performance appraisal, another list of competence areas that underpins management development activities, while there are still other lists used for external recruitment of executives. To be effective, the business needs a common language that all managers share and that forms the foundation for looking at all people-related issues from the moment someone is recruited to the time that they leave the business.

In my interviews with Heads of Human Resources in large businesses, I found that there was a general striving towards integration but that they were still some distance away from achieving this state of affairs.

These businesses had many of the necessary building blocks in place, but no one was happy that they had achieved the level of seamless talent development that they were striving for. It was especially hard for my sample businesses to integrate succession and career development with the 'normal' executive performance management process and with reward. They do, however, want to achieve one process, mapped on one sheet of paper that shows how everything works together:

We are really focused on trying to integrate things. We have a map of all of the components that we need in order to achieve our overall objective of having a choice of great people for key jobs, both existing and newly created. Some divisions will find it hard to give up 'ownership' of their most high-potential people. The key for me is to differentiate where we need consistency and where not. (Manufacturing business)

The Talent and Management Development Review type processes, including succession pipeline and development, are all integrated. The bits that are less integrated are performance reviews and the reward side, since our Remuneration Committee is different from the Management Development Review (MDR) group. We do have broad pay bands to support the MDR system – so that helps. The Executive Board is also now, for the first time, measured using the same performance management system, so that shows the importance of this issue. We will gradually integrate the last pieces. (Large retailer)

We want to be a one-stop shop for people's careers and we want to ensure that we manage careers effectively. We have an investment committee to look at buying businesses, but not to look at people and think through what kind of investment we need to have in order to keep the best people. This is of great importance and we want to focus on it more as we invest as much in a really high-potential person or group of people as we do in buying a small business. We need to be systematic in trying to build loyalty. It is critical to move toward integration. At the moment, our processes aren't necessarily linked, nor do they provide consistency of language and process. That is the goal we have set ourselves. We have all the support we need and we have many of the building blocks in place (score card, vision and values, employment brand) to be used as a launch pad for the talent management initiative to be integrated as one process. (Consumer services business)

We are reasonably integrated, surprisingly so, and I know that is fairly rare. In most organisations people 'do pay', 'do succession' and don't look at it as one process. We are helped by having integrated software systems. We are now moving into a total integration of these systems to have all the data about an individual in one place – not on separate systems. We have one calendar for all these processes though it isn't completely clear to everyone and we should clarify that on paper as a cycle. Sometimes the processes and systems take over too much and can reduce our flexibility, creativity and ability to step outside the box. We in HR need to ensure that managers understand that it's not a compliance issue. We have a lot of young sales-oriented people in our business and we need to show them we use these processes to support change – and deliver what we need – rather than to be driven by the processes. Our senior executives are very involved in this – they do their own 360°, and we have a staff survey that reports results for every business unit. So it's high-profile, but sometimes we put in too many processes. (Large retailer)

We need to become absolutely integrated. That is the next level of development for us. We have the processes and the business leaders are behind us but we need to connect the dots for people. In the past it was a very systemic process. Then, in the '90s, we stopped and told people that they need to take care of themselves and their own careers. Then we had another wave of large-scale business changes and that created a need for talent, which then opened doors for us to really do something well and take this process seriously. (Utility company)

Achieving the integration of all Human Resources processes that support talent management requires a focus on the core that underpins every one of these processes. This core is based on the following components:

- First, an understanding of jobs and the hierarchy of managerial positions that relates one job to the next across different job families.
- Second, the definition of managerial competencies that can be used to understand and develop performance within each management job level.
- Finally, culture and values are also at the core of all Human Resource services and, therefore, need to be integrated across them.

Figure 14.1 illustrates the kind of integration one would ideally strive to achieve across Human Resource processes and the place that talent management plays within it.

While the job levels, competencies and culture integrate all Human Resource services, from a talent management perspective it is important to understand how each service contributes to the implementation of effective talent management processes. This is outlined in Figure 14.2, which describes how each Human Resource process needs to contribute something to the overall efforts that focus on developing executive talent. From a 'Reward'

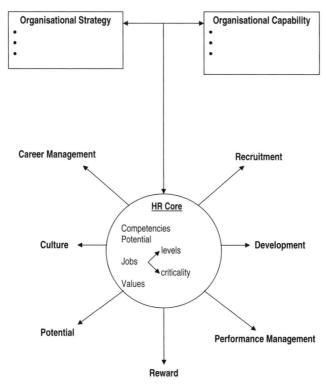

Figure 14.1 Chart of Human Resource processes.

perspective, it is important to have broad salary bands that make it possible for individuals to move from one part of the business to another and also to reward individuals who are especially capable by gradually expanding the breadth of responsibility that they are focused on. In addition, it is very important for high-potential executives to have a clear relationship between their performance and the kind of reward that they receive for it. Businesses that want to facilitate talent development need to create opportunities for significant differentiation according to performance so that executives who perform exceptionally well receive significantly larger bonuses than those who perform averagely.

Create a map that clarifies how each Human Resource management process 'participates' in the process of talent management. The following table may be useful.

Reward	Learning & Development	Developing Potential	Performance Management	Recruitment	Measurement	HR Planning	Organisation Culture
Broad salary bands Performance-related pay	Development plans Modular input Coaching Mentoring	Short-term projects Meeting the Exec. team Variety of job assignments to break 'silos'	Competencies and not just business objectives Feedback on potential Self-nominations for high-flyer programmes	Graduates Search firms External recruiters Internal job placements 'Branding' the need for talent Creating a talent 'bench' Diversity of talent pools Benchmarking	Assessment centres Employee surveys Exit interviews Scorecard Time taken to get to the top	Forecasting needs Assessing diversity Feedback from high potentials How many people, that we want to keep, leave us?	Branding talent Hard versus soft Diversity of talent pools

Figure 14.2 Best practice on the integration of talent management efforts.

From the 'Learning & Development' and 'Developing Potential' areas, it is important to create assessment processes in the form of assessment centres for middle managers and individual assessment for senior executives. These will provide validations to the ratings of potential provided by line managers as part of the performance management process. In addition, the assessment will provide executives in your talent pools with in-depth feedback about their strengths and weaknesses that they can use as a basis for continuing to develop their potential. The assessment data will then be used to guide in-depth development plans that will help high-potential executives to build on their strengths. The 'Learning & Development' area within Human Resources will then be responsible for offering a variety of input formats to assist high-potential managers in developing their capabilities. This will include modular training inputs, development programmes at key career junctions, coaching and mentoring processes, short-term project assignments, opportunities to engage with the senior executive team, career maps and career coaching (to help executives to understand where they would like to go), and a variety of job assignments that break silos and enable executives to develop a breadth of capability.

In terms of 'Performance Management', it is important that the system provides not only feedback on performance but also feedback on potential that enables the business to highlight individuals who are exceptional in terms of both. Some businesses also enable self-nominations for high-potential programmes so that executives who feel that they have the capability to rise to senior levels and are not recognised by their line managers have the opportunity to participate in assessment centres and prove their capability.

In terms of 'Recruitment', it is important that the business briefs executive search firms about the kind of talent it is looking for and uses the understanding of competence and job levels to identify the key characteristics of high-potential executives that it requires. Some businesses also have internal job placements where job opportunities are open to individuals who may see the value in crossing Divisional boundaries or functional areas in order to develop the breadth of their capability. These external and internal resourcing processes are based on clear branding that focuses on the kind of executive talent that the organisation needs. Relevant resourcing topics include having a talent bench that is available for new job openings, ensuring the diversity of the talent pool, and benchmarking external executive talent through talent scouting.

In terms of Human Resource 'Planning', it is important to forecast the need for talent by examining the natural turnover in executive ranks, analysing when executives are likely to retire and reviewing strategic business growth expectations and what they mean in terms of talent requirements across different parts of the business. In addition, 'Measurement' should focus on feedback from high-potential executives aimed at understanding what they value and to what degree different Divisions in the business are providing the desired opportunities for them. It is also important for Human Resources to track how many executives stay and how many leave from those identified as high-potential. This will assess the effectiveness of talent management processes in retaining and promoting talent. Other indicators include tracking movements across organisational silos and tracking the diversity of talent pools at various levels within the business.

Finally, under 'Organisation Culture', it is important for the business to be clear about the talent standards it requires and why those are critical for business success, to communicate the executive brand across the business in order to encourage people to join and to move internally from one part of the business to another, and finally, to address the whole question of transparency and the degree to which all executives understand what is required in order to be recognised as having the potential to reach senior executive levels. The 'Culture' also includes the ownership of executive talent and the degree to which business silos are allowed to retain their own internal talent instead of ensuring that key positions are owned at Group level, and facilitating the development of a broad experience base for exceptionally capable executives.

SUMMARY

This chapter has focused on the importance of ensuring that talent management processes are well integrated with other Human Resource processes. This will ensure that line managers understand why talent is important and how every aspect of Human Resource management contributes to the development of executive talent. Human Resource processes around 'Reward', 'Learning & Development', 'Performance Management', 'Measurement' and 'Organisation Culture' all contribute to the development of executives, since all individuals have talents and can make a significant contribution to the overall performance of the business.

In the context of this book, however, the focus is on only about 10% of the executive population, those who are perceived to have the underlying capability and potential to become future leaders. From this perspective, all Human Resource processes need to play their part in enabling the development of this top 10% of the talent pool, since by investing in a disproportionate manner in this small sub-population we will produce a dramatic result in terms of the leadership of the business as a whole. In this chapter I have outlined some of the areas within Human Resources that need to contribute to the implementation of talent management processes. It is not enough that there is an individual in Group Human Resources who is responsible for talent and that person provides individual attention to the top 100 high-potential executives, and facilitates annual talent reviews. All Human Resource functions need to understand the importance of talent management activities and how they can contribute to a focus on a small number of high-potential executives that will have a significant impact on the performance of the business as a whole.

CHAPTER 15

HOW ABOUT EXCEPTIONAL PERFORMERS?

*W*hen we think about executives with a significant amount of talent we are usually interested in those who have the potential to take on larger jobs within the foreseeable future. But there are other executives who may be considered to have talent which does not take the form of long-term potential. In every organisation there are individuals who are exceptional in their performance in their current jobs, even though they do not have the capability or the motivation to take on significantly larger jobs in the future. In many cases they occupy jobs that require a great deal of technical or professional expertise and over the years they have acquired an immense amount of experience that has become invaluable to the organisation. It is important, therefore, that we focus our talent management efforts not only on those people who are expected to rise through the managerial hierarchy, but also on those executives who are exceptional in terms of their current contribution in their current jobs.

In talent review meetings, many members of senior executive teams are afraid that by becoming transparent in identifying executive talent we will de-motivate the other executives in the business. Talent management usually involves around 10% of the executive population and the question is what happens with the other 90%. The picture, however, is much more complex. Many executives do not want to take on high-flying jobs because they do not have the ambition and long-term vision that pushes them to continuously move every 3 to 4 years to more and more demanding jobs. Many individuals prefer to stay in a role for much longer periods of time and to develop their expertise and experience within that role by gradually acquiring more in-depth ability to handle a variety of situations. Every job move has a significant amount of risk associated with it and high-potential executives enjoy this risk. Therefore, after being in the same position for 3 or 4 years they become restless and seek to take on a larger challenge that would test their capabilities. But that does not characterise all of the executive population in a business. Many do not want to take the risks associated with significant job changes and prefer to develop mastery within their current area of accountability. As a result, you will find that the key for motivating these executives is not to offer them a vision of continuous job changes associated with the potential to move up the organisational hierarchy. For them it is more important to provide recognition, the feeling that their contribution is valued and that they can influence what the business is doing in their area of expertise.

When I talk about 'exceptional performers' I do not mean the 90% of executives that were not covered by the talent management processes discussed so far in this book. Within this 90% there will be a relatively small group of executives who are exceptional in terms of their performance in their current job while not necessarily having the desire or the long-term potential to take on significantly larger positions. If we go back to the 'nine-box matrix' where managers, through the performance appraisal process, rate

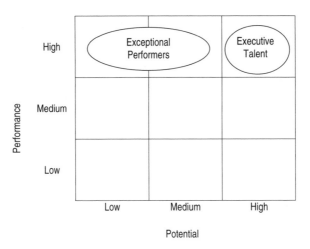

Figure 15.1

individuals in terms of their performance and their potential, the notion of 'exceptional performers' will involve executives in 'box three' and 'box six' (see Figure 15.1). 'Box three' executives are those who demonstrate highly effective performance, while they receive lower ratings in terms of their potential. Similarly, 'box six' individuals are also exceptional performers in their current jobs who receive average ratings on their long-term potential.

Everything that I have discussed so far in this book has focused on 'box nine' executives who are both exceptional performers and have exceptional potential to rise to the top of the organisation. You can expect that 'Exceptional Performers' in 'box three' and in 'box six' of the performance appraisal ratings (Figure 15.1) will include about 25% of the remaining executive population. This still leaves a significant group of executives, somewhere around the 65% mark, who demonstrate neither high potential nor superior performance in their current jobs. They may be good performers and may form the backbone of the executive population within your business. In this chapter I will focus on the performers who are still exceptional and, therefore, should be discussed within this book's focus on talent management.

Chapter 3 focused on the need to start talent management activities by defining critical jobs that have a disproportionate impact on the performance of your business. Similarly, when dealing with exceptional performers, we should focus on critical jobs. The first step in identifying exceptional performers is to examine the list of critical jobs and review the performance appraisal ratings that have been given to current job occupiers for these positions. This will be achieved by finding the 25% of executives in critical jobs who have received exceptional ratings of their performance, while not receiving very high ratings of their long-term potential. This population are the top performers in the business and it is critical for the ongoing effectiveness of talent management processes and the business as a whole to ensure that they are highly motivated and continue to develop their capabilities.

As we know from previous chapters, there may not be sufficient spread in your performance appraisal ratings. That will force you to get actual ranking on performance in order to identify this 'exceptional' population.

The first action that relates to exceptional performers is to ensure that they are reviewed in the annual talent management processes conducted with the senior executive team. It is important to review not only those executives who sit in the various talent pools because they have long-term potential, but also those executives who are in critical positions and are exceptional in their performance in these positions. The talent review in this case is not around possible moves and when they will happen. It is around what we should do for the exceptional performers to keep them motivated and to continue to improve their performance in their current jobs. Similar to players in the sports arena, also in business, executives who are very good in their job need to develop their expertise in order to stay on top. A lack of development will gradually make their expertise stale since they will not stay up-to-date on recent developments in the field, nor have the opportunity to exchange ideas and develop new approaches with experts in the field. The talent management review, therefore, should focus on risks associated with exceptional performers because their motivation is no longer what it used to be or on development opportunities that will enable them to continue to deepen their expertise.

It is essential to solicit direct input from your exceptional performers in order to find out what they think would help them to continue to do their jobs in as effective a way as they have been doing so far. This is not an area where feedback from Human Resources or from their direct line manager will be sufficient. When an executive does an exceptional job then their manager usually assumes that everything is fine and they tend to worry about others who may be facing some difficulties. Therefore, the best way to understand the needs of exceptional performers, both from an emotional-motivational point of view and a technical-expertise perspective is to ask them through a face-to-face interview.

In my experience, they will tell you that they are motivated by their expertise and by being recognised for their expertise. When I interviewed them, many have described that their satisfaction comes from continuing to learn and develop. In that sense they are similar to athletes, chess players, writers, musicians and others who gain their satisfaction and feeling of self-worth from a feeling of superior mastery in their chosen field of endeavour.

As a result, exceptional performers appreciate the opportunity to meet other exceptional performers in their content areas so that they can share ideas and think about things together. They also appreciate opportunities to go to conferences, read journals or books and otherwise deepen their expertise. Executives like these can be exceptionally loyal to your business if they perceive that the organisation continues to deepen their expertise in their specific content area and, thereby, enables them to feel that they are continuously improving. From an organisational point of view, this improvement may not have external visibility because they are not necessarily rising up the organisational hierarchy and becoming more important externally. But, this technical improvement is the foundation for deepening the knowledge base of the organisation and, therefore, enabling exceptional performers to access whatever they need in order to develop.

In addition to being motivated by refining their expertise, I found that exceptional performers were also focused on external recognition. Both within and outside the organisation, they appreciated the opportunity to be known for their expertise and receive acknowledgement that what they have invested has been worthwhile. The danger in most businesses is that the focus is on executives who have long-term potential. It is hard for a person who develops a lot of expertise not to feel that they are put in the corner and ignored, even though they think that they are making a very important and direct contribution to the effectiveness of the business. It is, therefore, critical to ensure that, as part of talent management activities, exceptional performers also receive public recognition for their contribution and expertise. This should be done by their direct line manager, their boss's boss and the Human Resource function, and ideally also through internal communication processes. Businesses that really understand the importance of technical expertise may have a monthly story in their intranet site, where the expertise of one of these exceptional performers is described and how he or she has provided the business with improved effectiveness because of certain technical elements that they have succeeded in implementing. This motivates the executive while also encouraging others to develop their expertise and receive recognition.

In addition to opportunities for deepening their expertise and for public recognition, exceptional performers are also useful in facilitating knowledge management activities across the business. It is important for the organisation to consolidate its knowledge base and as part of talent management activities to identify the small group of executives who have exceptionally deep levels of expertise across various content areas. Creating communities of knowledge around a small group of people with deep expertise will help the business to expand its knowledge base and, therefore, its competitive advantage in using this knowledge. Moreover, exceptional performers who participate in these internal forums will be motivated by the opportunity to interact with others, to share their expertise and brainstorm together.

In addition to meeting in technical forums, exceptional performers are useful in providing coaching to other executives. This may include coaching for high-potential executives who need to develop the breadth of their expertise, since their career so far may have restricted them to one part of the business. Creating a network of technical coaches that is available to expand the expertise of others benefits the learners who receive this coaching. It also enables the exceptional performer in their role as coach to feel recognised for their expertise. This level of personal recognition is what motivates exceptional performers to continue to deepen their expertise and, therefore, to increase their contribution to the business as a whole. It also motivates them to stay in the business and continue to contribute in an exceptional way as they have done so far.

The key in focusing on exceptional performers is to ensure that the talent management review processes with the senior executive team include a mapping that identifies them across the business and a quarterly review of what happens to them. Any danger signs involving these executives (such as when they leave and go to competitors) should be addressed immediately because it indicates that there is a fundamental problem in managing this type of talent. It is 'sexier' to focus on executives who have the potential to rise to the top of your business, but in terms of today's business performance the 25% of exceptional performers who do not necessarily have the potential to move or want to move will have a significant impact on the performance of the business in the short term. When a small number of these people leave your business and go to your competitors then you can assume that some of the basic motivational elements are not in place in terms of the management of executive talent. Either their direct line managers do not understand their importance and do not, therefore, give them the recognition that they deserve, or they feel that the business does not support their natural wish to continue to develop.

SUMMARY

The talent management activities described in this book focus on a small group of executives who have a disproportionate impact on the effectiveness of the business as a whole. Previous chapters focused on executives with the long-term potential to rise to the top or executives who sat in critical positions and it was, therefore, important to ensure that they were of the best calibre in the market. This chapter has focused on the small group of performers who are exceptional in terms of their contribution in their current jobs while not necessarily having the desire or potential to move to significantly larger jobs in the future.

Exceptional performers have a disproportionate impact on the performance of the business because their capability, expertise and experience are significantly better than the rest of the management population. It is important, therefore, to map out exceptional performers in critical jobs and to provide a regular review to the senior executive team in order to ensure that they know who the exceptional performers are and they focus on keeping them. The management of exceptional performers needs to focus on ensuring their level of motivation. This is derived from a combination of opportunities to continue to deepen their expertise and to be recognised publicly as executives who possess expertise. Exceptional performers can be used to support coaching activities across the business, thereby improving the capability of others and maintaining their own motivation that comes from being recognised.

CHAPTER 16

BUILDING SUPPORT
AT THE TOP

*T*he success of talent management activities in your business will depend to a large degree upon the support that they receive from the senior management team. When talent is perceived to be a priority for line management it becomes a hard-nosed, intensive process that is not different from the energy that is spent on financial performance, marketing and other functional topics that are perceived to be fundamental to gaining and maintaining competitive advantage in the marketplace. On the other hand, in many businesses that I have worked with, talent management is still very much an HR-led process. The Human Resource function has developed forms that are filled in by line management and discussed once a year by the senior executive team talking about the importance of improving leadership capability in the business. But, HR-led processes are never very effective in changing the behaviour of line managers as long as the latter do not see that these activities will actually help them to be more successful. In my interviews with a number of senior executives in large corporations they mentioned that talent management activities will not be effective as long as there is no fundamental buy-in from the senior team.

> The organisation could do more to facilitate the thought process for me to think about my development. HR is more geared up lower in the organisation. We don't have at a very senior level the guidance and input to facilitate my thinking. A minority of senior people may see that as a threat but I am open to that. Human Resources is supportive but we need to have a more assertive framework for people who want to use it.

> I want and need to develop continuously. The company supports us in a passive way and I would welcome more input and suggestions. I would respond positively to more formal development.

> The organisation is passive though supportive. Once I reached a certain level, organisational passivity happened. There would be no resistance if I identified something, so I took active charge of my own development.

In contrast to these quotes, it is interesting to read Jack Welch's book (*Jack: Straight from the Gut*; see Appendix 2) on his experience as the Chairman of General Electric, which is one of the largest diversified industrial corporations in the world. In his role as Chairman, he spent a very large proportion of his time in various aspects of talent management because, from his point of view, if you get the right people in leadership positions then everything else will take care of itself in terms of running the business.

So how do we build the support of the senior team? In any gathering of Human Resources professionals there are always complaints about the fact that the line managers do not understand the importance of Human Resource processes. This moaning usually comes instead of focused activities that enable line managers to really 'own' the need for certain processes by seeing how they will contribute to the effectiveness of what the line is trying to do. After all, it is the self-interest of executives in trying to do their jobs in the most effective way that will drive what they will focus on day-to-day. From this perspective, gaining support from the top has to be based on actions that involve the line in 'owning' the advantages that will come to them from implementing effective talent management activities.

The first action to take in enlisting senior management support is to talk with each individual in the senior team about the importance of having effective leadership, about what they see as the strength and weaknesses of the current leadership teams within each Division and Function in the business and what they consider to be the actions that will create more effective leadership across the business. In my experience, members of the senior executive team are very interested to ensure that there is effective leadership within the top teams in every part of the business since they see the relationship between the quality of leadership and performance. The problem is not in an abstract commitment to the importance of leadership but in how you transform the existing situation and improve the current leadership when compared with what is available in the external marketplace. Most senior executives do not see a way that will help them to improve the leadership capabilities of their senior teams. They are aware of business school programmes and they discuss issues at talent management meetings, but they do not see how one or another can really improve the quality of leadership, nor do they know of any other approach that will achieve that objective. Everyone shares a fantasy about the kind of leadership that they would like to have, but they are not aware of concrete steps that can be taken in order to improve leadership at the top. As Human Resource professionals our aim is not so much to talk about the final goal, which we all share, but to 'sell' concrete action plans that will enable the business to reach that goal.

In addition to interviewing members of the senior team, it is very useful to interview their direct reports and collect data about their perceptions about the various development opportunities that are currently available to them. As we have seen in earlier chapters, the top 50 senior executives are very interested in developing their own careers. They have concrete suggestions about what can be done to improve career progression within the business and how they as individuals would like to be supported to utilise their capabilities in the most effective way in order to be considered as candidates for a variety of posts. This information from in-depth interviews with the second-tier executives will be very useful when you provide feedback to the senior team. It will include concrete suggestions about what can be done to help their direct reports to become better leaders and, thereby, to improve the quality of leadership talent across the business. This information comes directly from 'the consumers' of development activities and is not, therefore, an interesting suggestion from the Human Resource function. Once you interview the top 50 senior executives it is relatively easy to get the support of the senior team to implement concrete approaches that will help to build better talent development across the business.

The third action that can be used to build support at the top for implementing effective talent management processes is to focus on the performance appraisal system. By aggregating performance appraisal data in terms of the distributions of the ratings for each management level and each Division, it is possible to focus on those business units that do not use performance appraisal as a way of differentiating between more and less effective executives. You will find that certain Divisions and Functions use only the top end of the scale and do not provide feedback to executives about the need to improve. When this data is brought to the senior executive team as part of a talent management review, it clarifies the need for having a defined performance standard as described in Chapter 2 of this book.

The senior executive team needs to discuss the importance of having superior leadership in the business when compared to its competitors. The distribution of performance appraisals in each Division is a very good starting point to contrast the reality with the vision of having a truly superior leadership team heading part of your business. If all executives are rated as 'very good' or 'superior', then we can assume that their managers are too weak to confront the reality that some people are much better than others. This discussion around the talent standard with the performance appraisal distribution will open the way to formulate a policy that ensures that performance appraisal ratings for executives across the Group follow a distribution where maybe 5% receive the top scores, then another 20% the next score, 50% in the middle, 20% less than average and 5% in the lowest rating. A Normal distribution like this (or a 'flatter' one with 10%, 30%, 40%, 30%, 10% ratings) will enable the senior executive team to focus on the most talented executives and develop their potential while also addressing the deficiencies at the lower end of the distribution.

If the culture of your organisation will not support a forced distribution of performance appraisal ratings then it may be possible to add one more extra rating at the top of the distribution (exceptional performer) and to ensure that rating is kept for not more than 10% of executives. This will have less of an effect overall, but at least will enable each Division and Function to identify the top 10% of its executive talent that can then become the focus of discussion for talent management efforts.

The next area that will have a significant impact on building support for talent management initiatives is how talent review meetings are conducted. In most organisations the senior executive team will devote one day a year to talk about executive talent. These meetings tend to be less than effective when they focus on individuals and where the top team sits and listens to Division heads presenting data that demonstrates that everyone in their own leadership team is fine and that there are only minor issues to be addressed. In reality, when there is an informal discussion we all know that most Division heads are not that happy with the quality of leadership across their direct reports but they are very hesitant to bring that data up to a Group forum since they do not want to look bad in front of their colleagues. It is, therefore, very important to prepare the talent management meeting in an effective way to deal with key issues and how they demonstrate themselves across different Divisions and Functions instead of talking about individuals who are not necessarily familiar to anyone else in the meeting. Key issues include performance appraisal distributions, the number of job openings that are filled externally versus internally, the number of senior executives who were rated as top talent who left the organisation in the previous year, the number of high-potential senior executives from one part of the business that have taken up internal positions in other silos, etc. These are all symptoms of a more general question around the effective management of executive talent as a Group resource across all parts of the business. The more the meeting of the top team is focused on these issues, the easier it is to get support for implementing significant initiatives across the business. As a Human Resource practitioner leading this meeting, the key is to have a clear objective up-front of what it is that you are trying to achieve. These objectives will come from every chapter in this book focusing on the need to create talent pools, use objective assessment of potential and facilitate movement across organisational silos in order to improve the quality of leadership across the Group.

The next area that enables us to build senior executive support for talent management activities is the individual involvement of members of the senior team. It is very different when I am sitting in a meeting and talking about a conceptual topic that does not require me to do anything specific, compared with situations where I am personally involved in doing something and understanding the implications of that action. In my experience, the best organisations in terms of managing executive talents involve each member of the executive team in mentoring high-potential executives from other parts of the business whom they do not relate to through their day-to-day management. As a Division or Function head, I would be mentoring two or three of the most promising executives in other parts of the business. This will enable me to get in touch with how talented these people are and to understand what will enable them to use their individual potential to the benefit of the Group as a whole as opposed to being limited by the conditions that they encounter in their own business unit or functional area. This direct involvement from senior executives in mentoring high-potential executives from the 'Top 100' group benefits not only the high-potential person but also the senior executives themselves. It enables them to be engaged in business activities at the level below on a more personal basis and helps them to feel young again and to have direct feedback from the field as a result of this activity. A one-to-one mentoring relationship creates an emotional bond between the senior executive and the person he or she is mentoring. It builds emotional support for the need to facilitate career development and cross-business transitions for the most talented people as a way of developing truly innovative leadership for the Group as a whole.

Another process that I have found to be very useful in building support at senior executive levels is to look at the results of employee surveys that are done throughout the organisation. It is important to put a question into the survey about career opportunities and the ability to use your potential in the way that will benefit the business. You would be surprised at the percentage of respondents who feel that the organisation is not helping them to utilise their own potential, and is not benefiting from the contribution that they can provide.

SUMMARY

This chapter has focused on building support in the executive team for talent management activities as a critical factor that will determine the effectiveness of what you are doing. It is easy for the Human Resource function to have a bureaucratic process that involves form-filling and an annual meeting with the senior team and to think that will cause things to change. But, if we measure change by the number of high-potential executives that move from one part of the business to another or the transformation of senior leadership teams within each Division by bringing in high-potential people from below them as opposed to always going outside to recruit, then we will see that it is much more difficult to implement talent management activities effectively. It is interesting to go back to the original survey that was done by the McKinsey consultants in the USA a few years ago as part of their *The War for Talent* book (see Appendix 2) and to review the findings shown in Figure 16.1.

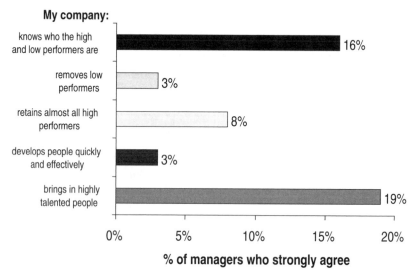

Figure 16.1 Most companies are poor at talent management.

Source: McKinsey & Company's *The War for Talent*, 1997 and 2000 surveys combined. Taken from 'Talent Management; A critical part of every leader's job.' (2001) *Ivey Business Journal*. Reproduced with permission.

In order to build support at the top, it is not enough to lecture people who sit in those positions, but we have to be able to demonstrate the benefits from implementing talent management activities. This will happen as a result of feedback from the senior executives who work for them and by getting the senior team personally involved in supporting high-potential executives so that they can see what can, in practice, be done. Throughout this book I have illustrated a broad array of activities that should be included within talent management. The problem is not so much about gaining support but about having a concrete plan that outlines everything that needs to be done and then comparing it to what is currently done in order to identify the key priorities for the coming years.

CHAPTER 17

HOW DO I MANAGE MY OWN CAREER?

So far, this book has focused on organisations and how the business as a whole implements talent management activities in order to develop its leadership capability. This chapter is focused on you as a consumer of talent management activities. Every executive has his or her own career to think about and this chapter will help you to go through that process. Are you sufficiently ambitious? What do you need to do to maximise your potential and build your career so that it matches your ambition?

The first question in managing your career is to understand your talents. This book is focused on the top 10% of the executive talent pool within an organisation and the question is, 'To what degree do you belong in this top 10%?' When we rate executives, we review their level of achievement and, therefore, the first question is, 'To what degree do you feel that your achievement within your current job is at the top 10% of executives who are doing similar jobs at similar levels within your part of the business?'

But the question of talent goes significantly deeper than that. As we have seen in earlier chapters, performance is best described in terms of competencies. Every executive has a profile of competencies where he or she is strong in some areas, average in others and also weak in other competence areas. Therefore, the most effective way to start to think about your own career is to understand your own profile of strengths and weaknesses. Typical competence areas include having a strategic vision, managing operations, managing people, interacting with others, working with clients and driving change and innovation. If you think of these six domains, how would you rate yourself? In what areas do you feel that you are exceptional (in the top 10%) when compared to the other executives that work in your business? In what areas do you feel that you are average and in what areas do you feel that you are weaker than others?

There is a great deal of research under the heading of Positive Psychology (see book reviews in Appendix 2) that provides strong indications about the benefit of building on your strengths as opposed to focusing on your weaknesses. Many people are naturally drawn to examine their weaknesses with the fantasy that 'if I can eliminate my weaknesses then I can become a much stronger executive'. But a more effective perspective focuses on competitive advantage. Even if I succeed in developing my areas of weakness, I can at best expect to become average. On the other hand, if I invest in developing my strengths then I have a realistic possibility of becoming exceptional in those areas and, thereby, gain competitive advantage compared to executives with similar backgrounds to mine. Therefore, as we see in a business environment, it is important to identify your areas of potential competitive advantage and to leverage those areas as means of building your capability and achieving the maximum of your potential.

This discussion around competencies and identifying your own profile of strengths and weaknesses is very important for building your career. But more significant for long-term success within a business environment is your motivation. In my work with senior executives in different countries and businesses I have often met individuals who were extremely successful owing to their high degree of motivation, ambition and tenacity and who, therefore, have utilised their capabilities to their utmost. Similarly, I have met senior executives who were exceptionally capable in terms of their intellectual ability, their depth of expertise and breadth of knowledge. But because their level of motivation, ambition, and tenacity was not as high, they did not achieve as much. So how motivated are you? What would you like to achieve?

To what degree do you want to achieve significantly more than you are achieving today? It is rare to find a person who thinks through their whole career chain and says that in 10 or 15 years' time they would like to be the Chief Executive. It is much more common, however, to see ambitious executives translate that ambition into wanting significantly more responsibilities than they currently have. Ambition, therefore, is best focused on the next step within the managerial hierarchy, rather than having an up-front, well-mapped plan for everything that will happen in the future. The world of business today is extremely volatile, and there is no point in working through an elaborate multi-step career development plan. It is much more effective to have a desire to expand your career, to scan the horizon and identify the next step which will be a significant challenge that you are capable of taking on. One step after another, you will move without necessarily having a long-term vision of where you want to get to.

In thinking about ambition, however, it is important to remember that career development is tied fundamentally with the process of change. Every time you leave your current job and take on a new position, you are taking a large risk associated with this change. While staying in your current job, you are assured that you are doing things well, you feel competent, gradually over time it will be easier to do things that would be more difficult for a newcomer; you have built a network of relationships that support you within the current environment. If you are performing well then there is a natural tendency to feel good and receive positive reinforcement for your work. These reinforcements in your current job are actually functioning as 'chains' that keep you tied down and act against any decision to take on a new position. In the new place, you will not know the people as well, it will not be as clear what you have to do in order to be successful and there may be some initial periods of hesitation where your performance will not be up to the standards that you are used to. In addition to these managerial risks, emotionally it is hard to feel very good about yourself when you are insecure about what you are doing and how successful it is going to be. These negative feelings associated with a new position act as deflectors, which again tend to encourage executives to stay in their current, relatively safe position.

There is, however, also significant drawing power towards a new position. First, there is the challenge of wanting to stretch yourself and to be able to use your capabilities to the utmost. Many executives, once they have done a job well for a few years, become bored and feel that they are not really using their capabilities. Like an athlete, superior performers need new challenges. Once they have surpassed a certain achievement level they look to the next level as a way of challenging themselves and getting the best out of what they are capable of doing (for the concept of 'flow', which characterises superior performers, see Appendix 2, *Beyond Boredom and Anxiety*). This notion of self-challenge and 'stretch' comes in addition to the recognition and reward that are associated with more senior jobs within the business. But for many ambitious executives, the external recognitions and financial rewards are experienced as symptoms of the fact that they have succeeded in challenging and stretching themselves and are performing at the level that they would like to be able to perform.

In general, any job change is a risk and, therefore, when I decide to leave the safety of my current position where I am doing well and take on the risk of moving to a new position where it is still unclear how well I will be doing, I am taking a gamble. In deciding whether to gamble I need to think of the relative value of the gain versus the value of the loss. I, for example, hate to gamble in casinos. For me, to win a certain sum of money is nice, but it does not make me feel great since I know that it has more to do with luck than skill. On the other hand, while losing that same sum of money will not be terrible financially, it does make me feel stupid. It is important for me to have control over what I do and to develop my expertise. By gambling I am just throwing money away on an activity where I have no perceived control. Therefore, for me, the value of the gain (if I win) is significantly smaller than the value of the loss (if I lose). A similar thought process exists in gambling on a move to a new position. To what degree are the benefits associated with the possibility of success in the new position larger than the losses associated with failure in the new position? Obviously there is no right answer here. This is a personal answer since each of us has a personal formula that determines how risk-seeking or risk-averse they will be in their career.

When dealing with motivation, we need to examine not only the motivation for moving up (which we have looked at so far), but also the motivation for staying where you are, if that is the decision that you reach. Are you deciding to stay because you enjoy what you are doing and, therefore, why change? Are you deciding to stay because you are afraid to take the risk that is associated with moving? It is perfectly acceptable for executives to find a job which they feel best utilises their capabilities and to spend a significant number of years honing their expertise and become 'exceptional performers' as described in Chapter 15. Not everyone feels the need to move every 3 or 4 years to a more senior position. Many executives get a great deal of pleasure from becoming experts in a specific area in a way that best utilises their capabilities. The most important question, therefore, in deciding to move or to stay is the nature of your motivation. Does this come from a positive motive? Are you staying because you want to develop your expertise? Are you moving because you want to have a larger challenge? Or, is the decision based on fear – are you not moving because you are afraid that you will fail?

This difference between positive and negative motivations relates to the area of perceived self-worth. All of us have a certain perception of how good we are, and that perception sometimes does and sometimes does not match the perception of others around us. People are sometimes surprised when others tell them how good they are, or how easy it seemed for them to achieve a certain level of success, while they themselves may not feel like that at all. In general, research on perceived self-worth has demonstrated that it is based on people's experience in utilising their capabilities. People with high self-worth are characterised by setting targets for themselves that are stretching and realistic and, therefore, gradually encouraging themselves to develop their capabilities. People with low self-worth are characterised by setting targets for themselves that are either too low, and then they do not use their capabilities, or too high, and then they set themselves up for failure. We are 'programmed' to build on our capabilities and, therefore, we feel better when we do so. People who are bored, or spend a lot of time without expressing themselves and their capabilities tend to feel depressed and have low self-esteem even though from an external point of view someone else may think that they are enjoying themselves sitting by the pool. It is very different to sit by the pool when you think that you have earned it because you have stretched your capability, as opposed to sitting by the pool knowing that you are doing so because there is nothing that you can do. Our ability to stretch ourselves and build our capability is impacted by our perceived self-worth. If we feel good about our capability, then we stretch ourselves. If we do not, then we are afraid to take on new challenges or we set ourselves up for failure. This process becomes a self-fulfilling prophecy. If we succeed, then we feel good about ourselves, set new stretching targets, succeed, etc. If we have low perceived self-worth, then we do not try and that just reinforces our negative self-image.

Assuming that you have identified within your profile of competencies those areas of strength where you have a realistic chance to achieve competitive advantage and you have identified a level of ambition and motivation that will drive you to build on these capabilities, then the rest of this chapter will deal with what you can do to develop your career further. How do you turn this level of capability and this level of ambition and motivation into concrete achievements in the business world? The following eight areas highlight significant actions that can help you to build your career.

1. Your boss is your client. When individuals talk about their line managers they tend to expect to be managed in a certain way and when their boss does not act according to those expectations they complain and feel that they do not receive what they deserve. This is a somewhat child-orientated perception of the manager/ direct report relationship. The manager is perceived, at least emotionally, as a paternal (or maternal) figure who is responsible for taking care of us and our needs. An alternative and more useful formulation would look at your manager as your client. In that case, in order to be successful, you need to understand what your manager expects from you, you need to try to satisfy those expectations and you need to measure that satisfaction in a similar fashion to what you would do with any other client. This different type of formulation is much more useful. We do not usually complain about our clients, since we depend on them and assume that they are right (from their perspective). We try to understand our clients and once we do, we try to satisfy them. When we check with our clients that they are satisfied it makes them even happier because we bothered to find out how they felt about our service. This positive cycle in servicing client needs also works well with managers when we switch our perception from thinking that it is their job to satisfy us, to understanding that they are paying us and it is our job to satisfy them. I describe this internal world of assumptions around the relationship between a direct report and their boss because the first requirement for developing your career is to ensure that your manager feels that you are doing an exceptional job and identifies you as having high potential. It is very rare that people who are mediocre or failing in their current job will have opportunities to do more senior jobs that will stretch them further. By understanding what it is that you are doing according to expectations and what you can do to go beyond your boss/client's expectation, you ensure that they are exceptionally happy with the service that you provide and, therefore, your current job will become a useful springboard for a new position.

2. Network. Many executives focus all of their attention on their current job and the relationships that are important for them to perform in their current job. Keeping your head down may be useful for performance today but it does not develop the exposure that is required in order to build on your capability and ambition and identify additional opportunities that may enable you to stretch your capabilities. Businesses are built around loose networks of contacts and the executives who have personal contacts in a broad area have better chances of being noticed by others, of identifying new job opportunities and going for them. Therefore, in order to develop your long-term career, you need to develop a network of contacts with individuals who work in other Divisions and Functional areas, to participate in task forces where others come from across the business, to attend executive courses where you will meet other people whom you did not know before, to introduce yourself to key job holders who may be relevant when positions become available, and to initiate knowledge-sharing forums where you will share expertise with other executives like yourself from other parts of the business, thereby getting to know each other well.

3. Step up. There is a story about a holy man who, when he was reaching retirement age, complained to God and asked why, despite all the good that he had done, he had never won the lottery. After a brief hesitation, a voice came back and asked him to provide a little help himself by first buying a ticket. This may sound obvious when dealing with the lottery, but when you talk about career opportunities, it is not unusual to find capable executives who are beavering away, doing an exceptional job in their current position, while expecting that someone will notice them and put their name forward without them doing anything active in that direction. If you want to be noticed, you need to speak up in meetings where other people can hear that you have something to say. You need to put forward to your boss and your boss's boss suggestions for improvements even in areas that are not directly within your realm of responsibility. You should ask key decision makers in Human Resources or in Divisional headquarters about job opportunities and let them know what you are looking for. The natural tendency is to assume that when people do not speak up they are probably OK where they are. Therefore, if you are interested in getting more, then you need to let other relevant people know that this is what you would like to see happen.

4. Don't overdo it. The suggestions described above are positioned within the assumption that you will be acting on them in an interpersonally sensitive manner. People appreciate executives who add value and, thereby, go beyond their day-to-day accountabilities and contribute in a way that demonstrates their capability and ambition to take on broader responsibilities. On the other hand, no one appreciates a 'know it all' who at every available opportunity stands up and shows everyone else how much smarter he is. In general, in executive career development, interpersonal skills are the most important foundation. It is important that you think through how to cause others to feel that you are adding value and to believe that you are exceptionally capable and ambitious without them feeling that you are overplaying your hand.

5. Build a diverse résumé. The natural steps of career progression in a business tend to happen within organisational silos. Once you start your career in a certain Division, you tend to see your opportunities for progress within that Division, other people who work there know you and recommend you for new openings etc. This may be a relatively easy route for making progress in the first few steps up the management hierarchy but gradually your silo becomes a sharp-tipped pyramid and the number of opportunities starts to reduce dramatically. You will find, therefore, at the senior levels of any Divisional silo, a large number of capable and ambitious executives who are waiting for a very small number of positions to open up. A more strategic approach to career development is to take on a broad array of diverse jobs. It is risky to move from one Division to another, or to move from one functional area to a line position. But these risks have significant advantages in the medium term. When a recruiting manager looks at a candidate's career path, they will appreciate the breadth of expertise that comes from playing in different business environments. But more significantly, by having a variety of functional and line jobs in different business environments, you become a realistic candidate for a much broader universe of potential job opportunities. You are, therefore, no longer limited by the small number of opportunities that typify the top of any Divisional pyramid within your business, since you can 'hunt' and be considered to be a relevant candidate for a number of different business silos.

6. Understand jobs. Just like any other business plan, it is not enough to have the capability and ambition. It is also important to research the terrain, understand what the opportunities are and what is required to succeed in each area. This principle also applies to career development. If you want to develop your career, it is important to understand the main steps in the managerial hierarchy across the whole business and what jobs sit within each step across each Division and Function. Because of our career history, we have a very myopic picture of job opportunities since we know very well the jobs that surround ours and we know less and less about other Divisions and Functions which we are not in contact with on a regular basis. If you want to develop your career, especially if diversity of opportunities will play a major role in that, it is important that you understand what could be available at the next level up from your current position in each of the silos of your business. The best way to find this out is to talk to Human Resource executives in different Divisions and Functional areas. Describe your job level, ask them to describe similar jobs in their own part of the organisation and what could be the natural progress from those jobs up the hierarchy. By becoming an 'educated consumer' of jobs, you will know what possible moves there are for you across Divisional silos. You can then start to plan systematically how to contact decision makers who look after those positions, get to know them and help them to get to know you, your capabilities and your ambition to work with them.

7. Frequency of moves. It is natural for executives to stay too long in their current positions. Once individuals reach a level of management where they feel that their capability has been recognised, there begins to be a more delicate balance between the pushes and pulls that are associated with moving on to a new position with the risks related to a move. Therefore, it is not unusual to find executives that move rapidly during their early years but then peak in their late 30s and 40s and stay 8 to 10 years in the same job. While being comfortable, the longer you stay the harder it is to move to the next job. You become more entrenched where you are and others stop thinking of you as a high-flyer who is ambitious and wants to move up the hierarchy. The other extreme is just as problematic, however. Some executives let their ambition overshadow their realism and then stay only 1 or 2 years in a position, while already starting to look outside at other alternatives that may be more seductive. As with interpersonal relationships, a 'wandering eye' means that people do not invest sufficiently in their current relationship. Therefore, when an individual starts to move every 2 years then they get labelled as 'not serious' since 2 years is too short a time to make a significant contribution to a job and the person is perceived to have moved before they had the opportunity to prove that they could add significant value. Being labelled a 'lightweight' because of frequent moves in your early career may prevent people from taking you seriously and offering you significant career development opportunities in the future. In my experience, a 3- to 5-year time in a given position is probably the ideal range. It will enable you to both invest and add significant value where you are and not become too stale before you move on to larger challenges.

8. Work–life balance. The final point concerns the fact that career development is a long-term marathon and not a quick sprint. It is, therefore, important to preserve your energy sources and to ensure that you do not invest so much in one position that you become depleted before it is time to move on. As human beings we receive energy not only from our own success and recognition at work but also from the social network around us, family and friends who provide us with emotional and sometimes concrete support. I am reminded of a person who told me about his friend who, after many years of intense competition, was nominated to become the Managing Partner of a large accounting firm in the northeast of the USA. When he drove home ecstatic to tell his family, he found an empty house: his wife had taken the kids and the furniture because by then she did not want to be with him. This may be an extreme example, but it illustrates that in developing our career we have to ensure that we also spend sufficient resources developing our social network that will 'feed us' emotionally and enable us to continue to regenerate the energy that will be required at later steps. A lot of this investment is also tied to an individual's perceptions of what it takes to be successful. In my experience, success requires work but hard work is turned into effective output based on its quality and not on its quantity. Staying late at night and working at weekends is something that characterises individuals who do not want to go home and spend time with their family as opposed to those who do what the job really requires. It is true that in some unique cases, for a restricted period of time, such as a business merger or acquisition, executives have to put in an unprecedented number of hours. However, these are relatively short periods of time and, if your support network has been 'fed' appropriately in the previous years, then they will understand why you may not be available for a specific period of time. Otherwise, it is much more important to think strategically about your work investment. Ensure that you work reasonable hours, and that you use these hours in an efficient way so that it leaves you with enough time and emotional energy to spend with family, friends and other contacts that will build your emotional resilience.

SUMMARY

This chapter has focused on what you can do to manage your own career using some of the concepts that have been outlined throughout this book. Thinking of your career starts with an in-depth understanding of the profile of your capabilities and a focus on those areas where you are already very good, so that with additional development you will become exceptional and, thereby, gain competitive advantage over other executives who may be vying for similar positions.

The second major area has to do with ambition: understanding your wish to move up to more challenging jobs and at the same time take the risks that are involved in leaving your comfort zone and trying new and unfamiliar things. Assuming that the analysis of talent and ambition points to the fact that you do want to progress up the hierarchy to more complex positions, the chapter identified eight concrete action areas that enable you to focus your energy on adding value and creating an awareness across your business that you are capable and have the ambition to take on larger challenges. By ensuring that others are aware of what you are trying to achieve and of your record of achievement, you will open up a large array of opportunities that should match your ambition.

CHAPTER 18

CONCLUSION

*E*very executive in your business has some talent and it is possible to think of talent management as something that concerns everyone. But within the context of this book, talent management is about developing the capability of a small elite group, since these very capable executives will benefit the business in a very significant way. The information provided here is based on interviews with Heads of Human Resources in large international businesses and on my experience with a variety of corporate clients who are in various stages of implementing sophisticated talent management processes. Through all of these contacts, it is clear that talent management has become a high priority for many large organisations. This reflects significant processes of organisational change that have taken place in the last 10 years, with an increased focus on the quality of leadership that guides large corporations. The average lifespan of Chief Executives has reduced dramatically. When a business is not performing according to shareholder expectations, it is not unusual to replace the Chief Executive and/or significant numbers of senior leaders. As a result, large businesses increasingly focus on the quality of leadership within their Divisional and Functional teams and on ensuring that they have the best executives in the marketplace who can guide the business towards competitive advantage.

Systematic talent management starts with clarity around the leadership standards that are required in this area. The success or failure of any talent management efforts will be based on the importance that the senior team puts on having the best executives that are available in their competitive environment. Once a business is clear that they want to have this level of leadership then it is able to move systematically to define what is meant by talent, to assess their current leadership by comparing the capability of their executives with what is required, to evaluate other executives that are available in the marketplace, and to act to ensure that the business has the leadership team that it desires. In this process of defining the talent strategy, the book highlighted the need to start with a leadership standard. What your business is trying to achieve in the next 3 years will have a direct impact on the type of leaders that it needs. A strategic definition of leadership characteristics, instead of just vague words about having the best leaders, will provide specific criteria for all talent management efforts to identify people, assess their capability, develop them and move them to more influential positions within your business.

When we think about executive talent, we always think about individuals. However, as we have seen in the first few chapters of this book, the key in any talent management effort is to start with jobs. What are the key jobs that have a significant impact on the performance of your business? By focusing on the top 10% or so of jobs, you can assess the executives who are occupying these positions, compare them and their capability to what is available in the marketplace and change leaders as required to ensure that the business has the best players in the most important positions.

An analysis of jobs leads to the question of succession management. Most large organisations have some form of systematic succession planning process, but in many cases these are very bureaucratic, owned by Human Resources, where managers identify direct reports who can replace them. This process may result in a large book with names against various positions, but it does not usually provide a real basis for action. Executives continue to go outside and recruit when an opening is available, and becoming a candidate for internal promotion still depends more on networking and personal contacts than on systematic succession management. As a result, businesses have moved from bureaucratic processes to managing succession through talent pools. Exceptional executives at various levels are identified and developed for their capability to take on a broad base of positions so that candidates can be used when a variety of different openings become available. Sophisticated organisations tend to develop three types of talent pools: one right below the executive team, which includes candidates for the most senior level; another pool with senior executives who can step up into a 'top 100' executive position, and a third pool of young, promising managers with the capability to step up into the executive ranks. Membership in the pool is based on line manager recommendations, backed up by independent assessment of potential. Each talent pool includes a small number of executives, since it is critical to be able to invest significant efforts in identifying their strengths and weaknesses, helping them to develop their capability and facilitating their career progression. Given the depth of the investment in these executives, it is important to have a small number of people in each talent pool, so that real action will take place that will transform them into the type of leaders that the business actually needs to have.

The book has also discussed the concept of talent scouting, which is still very new and implemented systematically only by a few businesses around the world. The concept, as in the sports arena, is to identify the best players in the marketplace, even if there are no positions available to recruit them into your business at this point in time. By getting to know the best executives and understanding what they are like, the senior executive team can gradually focus on what is possible and start to bring those executives into the business as a way of gradually upgrading the effectiveness of its leadership.

The book has also presented the processes for identifying executive potential early on and developing it. This starts with a definition of what we mean by potential, since we do not really have a useful language to describe it. Competencies are used to describe executives' performance in their current jobs; but what do we mean when we are talking about long-term potential? The key for understanding potential is to start with an analysis of the hierarchy of managerial jobs within your business, since potential is the ability to take on the challenges involved in more senior jobs. The book has identified seven key management transitions, all the way from one's first junior management position to being Chief Executive of a group of diverse businesses. The key in identifying these transitions is that at every step, executives need to change their behaviour in order to become effective. It is ironic that what has made someone successful in their current job will not be appropriate any more for them to be effective in a significantly larger job. Understanding management transitions across the hierarchy leads to the concept of career paths. The book has identified the need to focus on job families and the hierarchies of management jobs within each family. Career decisions around future jobs require the executive to understand what are possible positions, what is required to succeed in each of these, capability gaps between what they have and what is required in terms of skills and experience, and how to develop towards the new position. The key in career development is a combination of stretch and support. It is important to enable your highest-potential executives to stretch their capabilities and to build on their potential. But it is also important to support them and ensure that they do not fail by taking on positions that they will not be able to cope with. This led to a description of on-boarding processes that will help executives within the talent pool to succeed. Ensuring that your senior executive team trusts that the talent pool is an effective source for internal resourcing is key to the success of talent management efforts.

I then discussed the concept of building executive capability. There is always a danger that the business invests a great deal of resources in identifying the most talented executives and assessing their capability but fails to actually develop them. Ironically, in some organisations, the executives do not even know that they have been identified as being in the talent pool and, therefore, it is unlikely that they will develop their potential to be able to cope with future leadership challenges. The key for effective development is to start with transparency about strengths and weaknesses and then to follow that with a commitment to build on an executive's strengths and to help them to become exceptional. A range of development opportunities has been reviewed to ensure that what is provided for talented executives is tailored to their individual needs, as opposed to a business school programme that is supposed to address what everyone requires.

The main problems in making talent management an effective tool for leadership development are associated with business silos. Executives trust their direct reports and do not want to let them move to other areas, while also having relatively restricted views of what are legitimate career paths. Managers hesitate to recruit executives who come up the organisation by very different routes to what they themselves are used to. Moreover, candidates like to move in a familiar environment and hesitate to take on the risks associated with moving to a different Division or Functional area. The book discussed approaches to breaking down business silos. These focus on creating personal familiarity by members of the senior executive team with the best executive talent that is available across the business. By getting to know promising executives from different Divisions, recruiting executives will open their minds to people they would otherwise not have considered. At the same time, candidates will perceive that there are more diverse opportunities than what they see in their own business silo. The issue of organisational silos also relates to the topic of diversity. This is not a politically correct initiative, since without diversity we are restricting the talent pool from which we draw. It is also important to ensure that your business leadership teams are diverse in order to facilitate creativity and innovation and to be able to address diverse customer requirements.

Another topic that has been discussed in the book is the branding associated with talent management. Many businesses have devoted a great deal of resources to developing an employer brand in order to attract staff. It is now possible to segment this branding concept and to dedicate brands to specific executive populations that you want to draw into your business. Assessing the current perception of the business in terms of how attractive it is for certain kinds of high-potential executives and what needs to be done to make it more attractive will provide the foundation for developing a strong executive brand that will draw the best candidates in the market.

Talent management is an HR-led process focused on the top 10% of leaders within your business and to be effective it needs to integrate with all other Human Resource processes. Performance management, reward, internal communications, and training and development all need to contribute to the effectiveness of your attempt to develop the best leadership population.

In talent management, we naturally focus on executives who have the potential for taking on significantly larger jobs across the business. In every business, however, there are executives with a depth of expertise who are 'exceptional performers' that need to be motivated and can be used as resources for knowledge management and to coach others. Within your talent management reviews and development activities, it is important to focus on exceptional performers, and ensure that they are motivated and used effectively since they form the backbone of business performance.

The success of any talent management efforts depends to a large degree on support from the top. These processes will not be effective if they are seen as Human Resource bureaucracy and, therefore, they need to be perceived by the line to be activities that support business effectiveness. The book presented various ways that can ensure that the senior team takes ownership of talent management processes, starting with the definition of a talent standard and continuing with personal involvement in getting to know and developing the most talented leaders across the business.

The final chapter in the book focused on you, the reader, and your own career. How can you identify your talents and your level of motivation and what can you do to use talent management concepts to build your own career?

In general, talent management has focused attention in the last few years on the need to develop exceptional leaders that will be able to build the competitive advantage of your business. In many large organisations talent management is still too bureaucratic and line managers do not see it as a real tool to gain and sustain competitive advantage. This stems mostly from the hesitancy of senior executive teams to act decisively in the area of leadership development. The business may spend a lot of time and resources identifying high-potential executives, but when key positions become open it is quite typical to go outside to recruit candidates or to move people around based on their individual network and who they know. Businesses are still too tolerant of mediocre executives, since they do not see a clear route to improving the capability of their leadership teams.

Everything goes back to the beginning of the book, where the senior leadership team has to focus on the importance that they attribute to having the best players within their marketplace. Sports teams invest a great deal of effort to analyse the quality of their players, compare them to what is available in the marketplace and use that information to build the best team that they can afford. Similar processes are rare in large corporate environments. Those organisations that leverage talent management activities have a commitment to define the kind of leaders that they need in each Division and Function, assess the capability of existing people, and take the hard decisions associated with replacing and developing leaders to ensure that their business is in the forefront of performance.

APPENDIX 1

This appendix provides a sample of different types of competence frameworks. The first is just a list of headings. The second describes competence headings and how they will apply to different job levels. The third framework is the most elaborate with competence headings, then subheadings and definitions.

Consumer Products Business

The 12 Competencies

Big-Picture Thinking	Customer Focus
Change Management	Teambuilding
Innovation	Influencing
Making Things Happen	Partnering
Commercial Rigour	Leadership
Consumer & Brand Focus	Interpersonal Relationships

Competence Levels Required for Target Job

Different jobs require a different profile of competencies. A Marketing Director may need high-level strategic vision, an Operations Director may need a high level of people management competencies, etc. Please use this table to indicate, for each competence area, the level that is required in order to perform the job effectively.

		Strategic Vision	Managing Operations	Leading People	Teamwork & External Relationships	Commercial Acumen
LOW		General knowledge of business strategy & no specific strategy for own area of accountability	Follows general works processes with some operational performance issues	Manages the team in line with business policies	Co-operates with colleagues and external bodies as and when required	Able to function within a business context and to reach business decisions when required to do so
	2	Understands business strategy & establishes strategy for own area that is used to develop systematic plans and objectives for the team	Follows work processes & delivers expected operational performance	Leads own team effectively by encouraging input & building cohesion	Works well with colleagues and external bodies and is part of a co-operative approach to achieving common objectives	Understands the business decisions required and acts on business opportunities effectively to ensure the smooth operation of the unit
	3	Demonstrates in-depth understanding of business strategy & actively builds clear links to strategy & plans for own area of accountability	Demonstrates in-depth understanding of work processes & uses them to get the best possible operational performance	Provides very effective leadership for own team that enables them to maximise their contribution to business unit performance	Encourages cross-business unit and external co-operation & works closely with relevant others to ensure smooth operations & continuous improvement processes	Has a deep understanding of the nature of business decisions required to ensure the success of own unit and uses business opportunities to maximise the long-term impact of decisions
	4	Continuously develops strategy & plans for own area of accountability in light of overall business changes. Contributes to business strategy beyond own area	Continuous improvement of work processes leads to significant operational improvements & impacts business	Demonstrates exceptional leadership that enables team to maximise their potential & goes beyond own team in facilitating people development	Builds co-operation across business units and with external bodies and uses it to ensure that own area receives and provides the support needed by everyone to achieve significant business improvements	Demonstrated exceptional business acumen in identifying key business-decisions & opportunities, using them to significantly improve performance for own unit as well as others
	5	Assertive in planning & implementing transformational strategic initiatives within & beyond own area of accountability, thereby creating significant competitive advantage for the business as a whole	Transforms operational performance beyond own unit through the implementation of significant business processes improvements that are the standard for the industry as a whole	Demonstrates inspirational leadership within own team resulting in accountability for key business-wide people development processes that are in the forefront of the industry	Works very closely with key leaders across the business and in the external environment to ensure cross-fertilisation and significantly improve business integration as a tool for improved performance for the business as a whole	Due to exceptional business acumen, has direct responsibility for key business decisions that go beyond own area of accountability and uses that to identify significant business opportunities that impact performance
HIGH		Has direct impact on transforming the competitive environment through the development & implementation of significant strategic initiatives	Transforms the basic operational paradigms used in the business environment through the development & implementation of radically different operational processes	Transforms the key people management processes used in the sector as a basis for significant improvements in business performance	Has direct impact on transforming the nature of relationships across business units and with the external environment & thereby transforms business processes across the business & the sector as a whole	Transforms the nature of decisions made across the business & thereby the nature of opportunities that are acted upon and affect the business and the market as a whole

Large Retailer: Competence Framework

A. Analytical Thinking

Analytical Thinking is the ability to understand problems, situations and issues and to draw out their logical conclusions by breaking them down into their component parts. It implies the ability to understand cause and effect relationships.

What it looks like

1. Breaks things down logically
Breaks uncomplicated issues down into smaller parts. Identifies basic requirements.

2. Sees basic relationships
Takes problems apart. Links together pieces with a simple A-leads-to-B link. Makes comparisons. Weighs up options and ensures they are based on accurate information. Explains things in a clear step-by-step way. Establishes straightforward priorities.

3. Sees multiple relationships
Describes a complicated situation in a logical and structured manner. Breaks down a problem into smaller parts. Identifies both potential causes and outcomes and draws logical conclusions. Is able to hypothesise, e.g. A-could-lead-to-B, C or D – depending-on X, Y or Z. Thinks ahead about next steps.

4. Makes complex analyses
Uses a range of analytical techniques as appropriate to break apart complex problems into component parts. Identifies a range of solutions and weighs up the value of each. Evaluates whether arguments or cases are complete or sound. Identifies the key issues in ambiguous or inconsistent data.

5. Synthesises results of analyses
Rebuilds the results of complex analyses, potentially from different sources, to form a sound, sustainable case. Creates order out of information that may come from many unrelated sources by finding the key interdependencies.

B. Concern for Accuracy and Quality

Concern for Accuracy and Quality is the drive to reduce uncertainty by creating a well-ordered work environment. It implies the ability to manage and monitor own and others' work in order to ensure quality and timeliness and to check accuracy of information.

What it looks like

1. Organised

Maintains information and records so that they are up-to-date, accurate, accessible and in good order. Ensures things are organised so that others can find what they want.

2. Checks own work

Seeks to clarify and define own role and what is expected. Checks the accuracy of information and the quality of own work.

3. Uses monitoring systems

Uses systems, procedures or documents to monitor information. Maintains awareness of what is going on. Takes action to correct own or others' mistakes in order to minimise impact on quality standards and timescales.

4. Identifies issues and takes action

Sets high standards through quality of own work. Assesses validity of information, measures standards, identifies issues and takes corrective action. Where in a team/project leader role, ensures accuracy by checking that others are following procedures and delivering good work efficiently.

5. Develops monitoring systems

Develops and uses systems to organise and check information, to improve the quality of data, and to establish better tracking procedures. Ensures high level of accuracy and quality at all times.

C. Teamworking and Ownership

Teamworking and Ownership is sharing collective responsibility for all aspects of our Company business, including delivery of the Customer Promise. It is shown in behaviours which are supportive and collaborative.

What it looks like

1. Willingly works with others
Is proud to work for our Company. Sees working with others as essential – does not have a 'silo' mentality. Talks about 'we' not 'they'. Shares agenda with others. Accepts Group decisions. Shares information. Helps colleagues under pressure. Creates time to develop teamworking and relationships.

2. Actively contributes to achieve organisational objectives
Positively supports our Company. Works with others, regardless of functional boundaries. Understands colleagues' needs and is proactive in offering support in order to ensure delivery of organisational objectives and the Customer Promise.

3. Works to find common ground
Supports the decisions and work of colleagues, regardless of function, trusting their professionalism and integrity. Actively seeks long-term win–win outcomes even if there is a personal short-term cost. Admits failure or mistakes openly without apportioning blame elsewhere. Is committed to our Company.

4. Takes responsibility for team's work
Willingly accepts responsibility on behalf of their whole team. Identifies areas of potential conflict within the team and takes steps to resolve. Acts as an ambassador for our Company both internally and externally and takes responsibility for all aspects of the business.

5. Promotes the long-term interests of the Company
Promotes decisions that benefit the Company, even if they are unpopular or controversial. Probes decision making to ensure the interests of the Company are always protected. Raises key sensitive issues openly, impartially and honestly.

D. Understanding our Company

Understanding our Company is sensitivity to the way our Company works at an informal and cultural level to enable excellent management. It implies the ability to understand how people think, feel and interact as groups and individuals.

What it looks like

1. Understands formal structure
Is aware of both formal and major players in our Company. Understands how functions link together. Communicates with other functions where necessary. Understands formal power and formal rules. Uses existing contacts around business.

2. Understands informal structure
Is aware of both formal and informal structure and uses both to get things done. Develops sound working relationships with other functions and seeks to understand the feelings of colleagues in other functions. Understands how people in different parts of the organisation link together.

3. Understands climate and culture
Is sensitive to organisational climate. Identifies areas of organisational stress and recognises limitations. Recognises and uses influential people when it is appropriate to do so.

4. Understands channels of influence
Understands how different groups and individuals, internally and externally, affect and influence decisions and outcomes. Understands how different parts of our Company will react in certain circumstances. Builds relations with influential people.

5. Understands underlying organisational issues
Puts sustained effort into building influential relationships both inside and outside our Company. Is attuned to and addresses the underlying reasons for ongoing organisational behaviour. Identifies how external factors affect different parts of the business. Recognises and uses alliances across our Company.

E. Drive for Achievement

Drive for Achievement is the hunger to do things better and to be successful so that our Company achieves its objectives. It is shown in a pride in setting and exceeding one's own standards.

What it looks like

1. Works to meet targets
Delivers what is required to get the job done to standard and on time. Takes pride in work and makes an effort to avoid waste or inefficiency. Meets others' standards.

2. Sets own standards
Delivers more than is required. Sets personal standards for day-to-day activities which are above those set by others and uses own methods to measure outcomes against them. Rises to challenges. Seeks feedback in order to learn and repeat success.

3. Improves performance
Wants to make a difference. Sets longer-term goals beyond those required and strives to achieve them. Makes changes in systems or work methods to improve own performance and performance of the team. Uses feedback and learning to improve personal performance and to spread best practice.

4. Sets challenging goals
Sets challenging goals involving an element of appropriate risk for self and business area. Analyses costs v. benefits to enhance chances of success. Continuously looks for ways of doing things faster, better, more efficiently and ensures changes are captured so that they bring longer-term business benefits. Sets out to excel by benchmarking against the best.

5. Sets transformational business goals
Commits significant resources to setting and realising high-priority, strategic business goals. Looks for opportunities to transform business or process areas in order to improve performance. Strives to be leading-edge. Encourages and supports others to take calculated risks to achieve new standards of excellence and business performance.

F. Impact and Influence

Impact and Influence is the conscious use of one's capabilities to have a positive impact on the organisation and others. It implies a desire to influence others to achieve effectiveness as well as an understanding of one's own strengths and weaknesses. It is rooted in interpersonal sensitivity.

What it looks like

1. Thinks about self in relation to others
Intends to have a specific effect on others and is concerned about own ability to influence. Listens to others and checks understanding. Makes time for others. Observes to identify best approaches for dealing with them.

2. Uses impact consciously
Sets out to influence outcomes in an assertive way using simple and direct methods. Recognises the value that can be added in achieving or helping others to achieve objectives. Shows consideration for, and seeks to understand, the unspoken thoughts and feelings of others.

3. Adapts to increase impact
Adapts style or content of approach in accordance with the situation and persons involved. Anticipates the effect of own actions. Is at ease with others at all grades and across functional boundaries so that they, in turn, are at ease. Wants to make others feel and work better.

4. Uses complex influencing strategies
Uses chains of indirect influence and group process skills to achieve significant impact. Considers the value and belief sets of other parties. Uses a range of response tactics and deals with a variety of complex behaviours, values and motives.

5. Establishes influence across and outside the organisation
Creates an atmosphere of loyalty and influence at an organisational level. Has high personal impact which leads to 'role model' status. Builds alliances outside Company to benefit the Company at a strategic level.

G. Initiative into Action

Initiative into Action is the bias for taking action to deal with a current situation or in anticipation of a future circumstance. It implies the ability to think about future issues and to take action to either mitigate their impact or seize the opportunities they may bring to our Company. It is underpinned by initiative.

What it looks like

1. Responds to current issues
Takes responsibility for dealing with recognised problems and issues. Identifies possible solutions and takes action, having first sought confirmation.

2. Anticipates and acts
Takes advantage of opportunities and takes prompt action to solve problems. Identifies key issues and acts to optimise outcomes. Prepares ahead to make sure things go well.

3. Proactively deals with current and future issues
Acts quickly and decisively, using significant effort or resource – to deal with situations posing a threat of some scale. Anticipates and prepares for specific future opportunities and removes obstacles to specific business objectives.

4. Addresses longer-term issues
Anticipates and prepares for longer-term opportunities and removes less obvious obstacles to business objectives over the longer term. Understands the medium- to long-term implications of potential problems and acts to minimise effects. Ensures benefits of action or cost of inaction outweigh the risks involved.

5. Takes strategic action
Develops and acts on strategies to minimise threats, exploit opportunities, and secure the Company's long-term interests. Acts to create major opportunities. Understands the full implications of commercial threats and acts to secure Company's interests. Acts decisively to turn around inefficient or underperforming parts of the business.

H. Positive Approach to Change

Positive Approach to Change is the ability to initiate and support change and respond positively to changing requirements. It implies the desire to support continuous process or business improvement to deliver the Customer Promise. It is underpinned by flexibility and continuous learning to adapt to the knowledge and skills requirements for new situations.

What it looks like

1. Accepts change
Accepts new or different types of work when required to. Changes work plans or routines without complaint.

2. Responds positively to change
Works enthusiastically to adopt new initiatives. Willingly accommodates unforeseen changes and adapts behaviour accordingly. Looks for new ways of improving performance and takes necessary steps to acquire new skill and knowledge requirements.

3. Gains buy-in of others to change
Communicates the benefits and requirements of change clearly and positively and ensures that they are fully understood by others. Suggests and encourages new ideas or approaches. Works to ensure success of change initiatives.

4. Manages specific change projects
Identifies, initiates or implements significant change projects that will have a positive impact on the business. Considers the potential benefits to achievement of business objectives and delivery of the Customer Promise and balances these against the costs and potential risks. Ensures the benefits are realised, minimising disruption and maximising acceptance.

5. Champions change projects
Acts as a role model by championing strategic change projects and demonstrating commitment to an innovative environment where taking appropriate risks to drive continuous improvement is required.

I. Business Awareness

Business Awareness is the ability to scan widely in the industry in order to have a broad and deep knowledge base and clear understanding of what it takes to be a world class company. It implies the desire to understand all parts of our Company and the business environment in order to be able to prioritise effectively so that we deliver excellent customer service.

What it looks like

1. Asks questions
Asks questions about our Company, the industry and the marketplace. Gathers visible, easily obtainable information and checks its validity.

2. Probes for detail
Probes to get at facts. Challenges and questions information obtained. Uses a range of information sources to build up the picture. Makes an effort to obtain data, e.g. investigates off-site and in person when it is necessary to do so.

3. Undertakes relevant research
Prioritises areas for investigation. Ranges widely rather than becoming over-analytical. Challenges and questions information obtained. Is able to identify and explain the nature of external issues. Talks to a range of informed Company and industry contacts.

4. Systematically scans the market
Systematically scans the marketplace to identify market trends and their impact on our Company. Builds up market and company understanding over a sustained period. Builds network of key external information sources including managers from other leading companies outside the retail industry.

5. Scans the economic environment
Understands long-term political and economic agendas. Habitually gathers internal and external information to enable business decisions to be set in the context of current best practice and economic, social and cultural needs.

J. Developing Self and Others

Developing Self and Others is the ability to identify and maximise underlying potential to bring long-term benefit to the business and individuals. It implies that the manager demonstrates the value of continuous development by putting effort into his/her own development as well as that of his/her team.

What it looks like

1. Addresses obvious development needs
Assists individuals in meeting development needs identified in performance management process. Uses readily accessible training programmes. Assists with on-the-job learning by giving directions/demonstrations. Takes responsibility for ensuring own development needs are reviewed and met. Seeks and responds to feedback.

2. Coaches and develops
Assesses individuals and helps them to identify appropriate development opportunities. Spends time with individuals to train, coach and counsel. Values, nurtures and uses individuals' skill and knowledge. Encourages individuals to value personal development and take responsibility for their learning and models this by giving profile to his/her own development actions. Checks that individuals learn from their experiences, offering reassurance when mistakes are made.

3. Creates opportunities
Assesses team skills mix and takes responsibility for maximising team capability and performance in the context of current business requirements. Uses channels of influence to create learning opportunities for self and others outside the boundaries of current role and team. Spots high performers and encourages them to look around Company for further career development. Recognises tailing off of performance and works with the individual to identify the reasons and address them.

4. Establishes and meets future development needs
Plans longer-term capability requirements against business requirements and delivery of the Customer Promise. Identifies creative ways of fulfilling needs. Finds or creates stretching activities/roles for individuals, including cross-functional moves if appropriate. Willingly supports aspirations even at personal or team cost. Shows leadership in treating team mistakes as learning experiences, encouraging open discussion to agree future improvements and ways forward.

K. Goal Focus

Goal Focus is the ability to maintain an objective view of the overall goals so as to deliver high standards and results. It implies setting and monitoring against clear measures. Furthermore, it requires open-mindedness and detachment so that one can be decisive in making changes where effort is no longer focused in an appropriate way. It is rooted in a real sense of accountability.

What it looks like

1. Monitors performance
Sets and agrees clear, measurable standards and timescales. Monitors against these measures and feeds back constructively.

2. Focuses on outcomes
Encourages team members to look for lasting solutions which will take the business forward, not just quick fixes. Enables others to prioritise by making performance expectations clear. Role-models the need to work with others to achieve business targets. Monitors performance and feeds back in the context of overall goals.

3. Reviews and makes changes
Reviews priorities and updates plans accordingly. Monitors cost/benefit against clear objectives and reassesses if necessary. Recognises and deals with underperformance. Stops unproductive activities.

4. Creates a goal-focused culture
Encourages innovative thinking in the team to exceed goals. Sets and monitors long-term goals for teams and individuals. Takes tough decisions when addressing performance issues. Stops unproductive projects or processes.

5. Breaks the mould to achieve strategic goals
Makes significant contribution to organisation, infrastructure, resource allocation or people in order to achieve Company strategy.

L. Leadership

Leadership is the ability to make things happen through others by organising, motivating and inspiring them. It implies the desire and ability to establish clarity and organise resources to achieve the company vision. It is underpinned by the ability to communicate.

What it looks like

1. Clarifies tasks
Tells people clearly both what they have to do and why. Communicates fluently. Thinks about optimal use of people and resources. Shares information. Organises resources and acts to make things happen. Establishes delivery mechanisms and processes.

2. Clarifies objectives
Ensures that all team members have a clear understanding of how their roles and responsibilities contribute to short- and long-term performance. Shares problems and asks for input. Encourages participation in group decisions. Plans resource requirements.

3. Fosters shared responsibility
Fosters responsibility for team objectives. Creates ownership by establishing major outcomes but allowing team to decide how to get there. Assesses risk of delegation and passes on responsibility appropriately. Challenges inefficient resource utilisation.

4. Fosters disciplined freedom
Empowers others in significant ways: scale, resource, impact – within clear frameworks of authority and accountability. Makes people enthusiastic about the vision. Clearly communicates strategy across organisational levels and functions. Sees connections between processes, functions and levels and makes the most of resources.

5. Inspires ownership of the vision
Establishes, presents and communicates a clear strategic direction which inspires ownership across the business. Generates excitement, enthusiasm and commitment to the vision. Encourages people to think about resources as means to create value.

M. Strategic Thinking

Strategic Thinking is the ability to see opportunities and use conceptual thinking to adapt them creatively to the needs of our Company. It implies the capacity to develop a practical vision and identify solutions to business problems or issues.

What it looks like

1. Recognises connections and themes
Recognises when a situation is similar to a previous one. Makes connections and applies past experience or common sense.

2. Sees clearly through complexity
Sees patterns, trends or missing pieces. Applies past experience to identify potential benefits or problems. Pulls ideas, issues and observations together to clarify broad implications.

3. Applies and adapts complex concepts
Uses and modifies complex learned concepts or knowledge of past situations to identify and understand major issues from a mass of apparently unrelated data. Steps back from complex situations to avoid getting bogged down; takes a 'helicopter view'. Asks: 'What are the wider implications of exploiting this opportunity?'

4. Creates new models and frameworks
Cuts through complexity to create simple frameworks that others can easily understand. Helps others to change their perspective. Demonstrates an understanding of the consequences arising from complex situations or actions. Rethinks situations and identifies themes not obvious to others. Asks: 'What if . . . ?'

5. Creates concepts and strategies
Creates concepts through focused reflection on a holistic view of our Company. Creatively tests and adapts options against our Company's overall strategic framework. Modifies strategic thinking as a result of reflecting on our Company's positions in the market. Asks: 'Why not . . . ?'

N. Self-Confidence

Self-Confidence enables one to take personal risks for the benefit of the Company. It implies willingness to both challenge more senior managers and organisational norms and to ask for help when it might be difficult to do so. It is underpinned by integrity.

What it looks like

1. Demonstrates self-confidence
Appears confident and presents positive self-image. Calm and assured in familiar or routine situations. Works without needing supervision. Asks for help when necessary.

2. Acts independently
Makes decisions or takes action in spite of disagreement or opposition from others. States own views in an appropriately assertive and firm manner when in disagreement with more senior colleagues. Is willing to take the consequences of decisions. Admits failure without seeing this as a sign of weakness. Is not defensive about feedback.

3. States confidence in own ability
Expresses justified confidence in own expertise, capabilities or judgement, even in difficult situations and when the stakes are high. Addresses conflict. Is willing to listen to and take on board challenges from others (including more junior staff) as a positive contribution.

4. Chooses challenge
Confidently challenges the organisational view and the opinions of more senior people, using good judgement and timing. Readily accepts challenging and uncertain situations. Takes calculated risks where the potential benefits to the business justify this. Takes personal risks to achieve consensus. Asks for help from others even when it might be difficult to do so.

5. Confidence in the broader business context
Is prepared to go it alone and hold on to own well-founded ideas despite opposition from other senior people where our Company's best interests are at stake. Genuinely and justifiably believes in own capability to lead our Company forward. Deals confidently and assertively to represent our Company with senior people externally.

O. Tenacity

Tenacity is the determination to overcome obstacles in order to deliver what is required. It implies clarity of purpose and is underpinned by Drive for Achievement.

What it looks like

1. Sticks with it
Stays with the task or job even when it gets tedious, difficult or inconvenient. Continues even when feeling bored. Persists and is not too discouraged by routine obstacles.

2. Expresses optimism
Sees positive possibilities even in negative situations. Takes personal responsibility for seeing things through. Responds calmly and constructively under moderate pressure.

3. Takes action to overcome resistance or obstacles
Puts in effort to understand resistance and find a way round it. Tries an alternative approach in the event of failure. Takes steps to get past obstacles.

4. Takes repeated action to overcome resistance or obstacles
Persists in the face of numerous obstacles. Uses high energy, determination and resilience despite frequent rejections. Maintains composure and responds in an appropriate manner in high-pressure situations. Copes positively with setbacks.

5. Takes multiple actions to overcome resistance or obstacles
Addresses frequent and varied setbacks or obstacles with a number of different approaches. Deals calmly and assertively with individuals who pose a threat to achievement of personal and team objectives. Maintains objectivity even under severe pressure. Sustains significant effort over the long term.

APPENDIX 2

ARTICLES IN PROFESSIONAL JOURNALS

Atkinson, C (2002) 'Career management and the changing psychological contract', *Career Development International*, **7**, 14–23.

Backhaus, Kristin & Tikoo, Surinder (2004) 'Conceptualizing and researching employer branding', *Career Development International*, **9**, 501–517.

Behn, Bruce K, Riley, Richard A & Yang, Ya-wen (2005) 'The value of an heir apparent in succession planning', *Corporate Governance*, **13**, 168–177.

Byham, William (2002) 'Headstart: a new look at succession management', *Ivey Business Journal*, May/June, 10–12.

Cantor, Paul (2005) 'Succession planning: often requested, rarely delivered', *Ivey Management Services*, January/February, 1–10.

Clutterbuck, David (2005) 'Succession planning: a development approach', *Development and Learning in Organizations: An International Journal*, **19**, 11–13.

Crawshaw, Jonathan R (2006) 'Justice source and justice content: evaluating the fairness of organisational career management practices', *Human Resource Management Journal*, **16**, 98–120.

Dulewicz, V & Herbert, P (1999) 'Predicting advancement to senior management from competencies and personality data: a seven-year follow-up study', *British Journal of Management*, **10**, 13–22.

Guinn, SL (2000) 'Succession planning without job titles', *Career Development International*, **5**, 390–393.

Hall, DT (1999) 'Accelerate executive development – at your peril!', *Career Development International*, **4**, 23.

Hiltrop, JM (1999) 'The quest for the best: human resource practices to attract and retain talent', *European Management Journal*, **17**, 422–430.

Huang, T-C (2001) 'Succession management systems and human resource outcomes', *International Journal of Manpower*, **22**, 736–747.

Kakabadse, A & Kakabadse, N (2001) 'Dynamics of executive succession', *Corporate Governance: International Journal of Business in Society*, **1**, 9–14.

Kransdorff, A (1996) 'Succession planning in a fast-changing world', *Management Decision*, **34**, 30–34.

Mighty, EJ & Ashton, W (2003) 'Management development: hoax or hero', *The Journal of Management Development*, **22**, 14–31.

Ng, Eddy SW & Burke, Ronald J (2005) 'Person–organization fit and the war for talent: does diversity management make a difference?, *International Journal of Human Resource Management*, **16**, 1195–1210.

Pollitt, David (2005) 'Leadership succession planning "affects commercial success": chief executives crucial to developing high-potential employees', *Human Resource Management International Digest*, **13**, 36–38.

Sambrook, Sally (2005) 'Exploring succession planning in small, growing firms', *Journal of Small Business and Enterprise Development*, **12**, 579–594.

Stainton, Amanda (2005) 'Talent management: latest buzzword or refocusing existing processes?', *Competency & Emotional Intelligence Quarterly*, **12**, 39–45.

Van der Sluis-den Dikken, L & Hoeksema, LH (2001) 'The palette of management development', *The Journal of Management Development*, **20**, 168–179.

Watkin, C (2003) 'The talent management maze', *Competency & Emotional Intelligence Quarterly*, **11**, 20.

BOOKS

The War for Talent
by Ed Michaels, Helen Handfield-Jones and Beth Axelrod
Harvard University Press, 2001, 200 pages

This is the book that established talent management as a key strategic topic. McKinsey consultants Ed Michaels, Helen Handfield-Jones and Beth Axelrod argue that winning the war for leadership talent is about much more than frenzied recruiting tactics. It is about the timeless principles of attracting, developing and retaining highly talented managers – applied in bold new ways. And it is about recognising the strategic importance of human capital because of the enormous value that better talent creates.

Fortified by 5 years of in-depth research on how companies manage leadership talent – including surveys of 13,000 US executives at more than 120 companies and case studies of 27 leading companies – the authors propose a fundamentally new approach to talent management.

The Leadership Pipeline: How to Build the Leadership-Powered Company
by Ram Charan, Stephen Drotter and James Noel
Jossey-Bass, 2001, 248 pages

In this book, three consultants describe how businesses can develop leadership at every organisational level. Drawing from their experience at General Electric, Goodyear, Citibank, Ford and other top companies, they present a model for identifying future leaders, assessing their competence, planning their development and measuring the results. Moreover, they integrate their leadership development process with a succession planning process that enables companies to constantly renew leaders at all levels.

This book presents the notion of key leadership transitions which is essential for understanding and developing leadership potential.

Developing and Managing Talent
by Sultan Kermally
Thorogood Publishers, 2004, 110 pages

This book offers strategies and practical guidance for finding, developing and above all keeping talented individuals. After explaining what developing talent actually means to the organisation, the author explores the e-dimension and the global dimension. He summarises what the 'gurus' have to say on the development of leadership talent, and examines the 'softer approach'. Finally, he includes valuable case studies drawn from Hilton, Volkswagen, Unilever, Microsoft and others.

Effective Succession Planning (second edition)
by William J. Rothwell
AMACOM (American Management Association), 2001, 338 pages

This book provides information to help you establish, revitalise, or evaluate a succession planning and management (SP&M) programme for your firm. Case studies, self-assessment tools and planning guides are included. This book details a step-by-step approach to succession planning that allows you to:

- Identify competencies and clarify values for both planning and managing a succession programme.
- Plan for and fill crucial vacancies at all levels from top management to sales, administrative, technical and production positions.
- Develop and retain top talent, building and preserving your organisation's intellectual capital.
- Assess current needs and future resources for succession planning.
- Use on-line and other technology tools to organise and implement SP&M programmes.

Effective Succession Planning introduces and examines eight key trends that are influencing and framing the future of SP&M. These include predictions about the impacts of globalisation, real-time technological innovations, and the need for employees to balance their work and personal lives.

The Talent Management Handbook
edited by Lance A. Berger and Dorothy R. Berger
McGraw-Hill, 2004, 448 pages

This book focuses on how to connect organisational excellence to people management by systematically identifying, keeping and promoting your organisation's best people. Featuring the contributions of executives, Human Resources practitioners and consultants, this book presents a comprehensive approach to talent management and integrating your company's infrastructure of HR assessment, planning and development tools into a single cogent system. The Talent Management Handbook explains how to align your company's people with the current and future needs of the organisation by placing employees in positions that maximise their value.

This book also explains how to build all your HR disciplines on the 'building blocks' of organisational competencies, performance appraisal and forecast of employee/manager potential.

High-Impact Succession Management: From Succession Planning to Strategic Executive Talent Management
Corporate Executive Board, 2003, 107 pages

This report presents various approaches to talent management using case study examples from Johnson & Johnson, IBM, Shell, Duke Energy, Schlumberger, American Express and Marriott. The report focuses on the key issues in talent management and describes how each of these businesses approached the need to maximise its leadership capabilities.

The Employer Brand
by Simon Barrow and Richard Mosley
John Wiley, 2005, 214 pages

This book focuses on the development of an employer brand. Your most important brand relationship is unlikely to be your choice of breakfast cereal, your car or even your football team, but the brand you work for – your employer brand. How people feel about their employer brand is increasingly critical to business success or failure. Leading companies realise its importance in attracting and engaging the people they need to deliver profitable growth. They are also beginning to recognise that creating a positive brand experience for employees requires the same degree of focus, care and coherence that has long characterised effective management of the customer brand experience. This book provides a comprehensive guide to developing and managing this critical business asset.

The Strategic Development of Talent: A Framework for Using Talent to Support Your Organizational Strategy (second edition)
by William J. Rothwell and H.C. Kazanas
HRD Press, 2003, 577 pages

This book applies the principles of strategic business planning to the field that has had a variety of names: Training and Development, Human Resource Development (HRD), Human Performance Improvement, and Workplace Learning and Performance (WLP). Earlier versions of this book focused on strategic planning as applied to HRD. This edition has been completely revised and updated to move beyond HRD to apply the principles of strategic business planning to talent management and knowledge management.

The First 90 Days
by Michael Watkins
Harvard Business School Press, 2003, 252 pages

This book is designed to help executives who are moving into a new position. You have just been promoted to a new leadership position. You are not yet sure of the challenges ahead or how you will meet them. All you know is that you have 3 months to get on top of the job and move forward – or fail. This book provides a road map for taking charge quickly and effectively during critical career transition periods, whether you are a first-time manager or a new CEO. Written by Michael Watkins, *The First 90 Days* outlines strategies that are designed to shorten the time it takes to reach what Watkins calls the 'breakeven point': the point at which your organisation needs you as much as you need the job.

Based on 3 years of research into leadership transitions at all levels and hands-on work-designing transition programmes, Watkins provides examples and tools that will show you how to:

- assess your strengths and weaknesses and identify personal vulnerabilities
- diagnose your situation and understand its challenges and opportunities
- negotiate a productive working relationship with your boss
- secure early wins that establish credibility and create momentum
- build your team and connect with influential support coalitions

Refuting the pervasive belief that new leaders should be left to 'sink or swim', *The First 90 Days* details a proactive planning approach that can make an individual's career – and ensure an organisation's future.

Coaching and Buying Coaching Services
by Jessica Jarvis
The Chartered Institute of Personnel and Development, UK, 2006

This on-line report:

- provides an overview of the coaching industry
- outlines the different professional bodies and the current training and qualification options
- explains the different types of coaching
- discusses the business case for coaching
- considers when coaching is an appropriate intervention
- discusses the different interest groups in coaching (HR, line managers, the individual etc.)
- explains when the use of internal or external coaches may be appropriate
- provides guidance on what to look for in a coach during selection
- provides guidance and advice for HR on recruiting and matching coaches to your organisation.

This guide offers practical advice about how to gain full value from your use of external coaching services. By exerting pressure in terms of minimum expected standards, qualifications and outcomes, the CIPD aims to help its members 'raise the bar' in terms of standards and professionalism across the industry and ensure the potential benefits of coaching interventions are realised.

Jack: Straight from the Gut
by Jack Welch with John A. Byrne
Headline, 2001, 512 pages

Jack Welch is arguably the most famous CEO in the world. His 20-year reign as the head of General Electric brought the company from bureaucratic behemoth to dynamic and revered powerhouse. During his tenure, GE market value grew from $13 billion to $500 billion. In the process, Welch's management innovations made him the most influential CEO of his era. Many books have been written about him and his principles. In this book Jack Welch tells his own story. It is a candid, engaging account of Welch's rise to the top, his tenure there, and the perspectives and lessons he learned along the way. In the present context, Jack Welch focuses on the need to identify, develop and reward executive talent as a foundation for successful business performance.

Positive Psychology

Authentic Happiness: Using the New Positive Psychology to Realise Your Potential for Lasting Fulfilment
by Martin E. P. Seligman
Nicholas & Brealey, 2003, 326 pages

In this national bestseller Martin Seligman shows how Positive Psychology is shifting the profession's paradigm away from its narrow-minded focus on pathology, victimology and mental illness to positive emotion and mental health. Happiness, studies show, is not the result of good genes or luck. It can be cultivated by identifying and nurturing traits that we already possess – including kindness, originality, humour, optimism and generosity.

Seligman provides the tools for you to ascertain your most positive traits or strengths. Then he explains how, by frequently calling upon these 'signature strengths' in all the crucial realms of life – health, relationships, career – you will not only develop natural buffers against misfortune and negative emotion, but also achieve new and sustainable levels of authentic contentment, gratification and meaning.

Now Discover Your Strengths
by Marcus Buckingham and Donald O. Clifton
Free Press, 2002, 260 pages

This book is an example of the Positive Psychology movement in its application to executive development. The authors have created a programme to help readers identify their talents, build them into strengths and enjoy consistent performance. At the heart of the book is the Internet-based Strengths-Finder® Profile. This programme introduces 34 dominant themes that, when combined, can provide an insight into the reader's core abilities and how they can be translated into personal and career success.

Beyond Boredom and Anxiety: Experiencing Flow in Work and Play
by Mihaly Csikszentmihalyi
Jossey-Bass, 1975, 231 pages

This book provides an understanding of work-based motivation and how exceptional performers find satisfaction. Flow is a concentrated action in which the individual is aware of his actions but not aware of his awareness. *Beyond Boredom and Anxiety* is the book that introduced the world to 'flow'. This state of peak enjoyment, energetic focus and creative concentration experienced by people engaged in adult play has become the basis of a highly creative approach to living and working.

APPENDIX 3:
A RECOMMENDED APPROACH TO TALENT MANAGEMENT AND SUCCESSION PLANNING

BACKGROUND

- Talent management tends to be a bureaucratic process with little impact on business performance.
- High-potential employees (graduates & junior managers) are identified but their development process is too long and indirect.
- Succession planning produces lists of sometimes unrealistic candidates & doesn't contribute to breaking down business unit silos.
- Senior executives in roles with direct impact on business performance are not developed systematically.
- Assessment of potential is focused on current competence & not on the potential to perform effectively at the next management level.
- High-potential executives do not receive in-depth input around possible career paths & what they need to do to develop towards them.
- When executives take on more senior positions they don't always 'let go' of the behaviours that made them successful at the previous management level.

OUR OBJECTIVES

1. Focus talent development efforts on **jobs that have direct impact** on business performance.
2. Develop **talent 'pools'** with high-performance candidates who have the potential to take on significantly larger jobs in the near future (& use pool candidates to 'feed' succession planning).
3. Ensure that the **assessment of potential** focuses on the difference between an executive's current job and what is required for being effective at the next management level.
4. Assist high-potential executives to **develop their capabilities** in line with possible career paths.
5. Facilitate cross-business unit familiarity with executive talent that can be utilised to reduce the impact of **organisational silos**.
6. Build development processes that focus on **solid performers** who may not have the potential to progress.

1. Critical jobs
(as a focus for competence assessment & succession planning)

- Identify management position with significant impact on business performance.
- Use relevant competence frameworks to assess current incumbents' development needs.
- Use Talent Management committee meetings to discuss significant competence gaps and their implications.
- Provide tailored input in line with identified development needs.
- Focus succession planning processes on these jobs (using 'pool' candidates).
- In some organisations/sectors, use the same process to focus also on critical skills.

2. Talent pools
(versus traditional succession planning processes)

- It is more effective to develop talent pools than to identify individual successors for specific positions.
- 1st pool should include candidates for executive-level positions.
- 2nd pool should include candidates for critical senior management jobs (e.g. Division Heads, BU CEOs).
- 3rd pool should include junior managers with long-term potential.
- Pool nominations based on manager's submissions to Talent Management committee (& a self-nomination process for pool 3).
- Objective assessment of potential will be done individually for the first two pools and through assessment centres for the third pool.
- Special efforts should focus on creating pool diversity.
- Pool candidates should have priority when filling vacancies.

3. Assessing potential

- In large organisations, each management level requires very different behaviours and, therefore, competencies, in order to be effective.
- When an executive performs in a similar way to what he/she was used to at a lower level job then they will not be successful.
- Assessing the potential to progress to the next level needs to focus on the difference in requirements between what makes the executive successful now and what will be required in the future.
- On-boarding processes should be used to help executives to become effective in their new positions.

Key managerial transitions

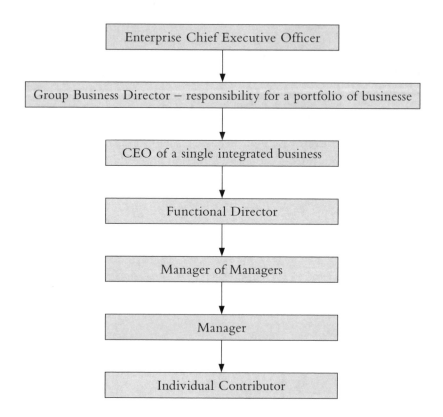

Characteristics of key management transitions

- Each step requires very different behaviours in order to be effective.
- When an executive performs in a similar way to what he/she was used to before then they will fail.
- Different managerial competencies are required in order to perform effectively at each level.
- Assessing the potential to progress to the next level needs to focus on the difference in requirements between what makes the executive successful now and what will be required in the future.

Some general rules, as you progress up the hierarchy:

■ You spend less time on your own work and **more time on managing others**: that increases at every transition.

■ There is an increased **broadening of thinking** at every transition, seeing the larger whole as a system with interdependencies.

■ Moving up requires you to identify and realise potential **synergies** between the component parts of the businesses below you.

■ You are less sure you have **all the information** you need, yet you have to take more **decisions that lack sufficient data support** for you to be entirely sure.

■ As you progress it becomes harder to **take the pulse** of a business.

■ Time spans change. You are **thinking more about the future** than about today and next year; although it has to be balanced and the present cannot be forgotten.

Key managerial transitions need to include both line and functional jobs

LINE	FUNCTIONAL
Enterprise CEO	
Group Business Director (Portfolio of companies)	
CEO of single business	Head of Group function
Division head	Head of function
Manager of managers	
Manager	Head of sub-function
Individual contributor	Individual contributor

Line and functional management job requirements

■ In general, line jobs require more accountability and a broader perspective than functional jobs

■ Functional jobs also form a managerial hierarchy where more senior positions require a broadened perspective & increased partnering with other functions.

■ Career paths should combine line and functional jobs in order to enable executives to be prepared for truly senior positions.

4. Developing high-potential executives

■ An objective assessment of strengths and development needs will provide a solid foundation for future action.

■ Development needs should focus on potential career paths and their implication in terms of competence requirements.

■ By 'owning' potential career paths and a development plan, executives will take responsibility for their own development.

■ Coaching, mentoring and participating in Group-wide strategic forums are perceived to be the best tools for development at senior management levels.

■ High-potential executives should 'feed' succession planning processes that focus on critical jobs with significant impact on business performance.

5. Breaking down silos

■ Organisation silos prevent best use of executive talent by restricting career paths & encouraging high-potential executives to look outside due to restricted opportunities.

■ Career paths should be 'mapped' across business units using the managerial hierarchy framework & then used for succession planning.

■ Career paths should be used to coach executives regarding possibilities for future jobs.

■ Executives take risks in appointing candidates from outside their silos. This can be reduced through cross-business unit mentoring of high-potential managers.

■ Cross-silo moves require more focused on-boarding processes to help candidates to acclimatise to the new setting.

6. Solid performers

■ Solid performers may not have the potential for significantly larger jobs but they contribute to current performance and, therefore, their development & motivation are key.

■ Solid performers should be identified through the performance management process and while there is no need for objective assessment, their names should still be validated through the Talent Management process.

■ Competence development contributes to job performance improvements directly but also by increasing motivation ('the organisation invests in me so I will invest back').

Summary of key points

■ Talent management & succession planning should focus on key individuals and on key jobs.

■ Objective assessment ensures effective development for managers in key jobs and unbiased views about potential.

■ Assessment of potential should focus on the difference in demands between current and future managerial positions.

■ Understanding the hierarchy of management positions enables effective career paths and facilitates activities to reduce management silos.

■ Creating pools with high-potential managers at different levels enables a more flexible approach than typical succession planning processes.

■ Talent management should also focus on solid performers.

INDEX